GOSPEL PRINCIPLES

Published by
The Church of Jesus Christ of Latter-day Saints
Salt Lake City, Utah

Comments and Suggestions

Your comments and suggestions about this manual are appreciated. Please submit them to—

Office of the Seventy
Attention: Curriculum Department
47 East South Temple Street
Salt Lake City, UT 84150
USA

Identify yourself by name, address, ward, and stake. Then identify the name of the manual, how you used it, your feelings about its strengths and weaknesses, and any recommended improvements.

CONTENTS

Hymns
(The hymns are listed by suggested use, but many of them could be used for more than one purpose. For instance, most of the opening and closing hymns could be used for either purpose.)

Special Topics

Children's Songs

INTRODUCTION

Gospel Principles was written both as a personal study guide and as a teacher's manual. Therefore, you can use this manual in many ways. It can help you —

• Build your knowledge and testimony of the gospel.
• Answer questions about the gospel.
• Study scriptures by topics.
• Prepare talks.
• Prepare lessons for family home evening.
• Prepare lessons for Church meetings.

As you study this manual, seek the Spirit of the Lord. The Holy Ghost will increase your understanding and testimony of Jesus Christ, his atonement, and the restoration of the gospel. Through your study of this text and its related scriptures, you can find answers to life's questions, gain an assurance of your purpose and self-worth, and solve personal difficulties. Many of the instructions for teachers listed below are also important when you use this manual as a personal study guide.

Instructions for Teaching at Church and at Home

In one way or another, everyone is a teacher. Being a teacher is a great opportunity and responsibility. The most important things you will ever teach are the doctrines of Christ as revealed through the scriptures and modern prophets and as confirmed by the Holy Ghost. To do this effectively, you must obtain the Spirit of the Lord. "The Spirit shall be given unto you by the prayer of faith," said the Lord, "and if ye receive not the Spirit ye shall not teach" (D&C 42:14). The Holy Ghost is the real teacher, so it is important to create an environment in which the Lord's Spirit can be present.

You can do many things to bring the Spirit into your class or home. The following suggestions will help you be a better teacher:

• Pray continually for divine understanding and guidance.
• Establish a habit of daily scripture study.
• Testify of the truthfulness of the gospel to your family and friends.
• Let sacred, uplifting music help you focus your thoughts and moods.
• Keep yourself free from sin, repenting when necessary and striving always to improve.
• Express your love to others and to your Heavenly Father.
• Rely on priesthood authority and its power to bless.

Related to these suggestions are some other ways to come unto Christ by drawing upon the Spirit. Consider fasting. It can give you spiritual strength and confidence. Attend the temple as often as possible. Ponder the covenants you have made, the ordinances you have entered into, and the gospel truths you are learning. As you draw close to the Lord, you and those you teach will receive more than mere intellectual understanding; you will receive a knowledge of truth that only the Spirit can give. You will experience the love of God and the benefits of living the gospel, which will greatly enhance your capacity to teach.

Obtain divine knowledge and spiritual guidance through careful study, prayerful preparation, and righteous living. Never speculate about Church doctrine. Teach only what is supported by the scriptures and the Holy Spirit.

Read and teach from the scriptures regularly. Remind those you are teaching to use their scriptures at home and in class. If necessary, obtain extra copies of the scriptures so that all may refer to them. Help others become more familiar and confident with the scriptures. Give scriptural references clearly and, if needed, provide help in finding them. Lesson discussions should lead participants to read and ponder the scriptures personally and with their families each day. Emphasize that the home is the main setting for gospel learning.

Become familiar with the teaching resources in this manual and, if available, the materials in your meetinghouse library. There are visual aids, music, audiovisual materials, general conference addresses, Church magazines, and other resources. Find out what they are and use them when the Spirit impresses you to do so.

As you teach, help others see how gospel principles apply to daily living. Encourage discussions on how these principles can affect our feelings about God, ourselves, our families, and our neighbors. Challenge participants to live according to the principles.

Try to involve as many people as possible in the lessons. You can do this by inviting them to read aloud, answer questions, or share experiences, but do so only when you are sure it will not embarrass them. You may want to make special assignments to class members while preparing the lessons. Be sensitive to the needs and feelings of others. You may need to talk privately with individuals before the lesson and ask how they feel about participating.

Some of the people you teach may need special attention. Be sensitive to those with language, cultural, social, or age differences; hearing, sight, physical, or speech difficulties; or mental, emotional, or learning disabilities. In some cases, you may want to talk with a person's family members or with Church leaders. When appropriate, speak to the person directly about any special concerns.

The Lord's Spirit will be present when love and unity exist. The Lord said, "Where two or three are gathered together in my name, there am I in the midst of them" (Matthew 18:20).

When the Spirit of the Lord is present, you will see significant results. The Lord promised that "every good tree bringeth forth good fruit" (Matthew 7:17). The following list suggests some of the fruits that you and those you teach will enjoy:

• Knowledge and understanding
 The desire to search for eternal truths.
 The desire to live according to the word of God.
 (See D&C 1:37–38.)

• Faith
 The desire to believe.
 The desire to draw closer to God.
 The desire to act in faith.
 (See Alma 22:16; D&C 11:17; 88:63.)

• Prayer
 The desire to worship God.
 The desire to communicate more with him.
 The desire to give thanks.
 The desire to seek direction.
 (See 1 Nephi 15:8; 18:3; Alma 33:1–11; Moroni 10:4–5.)

• Humility
 The desire to submit to the Lord.
 The desire to seek the Lord's will and glory.
 The desire to remove pride.
 (See John 6:38; Mosiah 3:19; Alma 34:38; D&C 5:24, 28.)

• Repentance
 The desire to repair any wrongs against others.
 The desire not to judge.
 The desire to change.
 The desire to acknowledge unworthiness.
 The desire to do good works.
 The desire to live according to the doctrines of Christ.
 (See Alma 26:21–22; 34:32–35; 38:14.)

• Covenants
 The desire to obtain all the saving ordinances.
 The desire to keep and renew covenants through priesthood ordinances.

The desire to obtain spiritual strength and power through priesthood ordinances. (See Ezekiel 11:19–20; D&C 84:19–21; 136:4.)

As you draw close to the Lord, you will find happiness and the fulfillment of Paul's words in Ephesians 4:13–15:

"[We will] come in the unity of the faith, and of the knowledge of the Son of God, unto a perfect man, unto the measure of the stature of the fulness of Christ: that we henceforth be no more children, tossed to and fro, and carried about with every wind of doctrine, by the sleight of men, and cunning craftiness, whereby they lie in wait to deceive; but speaking the truth in love, may grow up into him in all things, which is the head, even Christ."

OUR PREMORTAL
LIFE WITH GOD

Unit One

OUR FATHER IN HEAVEN

Chapter 1

There Is a God
Alma, a Book of Mormon prophet, wrote, "All things denote there is a God; yea, even the earth, and all things that are upon the face of it, yea, and its motion, yea, and also all the planets which move in their regular form do witness that there is a Supreme Creator" (Alma 30:44). We can look up at the sky at night and have an idea of what Alma meant. There are millions of stars and planets all in perfect order. They did not get there by chance. We can see the work of God in the heavens and on the earth. The many beautiful plants, the many kinds of animals, the mountains, the rivers, the clouds that bring us rain and snow—all these testify to us that there is a God.

Discussion
• Have someone read the first article of faith.
• What are some of the things around us that show us there is a God?

God Is the Ruler of Heaven and Earth
The prophets have taught us that God is the almighty ruler of the universe. God dwells in heaven (see D&C 20:17). Through his Son, Jesus Christ, he created heaven and earth and all things that are in them (see Moses 2:1). He made the moon, the stars, and the sun. He organized this world and gave it form, motion, and life. He filled the air and the water with

---

living things. He covered the hills and plains with all kinds of animal life. He gave us day and night, summer and winter, seedtime and harvest. He made man in his own image to be a ruler over his other creations (see Genesis 1:26–27).

Discussion

• Read Mosiah 4:9. What things did God create?

God is the one supreme and absolute being in whom we believe and whom we worship. He is the Creator, Ruler, and Preserver of all things (see *Discourses of Brigham Young,* pp. 18–23).

What Kind of Being Is God?

The Prophet Joseph Smith said: "If the veil were rent today, and the great God who holds this world in its orbit, and who upholds all worlds and all things by his power, was to make himself visible—I say, if you were to see him today, you would see him like a man in form" (*Teachings of the Prophet Joseph Smith,* p. 345). God is a glorified and perfected man, a personage of flesh and bones (see D&C 130:22). Inside his tangible body is an eternal spirit.

God is perfect. He is a God of love, mercy, charity, truth, power, faith, knowledge, and judgment. He has all power. He knows all things. He is full of goodness.

All good things come from God. Everything that he does is to help his children become like him—a god. He has said, "Behold, this is my work and my glory—to bring to pass the immortality and eternal life of man" (Moses 1:39).

Discussion

• Ask class members to read the following scriptural references and discuss what each one teaches about our Heavenly Father: Abraham 3:18–19; John 3:16; Mormon 9:9; 2 Nephi 9:17; Alma 26:35; D&C 109:77.

Why Should We Try to Know God?

Knowing God is so important that the Savior said, "This is life eternal, that they might know thee the only true God, and Jesus Christ, whom thou hast sent" (John 17:3).

The first and greatest commandment tells us, "Thou shalt love the Lord thy God with all thy heart" (Matthew 22:37).

The more we know God, the more we love him and keep his commandments (see 1 John 2:3). By keeping his commandments we can become like him.

Discussion
• Why is it important to know God?

How Can We Know God?

We can know God if we will—

1. Believe that he exists and that he loves us (see Mosiah 4:9).
2. Study the scriptures (see 2 Timothy 3:14–17).
3. Pray to him (see James 1:5).
4. Obey all his commandments as best we can (see John 14:21–23).

As we do these things, we will come to know God and eventually have eternal life.

Discussion
• What are some of the ways we can come to know God?
• How can each of us do these things in our lives?

Additional Scriptures
• Acts 7:55–56 (Son at the right hand of the Father)
• D&C 88:41–44 (qualities of God)
• Psalm 24:1 (the earth is the Lord's)
• Moses 1:30–39 (Creation)
• Alma 7:20 (God cannot do wrong)
• Joseph Smith—History 1:17 (Father and Son are separate)
• Alma 5:40 (good comes from God)
• John 14:6–9 (Son and Father are alike)
• Mormon 9:15–20 (God of miracles)

OUR HEAVENLY FAMILY

Chapter 2

We Are Children of Our Heavenly Father

God is not only our ruler and creator; he is also our Heavenly Father. "All men and women are . . . literally the sons and daughters of Deity. . . . Man, as a spirit, was begotten and born of heavenly parents, and reared to maturity in the eternal mansions of the Father, prior to coming upon the earth in a temporal [physical] body" (Joseph F. Smith, "The Origin of Man," *Improvement Era*, Nov. 1909, pp. 78, 80).

Every person who was ever born on earth was our spirit brother or sister in heaven. The first spirit born to our heavenly parents was Jesus Christ (see D&C 93:21), so he is literally our elder brother (see *Discourses of Brigham Young*, p. 26). Because we are the spiritual children of our heavenly parents, we have inherited the potential to develop their divine qualities. If we choose to do so, we can become perfect, just as they are.

Discussion
• Who is the Father of our spirits?
• Where did we live before we were born on earth?
• What is our relationship to God and to each other? Read Hebrews 12:9.
• Who was the first spirit born to our heavenly parents?
• How are we like our heavenly parents?

Our Father provided us a heavenly home more glorious and beautiful than any place on earth.

We Developed Personalities and Talents While We Lived in Heaven

The scriptures teach us that the prophets prepared themselves to become leaders on earth while they were still spirits in heaven (see Alma 13:1–3). God foreordained (chose) them to be his leaders on earth before they were born into mortal bodies. Jesus, Adam, and Abraham were some of these leaders. (See Abraham 3:22–23.) Joseph Smith taught that everyone who has a calling to lead people on earth in the Church was foreordained to do so (see *Teachings of the Prophet Joseph Smith,* p. 365). However, everyone is free on earth to accept or reject the calling.

We were not all alike in heaven. We were given different talents and abilities, and we were called to do different things on earth. (See *Discourses of Brigham Young,* p. 51.) We can learn more about our talents and callings when we receive our patriarchal blessings (see Harold B. Lee, *Stand Ye in Holy Places,* p. 117).

Even though we have forgotten, our Father in Heaven remembers who we were and what we did before we came here (see *Discourses of Brigham Young,* p. 50). He has chosen the time and place for each of us to be born so we can learn the lessons we personally need and do the most good with our individual talents and personalities.

Discussion
• What was our premortal life like?

Our Heavenly Parents Desired to Share Their Joy with Us

Our heavenly parents provided us with a celestial home more glorious and beautiful than any place on earth. We were happy there. Yet they knew we could not progress beyond a certain point unless we left them for a time. They wanted us to develop the godlike qualities that they have. To do this, we needed to leave our celestial home to be tested and to gain experience. We needed to choose good over evil. Our spirits needed to be clothed with physical bodies. We would need to leave our physical bodies at death and reunite with them in the Resurrection. Then we would receive immortal bodies like those of our heavenly parents. If we passed our tests, we would receive the fulness of joy that our heavenly parents have received. (See D&C 93:30–34.)

Discussion

• How does earth life help prepare us to become like our heavenly parents?

Our Heavenly Father Presented a Plan for Us to Become like Him

Since we could not progress further in heaven, our Heavenly Father called a Grand Council to present his plan for our progression (see *Teachings of the Prophet Joseph Smith,* pp. 348, 349, 365). We learned that if we followed his plan, we would become like him. We would have a resurrected body; we would have all power in heaven and on earth; we would become heavenly parents and have spirit children just as he does (see D&C 132:19–20).

We learned that he would provide an earth for us where we would be tested (see Abraham 3:24–26). A veil would cover our memories, and we would forget our heavenly home. This would be necessary so we could choose good or evil without being influenced by the memory of living with our Heavenly Father. Thus we could obey him because of our faith in him, not because of our knowledge or memory of him. He would help us recognize the truth when we heard it again on earth (see John 18:37).

At the Grand Council we also learned the purpose for our progression: to have a fulness of joy. However, we also learned that not all of our Father's children would want to receive a fulness of joy. Some of us would be deceived, choose other paths, and lose our way. We learned that all of us would have trials in our lives: sickness, disappointment, pain, sorrow, and death. But we understood that these would be given to us for our experience and our good (see D&C 122:7). If we allowed them to, these trials would purify us rather than defeat us. They would teach us to have endurance, patience, and charity (see Spencer W. Kimball, *Faith Precedes the Miracle,* pp. 97–98).

At this council we also learned that because of our weakness, all of us would sin. We learned that a Savior would be provided for us so we could overcome our sins and overcome death with resurrection. We learned that if we placed our faith in him, obeying his word and following his example, we would be exalted and become like our heavenly parents. We would receive a fulness of joy.

Discussion

• What plan did our Heavenly Father present to us?
• What did we learn would happen to us on earth?
• Why would our Father in Heaven permit us to experience suffering and death on earth?

Additional Scriptures

• Hebrews 12:9 (God is the father of our spirits)
• Job 38:4–7 (premortal life implied)
• Abraham 3:22–28 (vision of premortal life)
• Jeremiah 1:5 (vision of premortal life)
• D&C 29:31–38 (vision of premortal life)
• Moses 3:4–7 (spiritual then temporal creations)
• 1 Corinthians 15:44 (spiritual and temporal creations)
• D&C 76:23–24 (begotten sons and daughters)
• D&C 132:11–26 (plan for progression)

Under Heavenly Father's direction,
Jehovah (Jesus Christ) created the earth.

JESUS CHRIST, OUR CHOSEN LEADER AND SAVIOR

Chapter 3

A Savior and Leader Was Needed

When the plan for our salvation was presented to us in the spirit world, we were so happy that we shouted for joy (see Job 38:7).

We understood that we would have to leave our heavenly home for a time. We would not live in the presence of our heavenly parents. While we were away from them, all of us would sin and some of us would lose our way. Our Heavenly Father knew and loved each one of us. He knew we would need help, so he planned a way to help us.

We needed a Savior to pay for our sins and teach us how to return to our Heavenly Father. Our Father said, "Whom shall I send?" (Abraham 3:27). Two of our brothers offered to help. Our oldest brother, Jesus Christ, who was then called Jehovah, said, "Here am I, send me" (Abraham 3:27).

Jesus was willing to come to the earth, give his life for us, and take upon himself our sins. He, like our Heavenly Father, wanted us to choose whether we would obey Heavenly Father's commandments. He knew we must be free to choose in order to prove ourselves worthy of exaltation. Jesus said, "Father, thy will be done, and the glory be thine forever" (Moses 4:2).

Satan, who was called Lucifer, also came, saying, *"Behold, here am I, send me, I will be thy son, and I will redeem all mankind, that one soul shall not be lost, and surely I will do it; wherefore give me thine honor"* (Moses 4:1). Satan wanted to force us all to do his will. Under his plan, we would not be allowed to choose. He would take away the freedom of choice that our Father had given us. Satan wanted to have all the honor for our salvation.

Discussion
• Who is our leader and Savior?
• Who besides Jesus wanted to be our leader?

Jesus Christ Became Our Chosen Leader and Savior
After hearing both sons speak, Heavenly Father said, *"I will send the first"* (Abraham 3:27).

Jesus Christ was chosen and ordained to be our Savior. Many scriptures tell about this. One scripture tells us that long before Jesus was born, he appeared to the brother of Jared, a Book of Mormon prophet, and said: *"Behold, I am he who was prepared from the foundation of the world to redeem my people. Behold, I am Jesus Christ. . . . In me shall all mankind have life, and that eternally, even they who shall believe on my name"* (Ether 3:14).

When Jesus lived on earth, he taught: *"I came down from heaven, not to do mine own will, but the will of him that sent me. . . . And this is the will of him that sent me, that every one which seeth the Son, and believeth on him, may have everlasting life: and I will raise him up at the last day"* (John 6:38, 40).

Discussion
• Ask each person to tell something about Jesus.

The War in Heaven
Because our Heavenly Father chose Jesus Christ to be our Savior, Satan became angry and rebelled. There was war in heaven. Satan and his followers fought against Jesus and his followers.

In this great rebellion, Satan and all the spirits who followed him were sent away from the presence of God and cast down from heaven. One-third of the spirits in heaven were punished for following Satan: they were denied the right to receive mortal bodies.

Because we are here on earth and have mortal bodies, we know that we chose to follow Jesus Christ and our Heavenly Father. Satan and his followers are also on the earth, but as spirits. They have not forgotten who we are, and they are around us daily, tempting us and enticing us to do things that are not pleasing to our Heavenly Father. In our premortal life, we chose the right. We must continue to choose the right here on earth. Only by following Jesus can we return to our heavenly home.

Discussion
• How do we know that we chose to follow Jesus?

We Have the Savior's Teachings to Follow
From the beginning, Jesus Christ has revealed the gospel, which tells us what we must do to return to our Heavenly Father. At the appointed time he came to earth himself. He taught the plan of salvation and exaltation by his word and by the way he lived. He established his Church and his priesthood on the earth. He took our sins upon himself.

By following the Lord's teachings, we can return to live with him and our heavenly parents in the celestial kingdom. He was chosen to be our Savior when we all attended the great council with our heavenly parents. When he became our Savior, he did his part to help us return to our heavenly home. It is now up to each of us to do our part and become worthy of exaltation.

Discussion
• What are some of the things we must do to follow Jesus?
• Bear testimony of the Savior.

Additional Scriptures
- Moses 4:1–4 (Council in Heaven)
- Abraham 3:22–28 (Council in Heaven)
- D&C 76:24–29 (War in Heaven)
- Revelation 12:7–9 (War in Heaven)
- Isaiah 14:12–15 (why Lucifer was cast out)
- 2 Nephi 9:6–26; 3 Nephi 27:13–20 (purpose of the Atonement)

FREEDOM TO CHOOSE

Chapter 4

"Thou mayest choose for thyself, for it is given unto thee" (Moses 3:17).

God has told us through his prophets that we are free to choose between good and evil. We may choose liberty and eternal life by following Jesus Christ. We are also free to choose captivity and death by following Satan. (See 2 Nephi 2:27.) The right to choose between good and evil is called *agency.*

Agency Is an Eternal Principle

In the premortal life we were free agents. That means we had power to act for ourselves (see D&C 93:29–30). One purpose of earth life is to show what choices we will make (see 2 Nephi 2:15–16). If we were forced to choose the right, we would not be able to show what we would choose for ourselves. Also, we are happier doing things when we have made our own choices.

Agency may have been one of the first issues to arise in the premortal council in heaven. It was one of the main causes of the conflict between the followers of Christ and the followers of Satan. Satan said he would bring all of us back to our Father's presence, but he would have taken away our agency. When his offer was rejected, he rebelled and was cast out of heaven with his followers (see D&C 29:36–37).

Discussion
- Ask class members to compare the feelings the words *force* and *choice* bring to mind.

Agency Is a Necessary Part of the Plan of Salvation

Agency makes our life on earth a period of testing. When planning the mortal creation of man, God said, "We will prove [test] them herewith, to see if they will do all things whatsoever the Lord their God shall command them" (Abraham 3:25). Without the gift of agency, we would have been unable to show our Heavenly Father whether we would do all that he commanded us. Because we are able to choose, we are responsible for our actions (see Helaman 14:30–31).

When we choose to live according to God's plan for us, our agency is strengthened. Right choices increase our power to make more right choices.

As we obey each of our Father's commandments, we grow in wisdom and strength of character. Our faith increases. We find it easier to make right choices.

We began to make choices as spirit children in our Heavenly Father's presence. Our choices there made us worthy to come to earth. Our Heavenly Father wants us to grow in faith, power, knowledge, wisdom, and all other good things. If we keep his commandments and make right choices, we will learn and understand. We will become like him. (See D&C 93:28.)

Discussion
- Read Moses 3:17 and Joshua 24:14–15. What choices have you made this week? Did these choices bring you closer to the Lord?
- Why is agency necessary?
- Read 2 Nephi 28:30. How does making right choices help us make more right choices?

Agency Requires That There Be a Choice

We cannot choose unless the opposites of good and evil are placed before us. Lehi, a great Book of Mormon prophet, told his son that in order to bring about the eternal purposes of God, there must be "an opposition in all things. If not so, . . . righteousness could not be brought to pass, neither wickedness, neither holiness nor misery, neither good nor bad" (2 Nephi 2:11).

God allows Satan to oppose the good. God said of Satan:

"I caused that he should be cast down;

"And he became Satan, yea, even the devil, the father of all lies, to deceive and to blind men, and to lead them captive at his will, even as many as would not hearken unto my voice" (Moses 4:3–4).

Satan does all he can to destroy God's work. He seeks "the misery of all mankind, . . . for he seeketh that all men might be miserable like unto himself" (2 Nephi 2:18, 27). He does not love us. He does not want any good thing for us. He does not want us to be happy. He wants to make us his slaves. He uses many disguises to capture us.

When we follow the temptations of Satan, we limit our choices. The following example suggests how this works. Imagine seeing a sign on the seashore that reads: "Danger — whirlpool. No swimming allowed here." We might think that is a restriction. But is it? We still have many choices. We are free to swim somewhere else. We are free to walk along the beach and pick up seashells. We are free to watch the sunset. We are free to go home. We are also free to ignore the sign and swim in the dangerous place. But once the whirlpool has us in its grasp and we are pulled under, we have very few choices. We can try to escape, or we can call for help, but we may drown.

Even though we are free to choose our course of action, we are not free to choose the consequences of our actions. The consequences, whether good or bad, follow as a natural result of any choice we make (see Revelation 22:12). If we touch a hot flame, for example, we are burned.

Heavenly Father has told us how to escape the captivity of Satan. We must watch and pray always, asking God to help us withstand the temptations of Satan (see 3 Nephi 18:15). Our Heavenly Father will not allow us to be tempted beyond our power to resist (see 1 Corinthians 10:13).

God's commandments direct us away from danger and toward eternal life. By choosing wisely, we will gain exaltation, progress eternally, and enjoy perfect happiness (see 2 Nephi 2:27–28).

Discussion
- Place a treat within the reach of someone. Loosely wrap a cord around him, binding his arms to his body. Ask him if he can reach the treat. Tighten the cord so the person is bound. Explain that sin and ignorance also interfere with agency and prevent us from receiving blessings from God. Discuss how repentance and righteous living free us from the bondage of sin.
- Why is opposition necessary? See 2 Nephi 2:15–16.
- Read 2 Nephi 2:28. How can you choose eternal life?

Additional Scriptures
- Moses 7:32 (freedom of choice)
- Abraham 3:24–25 (earth life a test)
- Moroni 7:5–6 (works judged)
- 2 Nephi 2:11–16 (opposition is necessary)
- Moroni 7:12–17 (choosing good and evil)
- 2 Peter 2:19; John 8:34 (sin is bondage)
- 2 Nephi 2:28–29; Alma 40:12–13 (reward according to works)

LEAVING THE PRESENCE OF GOD

Unit Two

Jehovah created a beautiful world for us.

THE CREATION

When we lived as spirit children with our heavenly parents, our Heavenly Father told us about his plan for us to become more like him. We shouted for joy when we heard his plan (see Job 38:7). We were eager for new experiences. In order for these things to happen, we needed to leave our Father's presence and receive mortal bodies. We needed another place to live where we could prepare to become like him. Our new home was called *earth.*

Who Created the Earth for Us?

Jesus Christ created this world and everything in it. He also created many other worlds. He did so through the power of the priesthood, under the direction of our Heavenly Father. God the Father said, "Worlds without number have I created; . . . and by the Son I created them, which is mine Only Begotten" (Moses 1:33). We have other testimonies of this truth. Joseph Smith and Sidney Rigdon saw Jesus Christ in a vision. They testified "that by him, and through him, and of him, the worlds are and were created, and the inhabitants thereof are begotten sons and daughters unto God" (D&C 76:24).

Discussion
• Who created the earth? Read Hebrews 1:1–2 and Moses 1:33.

Carrying Out the Creation

The earth and everything on it were created spiritually before they were created physically (see Moses 3:5). In planning to create the physical earth, Christ said to those who were with him, "We will go down, for there is space there, . . . and we will make an earth whereon these [the spirit children of our Father in Heaven] may dwell" (Abraham 3:24).

Under the direction of the Father, Christ formed and organized the earth. He divided light from darkness to make day and night. He formed the sun, moon, and stars. He divided the waters from the dry land to make seas, rivers, and lakes. He made the earth beautiful and productive. He made grass, trees, flowers, and other plants of all kinds. These plants contained seeds from which new plants could grow. Then he created the animals—fish, cattle, insects, and birds of all kinds. These animals had the ability to reproduce their own kind.

Now the earth was ready for the greatest creation of all—mankind. Our spirits would be given bodies of flesh and blood so they could live on earth. "And I, God, said unto mine Only Begotten, which was with me from the beginning: Let us make man in our image, after our likeness; and it was so" (Moses 2:26). And so the first man, Adam, and the first woman, Eve, were formed and given bodies that resembled those of our heavenly parents. "In the image of God created he him; male and female created he them" (Genesis 1:27). When the Lord finished his creations, he was pleased and knew that his work was good, and he rested for a time.

Discussion
• Show a food recipe or a dress pattern. What is another word for *recipe* and *pattern*? (*Plan*.) Read Abraham 3:24 to show that God plans for all of his creations.

God's Creations Show His Love

We are now living in this beautiful world. Think of the sun, which gives us warmth and light. Think of the rain, which makes plants grow and makes the world feel clean and fresh. Think of how good it is to hear a bird singing or a friend laughing. Think of how wonderful our bodies are—how we can work and play and rest. When we consider all of these creations, we begin to understand what wise, powerful, and loving beings Jesus Christ and our Heavenly Father are. They have shown great love for us by providing for all of our needs.

Plant life and animal life were also made to give us joy. The Lord said, "Yea, all things which come of the earth, in the season thereof, are made for the benefit and the use of man, both to please the eye and to gladden the heart; yea, for food and for raiment, for taste and for smell, to strengthen the body and to enliven the soul" (D&C 59:18–19). Even though God's creations are many, he knows and loves them all. He said, "All things are numbered unto me, for they are mine and I know them" (Moses 1:35).

Discussion

• Discuss how we can show reverence for plants and animals.
• Discuss the purpose of God's creations (see D&C 59:18–19).
• How do God's creations show that he loves us?
• To help develop an appreciation for the beauty of God's creations, you might do the following activities for home evenings: plan a picnic, plant a garden, take a nature walk, enjoy a sunrise or sunset.

Additional Scriptures

• Genesis 1:1–2:7; Abraham 3:22–23 and chapters 4–5; Moses 1:27–42 and chapters 2–3 (accounts of the Creation)
• Hebrews 1:1–3; Colossians 1:13–17; D&C 38:1–3 (Jesus the Creator)
• D&C 59:18–20; Moses 2:26–31; D&C 104:13–17; Matthew 6:25–26 (Creation shows God's love)

Adam and Eve kneeling at an altar.

THE FALL OF ADAM AND EVE

Chapter 6

Adam and Eve Were the First to Come to Earth

God prepared this earth as a home for his children. Adam and Eve were chosen to be the first people to live on the earth (see Moses 1:34). Their part in our Father's plan was to bring mortality into the world. They were to be the first parents. (See D&C 107:54–56.)

Discussion

• Read D&C 107:54–56. Who was Adam? What was he chosen to do?

Adam and Eve Were Valiant Spirits

Adam and Eve were among our Father's noblest children. In the spirit world Adam was called Michael the Archangel (see D&C 27:11; Jude 1:9). He was chosen by our Heavenly Father to lead the righteous in the battle against Satan (see Revelation 12:7–9). Adam and Eve were foreordained to become the parents of the human race. The Lord promised Adam great blessings: "I have set thee to be at the head; a multitude of nations shall come of thee, and thou art a prince over them forever" (D&C 107:55).

Although the scriptures do not tell us anything about Eve before she came to earth, she must have been a choice daughter of God. She was called Eve because she was the mother of all living (see Moses 4:26). She was given to Adam because

God said *"*it was not good that the man should be alone*"* (Moses 3:18). She shared Adam's responsibility and will also share his eternal blessings.

Discussion

• Read Revelation 12:7–9. How did Adam (Michael) prove that he was a valiant spirit?
• Why was Eve given to Adam?

The Garden of Eden

When Adam and Eve were placed in the Garden of Eden, they were not yet mortal. They were not able to have children. There was no death. They had *physical* life because their spirits were housed in physical bodies made from the dust of the earth (see Abraham 5:7). They had *spiritual* life because they were in the presence of God (see Bruce R. McConkie, *Mormon Doctrine,* p. 268). They had not yet made a choice between good and evil.

God commanded them to have children and to learn to control the earth. He said, *"*Be fruitful, and multiply, and replenish the earth, and subdue it, and have dominion over . . . every living thing that moveth upon the earth*"* (Moses 2:28). God told them they could freely eat of every tree in the garden except one, the tree of knowledge of good and evil. Of that tree God said, *"*In the day thou eatest thereof thou shalt surely die*"* (Moses 3:17).

Satan, not knowing the mind of God but seeking to destroy God's plan, came to Eve in the Garden of Eden. He tempted her to eat of the fruit of the tree of knowledge of good and evil. He assured her that she would not die, but that she would *"*be as gods, knowing good and evil*"* (Moses 4:11). Eve yielded to the temptation and ate the fruit. When Adam learned what had happened, he chose to partake also. The changes that came upon Adam and Eve because they ate the fruit are called the *Fall.*

Discussion
- Read <u>Moses 4:6–32</u>. How was the Garden of Eden different from the world as we know it?
- Discuss the conditions of Adam and Eve in the Garden of Eden.

Adam and Eve's Separation from God

Because Adam and Eve had eaten the fruit of the tree of knowledge of good and evil, the Lord sent them out of the Garden of Eden into the world as we now know it. Their physical condition changed as a result of their eating the forbidden fruit. As God had promised, they became mortal. They were able to have children. They and their children would experience sickness, pain, and physical death.

Because of their transgression, Adam and Eve also suffered spiritual death. This meant they and their children could not walk and talk face to face with God. Because Satan had introduced evil into the world, Adam and Eve and their children were separated from God both physically and spiritually.

Discussion
- As a result of their transgression, what physical change occurred in Adam and Eve? What spiritual change occurred?
- Read <u>Moses 5:1–5</u>. What was life like for Adam and Eve outside the Garden of Eden?

Great Blessings Resulted from the Transgression

Some people believe Adam and Eve committed a serious sin when they ate of the tree of knowledge of good and evil. However, latter-day scriptures help us understand that their fall was a necessary step in the plan of life and a great blessing to all of us. Because of the Fall, we are blessed with physical bodies, the right to choose between good and evil, and the opportunity to gain eternal life. None of these privileges would have been ours had Adam and Eve remained in the garden.

After the Fall, Eve said, "Were it not for our transgression we never should have had seed [children], and never should have known good and evil, and the joy of our redemption, and the eternal life which God giveth unto all the obedient" (Moses 5:11).

The prophet Lehi explained:

"And now, behold, if Adam had not transgressed he would not have fallen [been cut off from the presence of God], but he would have remained in the Garden of Eden. And all things which were created must have remained in the same state in which they were after they were created; . . .

"And they would have had no children; wherefore they would have remained in a state of innocence, having no joy, for they knew no misery; doing no good, for they knew no sin.

"But behold, all things have been done in the wisdom of him who knoweth all things.

"Adam fell that men might be; and men are, that they might have joy" (2 Nephi 2:22–25).

Discussion
- Read Moses 5:6–12. After the Fall, how did Adam and Eve feel about their transgression and the Lord's promise to redeem them?

Additional Scriptures
- 1 Nephi 5:11; 2 Nephi 2:20 (Adam and Eve first parents, family)
- 2 Nephi 2:14–21 (opposition and the Fall; life a probation)
- 2 Nephi 2:22–26 (Fall part of the plan of salvation)

COMMUNICATION BETWEEN GOD AND MAN

Unit Three

THE HOLY GHOST

Chapter 7

After Adam and Eve left the Garden of Eden, they began to till the earth and work at other tasks for their living. They had many children, and their sons and daughters also married and had children (see Moses 5:1–3). Thus, spirit children of our Heavenly Father began leaving his presence to come to the earth as they had been promised. As they came to earth, the memory of their heavenly home was taken from them. But our Father did not shut them away from his influence. He sent the Holy Ghost to comfort and help and guide all of his spirit children.

Why Did the Holy Ghost Come to Adam?

Adam and Eve called upon Heavenly Father in prayer. He spoke to them and gave them commandments, which they obeyed. (See Moses 5:4–5.) An angel of the Lord came and taught Adam and Eve the plan of salvation. The Lord sent the Holy Ghost to testify of the Father and of the Son and to teach Adam and Eve the gospel (see Moses 5:9).

Through the power of the Holy Ghost, Adam "began to prophesy concerning all the families of the earth, saying: Blessed be the name of God, for because of my transgression my eyes are opened, and in this life I shall have joy, and again in the flesh I shall see God" (Moses 5:10). Because of the witness of the Holy Ghost to Eve, she said, "Were it not for our transgression we never should have had seed, and never should have known good and evil, and the joy of our redemption, and the eternal life which God giveth unto all the obedient" (Moses 5:11).

Discussion
• Read the account of the Holy Ghost being sent to Adam and Eve (see Moses 5:4–11).
• Discuss why the Holy Ghost was sent to them.

Who Is the Holy Ghost?
The Holy Ghost is a member of the Godhead (see 1 John 5:7; D&C 20:28). He is a spirit that has the form and likeness of a man (see D&C 130:22). He can be in only one place at a time, but his influence can be everywhere at the same time.

Heavenly Father, Jesus Christ, and the Holy Ghost are called the *Godhead.* They are unified in purpose. Each has an important assignment in the plan of salvation. Our Heavenly Father is our Father and ruler. Jesus Christ is our Savior. The Holy Ghost is the revealer and testifier of all truth.

The Holy Ghost is our Heavenly Father's messenger and is a special gift to us. How we can receive the Holy Ghost will be discussed in chapter 21.

Discussion
• Read D&C 130:22. Discuss how the Holy Ghost differs from the Father and the Son.
• How are the Father, Son, and Holy Ghost one? To answer, use the example of a father, mother, and children working for one same purpose. Relate examples.
• How can the influence of the Holy Ghost be in many places at one time? To answer, compare the Holy Ghost to the sun. There is just one sun, but its light and warmth are felt by everyone on earth.

Why Is the Holy Ghost Necessary?
The mission of the Holy Ghost is to bear witness of the Father and the Son and of the truth of all things.

The Holy Ghost will witness to us that Jesus is our Savior and Redeemer (see 3 Nephi 28:11; D&C 20:27; Hebrews 10:15). He will reveal to us that our Heavenly Father is the Father of our spirits. He will help us understand that we can become exalted like our Heavenly Father. (See Romans 8:16–17.) The prophets of the Lord have promised, "By the power of the Holy Ghost ye may know the truth of all things" (Moroni 10:5).

Without the Holy Ghost, we could not know that Jesus is the Christ. The Apostle Paul wrote, "No man can say that Jesus is the Lord, but by the Holy Ghost" (1 Corinthians 12:3). The Savior himself said, "And this is life eternal, that they might know thee the only true God, and Jesus Christ, whom thou hast sent" (John 17:3). It is by the power of the Holy Ghost that we are led to understand and live the gospel of Jesus Christ.

The convincing power of the Holy Ghost is so great that there can be no doubt that what it reveals to us is true. President Joseph Fielding Smith said:

"When a man has the manifestation from the Holy Ghost, it leaves an indelible impression on his soul, one that is not easily erased. It is Spirit speaking to spirit, and it comes with convincing force. A manifestation of an angel, or even the Son of God himself, would impress the eye and mind, and eventually become dimmed, but the impressions of the Holy Ghost sink deeper into the soul and are more difficult to erase" (*Answers to Gospel Questions,* 2:151).

President Smith also said, "Through the Holy Ghost the truth is woven into the very fibre and sinews of the body so that it cannot be forgotten" (*Doctrines of Salvation,* 1:48).

As members of The Church of Jesus Christ of Latter-day Saints, we should make ourselves worthy to receive this special messenger and witness of our Heavenly Father and Jesus Christ.

Discussion
- Why is the Holy Ghost necessary? Read again the statement by President Joseph Fielding Smith.
- Encourage the members to tell how they felt when the Holy Ghost bore witness to them of the truthfulness of the gospel.

Additional Scriptures
- Moses 5 (story of Adam's family)
- 2 Nephi 31:21 (Holy Ghost identified)
- Moroni 10:6–7 (Holy Ghost will witness of Jesus Christ)
- John 14:26; 15:26; 16:13; Luke 12:12; D&C 8:2–3; 11:12–13; 20:26 (Holy Ghost as comforter, teacher, testator of Christ, guide to all truth, revelator, companion, leader, guide, source of inspiration)

We should pray individually and as families morning and night.

PRAYING TO OUR HEAVENLY FATHER

Chapter 8

Jesus taught, "Ye must always pray unto the Father in my name" (3 Nephi 18:19).

Prayer is one of the greatest blessings we have while we are here on earth. Through prayer we can communicate with our Heavenly Father and seek his guidance daily.

What Is Prayer?

Prayer is a sincere, heartfelt talk with our Heavenly Father. We should pray to God and to no one else. We do not pray to any other being or to anything made by man or God (see Exodus 20:3–5).

Why Do We Pray?

Prayer has been an important part of the gospel from the beginning of the world. An angel of the Lord commanded Adam and Eve to repent and call upon God in the name of the Son (see Moses 5:8). This commandment has never been taken away. Nothing will help us draw closer to God than prayer. All of our thoughts, our words, and our actions are influenced by our prayers.

We should pray for strength to resist the temptations of Satan and his followers (see 3 Nephi 18:15; D&C 10:5). We should pray to confess our sins to God and ask him to forgive us (see Alma 38:14).

We should pray for the Lord's guidance and help in our daily lives. We need to pray for our families and friends, our neighbors, our crops and our animals, our daily work, and our other activities. We should pray for protection from our enemies. (See Alma 34:17–25.)

We should pray to express love to our Heavenly Father and to feel closer to him. We should pray to our Father to thank him for our welfare and comfort and for all things he gives us each day (see 1 Thessalonians 5:18). We need to pray to ask our Heavenly Father for strength to live the gospel.

We should pray so we can keep on the straight and narrow path that leads to eternal life. We must pray to God, the author of all righteousness, so we may be righteous in our thoughts, words, and actions.

Discussion
• How has prayer helped you grow closer to our Heavenly Father?
• Tell the story of Daniel to the class (see Daniel 6:1–23).
• How did Daniel pray?
• How important was prayer to Daniel?

When Should We Pray?
We can pray whenever we feel the need to communicate with our Heavenly Father, whether silently or vocally. Sometimes we need to be alone where we can pour out our souls to him (see Matthew 6:6). In addition, we can pray during our daily activities. We can pray while we are in a Church meeting, in our house, walking down a path or street, working, preparing a meal, or wherever we may be and whatever we may be doing. We can pray any time of the day or night. We can pray when we are alone or when we are with other people. We can keep our Heavenly Father in our thoughts at all times (see Alma 34:27).

At times we may not feel like praying. We may be angry or discouraged or upset. At these times we should make a special effort to pray.

We should each pray privately at least every night and every morning. The scriptures speak of praying morning, midday, and evening (see Alma 34:21).

We are commanded to have family prayers so that our families may be blessed (see 3 Nephi 18:21). Our Church leaders have counseled us to pray as families each morning and night.

We also have the privilege of praying to give thanks and ask a blessing on the food before each meal.

We open and close all of our Church meetings with prayer. We thank the Lord for his blessings and ask for his help so we may worship in a manner that pleases him.

Discussion
• Ask someone to read the story of Enos (see Enos 1:1–12).
• What words did Enos use to describe how he prayed?

How Should We Pray?
No matter where we are, whether we stand or kneel, whether we pray vocally or silently, whether we pray privately or in behalf of a group, we should always pray in faith, "with a sincere heart, with real intent" (Moroni 10:4).

As we pray to our Heavenly Father, we should tell him what we really feel in our hearts, confide in him, ask him for forgiveness, plead with him, thank him, express our love for him. We should not repeat meaningless words and phrases (see Matthew 6:7–8). We should always ask that his will be done, remembering that what we desire may not be best for us (see 3 Nephi 18:20). At the end of our prayer, we close in the name of Jesus Christ (see 3 Nephi 18:19).

How Are Prayers Answered?
Our sincere prayers are always answered. Sometimes the answer may be no, because what we have asked for would not

be best for us. Sometimes the answer is yes, and we have a warm, comfortable feeling about what we should do (see D&C 9:8–9). Sometimes the answer is "wait a while." Our prayers are always answered at a time and in a way that the Lord knows will help us the most.

Sometimes the Lord answers our prayers through other people. A good friend, a husband or wife, a parent or other family member, a Church leader, a missionary—any of these individuals may be inspired to perform acts that will answer our prayers. An example of this is the experience of a young mother whose baby was injured in an accident at home. She had no way to get the baby to a doctor. She was new in the neighborhood and did not know her neighbors. The young mother prayed for help. In a few minutes, a neighbor lady came to the door, saying, "I had a feeling I should come and see if you needed any help." The neighbor helped the young mother get the baby to a doctor.

Often God gives us the power to help answer our own prayers. As we pray for help, we should do all we can to bring about the things we desire.

As we live the gospel of Jesus Christ and pray always, we will have joy and happiness. "Be thou humble; and the Lord thy God shall lead thee by the hand, and give thee answer to thy prayers" (D&C 112:10).

Discussion
• Are we always given what we ask for? Why not?
• Read D&C 46:30. Why is it important to pray "if it be thy will"?
• Ask members to share experiences of when and how the Lord has answered their prayers.
• Close with your own testimony of prayer.
• Encourage prayers in the family, blessings on the food, and individual prayer.

Additional Scriptures

- James 1:5 (what to pray for)
- 1 Thessalonians 5:17; Psalm 55:17; 2 Nephi 32:9 (when to pray)
- Alma 34:26 (where to pray)
- 3 Nephi 19:6, 24; 1 Timothy 4:15 (how to pray)
- D&C 88:63–65 (how prayers are answered)
- Moroni 10:3–5; Alma 37:37 (promises for prayer)

Joseph Smith

Brigham Young

John Taylor

Wilford Woodruff

Lorenzo Snow

Joseph F. Smith

Heber J. Grant

George Albert Smith

David O. McKay

Joseph Fielding Smith

Harold B. Lee

Spencer W. Kimball

Howard W
Hunter
6-94

Ezra Taft Benson

The Lord has sent prophets in our own day.

PROPHETS
OF GOD

Chapter 9

"Surely the Lord God will do nothing, but he revealeth his secret unto his servants the prophets" (Amos 3:7).

Many people live in darkness, unsure of God's will. They believe that the heavens are closed and that people must face the world's perils alone. How fortunate are the latter-day Saints! We know that God communicates to the Church through his prophet. With grateful hearts, Saints the world over sing the hymn, "We thank thee, O God, for a prophet to guide us in these latter days."

Discussion
• Who is the prophet who guides us? What are his powers and gifts? How can we sustain him?

What Is a Prophet?

A prophet is a man called by God to be his representative on earth. When a prophet speaks for God, it is as if God were speaking. A prophet is also a special witness for Christ, testifying of His divinity and teaching His gospel. A prophet teaches truth and interprets the word of God. He calls the unrighteous to repentance. He receives revelations and directions from the Lord for our benefit. He may see into the future and foretell coming events so that the world may be warned.

A prophet may come from various stations in life. He may be young or old, highly educated or unschooled. He may be a farmer, a lawyer, or a teacher. Ancient prophets wore tunics and carried staffs. Modern prophets wear suits and carry briefcases. What, then, identifies a true prophet? A true prophet is always chosen by God and called through proper priesthood authority.

Latter-day Saints sustain the First Presidency and the Twelve Apostles as prophets. However, when we speak of "the prophet of the Church," we mean the President of the Church, who is President of the high priesthood.

Through the Ages God Has Called Prophets to Lead Mankind

There have been prophets on the earth since the days of Adam. Experiences of these great men excite and inspire us. Moses, an Old Testament prophet, led thousands of his people out of Egypt and slavery into the promised land. He wrote the first five books of the Old Testament and recorded the Ten Commandments. Nephi, a Book of Mormon prophet, sailed from Jerusalem to the American continent about six hundred years before the birth of Christ. This great leader and colonizer gave us many important writings in the Book of Mormon. John the Baptist was chosen to prepare the world for the coming of the Lord Jesus Christ. Through Joseph Smith, a latter-day prophet, the Lord restored the Church. Joseph Smith also translated the Book of Mormon while a young man.

Discussion
• What is a prophet?
• What power does he have?
• What does he do?
• What office does he hold in the Church?

We Have a Living Prophet on the Earth Today

We have a prophet living on the earth today. This prophet is the President of The Church of Jesus Christ of Latter-day Saints. He has the right to revelation for the entire Church. He holds the "keys of the kingdom," meaning that he has the right to control the administration of the ordinances (see Matthew 16:19). No person except the chosen prophet and president can receive God's will for the membership of the Church.

We should do those things the prophets tell us to do. President Wilford Woodruff said that a prophet will never be allowed to lead the Church astray:

"I say to Israel, the Lord will never permit me or any other man who stands as president of this Church to lead you astray. It is not in the program. It is not in the mind of God. If I were to attempt that the Lord would remove me out of my place, and so he will any other man who attempts to lead the children of men astray from the oracles of God and from their duty. God bless you" (*The Discourses of Wilford Woodruff*, pp. 212–13).

Discussion
• Ask class members to name as many prophets as they can.
• Have a class member tell about the living prophet of the Church.

We Should Sustain the Lord's Prophet
Many people find it easy to believe in the prophets of the past. But it is much greater to believe in and follow the living prophet. We raise our hands to sustain the President of the Church as prophet, seer, and revelator.

How can we sustain the prophet? We should pray for him. His burdens are heavy, and he needs to be strengthened by the prayers of the Saints.

We should study his words. We can listen to his conference addresses or read them in Church publications.

We should follow his inspired teachings completely. We should not choose to follow part of his inspired counsel and discard that which is unpleasant or difficult. The Lord commanded us to follow the inspired teachings of his prophet:

*Thou shalt give heed unto all his [the prophet's] words and commandments which he shall give unto you as he receiveth them, walking in all holiness before me;

"For his word ye shall receive, as if from mine own mouth, in all patience and faith* (D&C 21:4–5).

The Lord will never allow the President of the Church to lead us astray.

Discussion
• Discuss what we can do to follow and sustain the prophet.
• Where can we learn of his counsel today?

Great Blessings Follow Obedience to the Prophet
If we obey, the Lord promises, *The gates of hell shall not prevail against you; yea, and the Lord God will disperse the powers of darkness from before you; and cause the heavens to shake for your good, and his name's glory* (D&C 21:6).

When we do as our prophet directs, blessings pour down from heaven. A story from the life of Lorenzo Snow, the fifth president of the restored Church, shows how God rewards his people for their obedience. In those days the Church was suffering great financial trouble and had little money to pay its debts. Then more trouble came. A great drought afflicted many of the Saints. President Snow went to the Lord and prayed for relief. One day as the prophet was speaking in the St. George Tabernacle in Utah, the Holy Ghost inspired him to promise the Saints that they would receive rain if they would pay a full tithe. He quoted Malachi: *Bring ye all the tithes into the storehouse, . . . and prove me now herewith, saith the Lord of hosts, if I will not open you the windows of heaven, and pour you out a blessing, that there shall not be room enough to receive it" (Malachi 3:10). The people obeyed their prophet, and the rains fell on the parched crops.

In order to stand, the true Church must be built upon the foundation of prophets (see Ephesians 2:20). We are blessed in this insecure world to have a prophet through whom the Lord reveals his will.

Discussion
• Have someone share an experience in which obedience to the counsel of the prophet was a blessing.

Additional Scriptures
• Numbers 12:6 (God speaks through prophets)
• 1 Samuel 9:9 (prophet called a seer)
• Luke 1:70 (God speaks through prophets)
• D&C 45:10, 15 (God speaks today as in days of old)
• 1 Nephi 22:2 (by the Spirit things are made known to prophets)
• D&C 68:3–5 (when the Lord's servants speak as moved by the Holy Ghost, it is the mind, will, and voice of the Lord)
• D&C 107:65–67, 91–92 (duties of the President of the Church)
• D&C 43:1–7 (only the prophet is authorized to receive revelations for the Church)

SCRIPTURES

Chapter 10

When the Lord's servants speak or write under the influence of the Holy Ghost, their words become scripture (see D&C 68:4). From the beginning, the Lord has commanded his prophets to keep a record of his revelations and his dealings with his children. He said: "I command all men, both in the east and in the west, and in the north, and in the south, and in the islands of the sea, that they shall write the words which I speak unto them; for out of the books which shall be written I will judge the world, every man according to their works, according to that which is written" (2 Nephi 29:11).

What Scriptures Do We Have Today?
The Church of Jesus Christ of Latter-day Saints accepts four books as scripture: the Bible, the Book of Mormon, the Doctrine and Covenants, and the Pearl of Great Price. These books are called the standard works of the Church. The inspired words of our living prophets are also accepted as scripture.

The Bible is a collection of sacred writings containing God's revelations to man. These writings cover many centuries, from the time of Adam through the time when the Apostles of Jesus Christ lived. They were written by many prophets who lived at various times in the history of the world.

The Bible is divided into two sections: the Old Testament and the New Testament. Many prophecies in the Old Testament foretell the coming of a Savior and Redeemer. The New Testament tells of the life of that Savior and Redeemer, who is Jesus Christ. It also tells of the establishing of his Church in that day. *"*We believe the Bible to be the word of God as far as it is translated correctly*"* (Articles of Faith 1:8.)

We grow closer to God and each other as we read and ponder the scriptures together.

The Book of Mormon is a sacred record of some of the people who lived on the American continents between about 2,000 B.C. and A.D. 400. It contains the fulness of the gospel of Jesus Christ (see D&C 20:9; 42:12; 135:3). The Book of Mormon tells of the visit Jesus Christ made to the people in the Americas soon after his resurrection.

Joseph Smith translated the Book of Mormon into English through the gift and power of God. He said that it is *"*the most correct of any book on earth, and the keystone of our religion, and a man would get nearer to God by abiding by its precepts, than by any other book*"* (*History of the Church*, 4:461).

President Ezra Taft Benson helped us understand how the Book of Mormon is the keystone of our religion. He said:

*"*There are three ways in which the Book of Mormon is the keystone of our religion. It is the keystone in our witness of Christ. It is the keystone of our doctrine. It is the keystone of testimony.

"The Book of Mormon is the keystone in our witness of Jesus Christ, who is Himself the cornerstone of everything we do. It bears witness of His reality with power and clarity. . . .

"[It] broadens our understandings of the doctrines of salvation. The Book of Mormon . . . was written for our day. In [it] we find a pattern for preparing for the Second Coming. . . .

"The Book of Mormon teaches us truth [and] bears testimony of Jesus Christ. . . . But there is something more. There is a power in the book which will begin to flow into your lives the moment you begin a serious study of the book. You will find greater power to resist temptation. You will find the power to avoid deception. You will find the power to stay on the strait and narrow path. The scriptures are called 'the words of life,' and nowhere is that more true than it is of the Book of Mormon. . . . 'Every Latter-day Saint should make the study of this book a lifetime pursuit' " (in Conference Report, Oct. 1986, pp. 4–7; or *Ensign*, Nov. 1986, pp. 5–7).

The Doctrine and Covenants is a collection of modern revelations. In section 1 of the Doctrine and Covenants, the Lord reveals that the book is published to the inhabitants of the earth to prepare them for his coming:

"Wherefore the voice of the Lord is unto the ends of the earth, that all that will hear may hear:

"Prepare ye, prepare ye for that which is to come, for the Lord is nigh" (1:11–12).

This book contains the revelations regarding the Church of Jesus Christ as it has been restored in these last days. Several sections of the book explain the organization of the Church and define the offices of the priesthood and their functions. Other sections, such as sections 76 and 88, contain glorious truths that were lost to the world for hundreds of years. Still others, such as sections 29 and 93, shed light on teachings in the Bible. In addition, some sections, such as section 133, contain prophecies of events to come. God has commanded us to study his revelations in this book: "Search these commandments, for they are true and faithful, and the prophecies and promises which are in them shall all be fulfilled" (D&C 1:37).

The Pearl of Great Price contains the Book of Moses, the Book of Abraham, and some inspired writings of Joseph Smith. The Book of Moses contains an account of some of the visions and writings of Moses, revealed to the Prophet Joseph Smith in June and December 1830. It clarifies doctrines and teachings that were lost from the Bible and gives added information concerning the creation of the earth.

The Book of Abraham was translated by the Prophet Joseph Smith from a papyrus scroll taken from the Egyptian catacombs. This book contains valuable information about the Creation, the gospel, the nature of God, and the priesthood.

The writings of Joseph Smith include part of Joseph Smith's inspired translation of the Bible, selections from his *History of the Church,* and the Articles of Faith.

Words of Our Living Prophets

In addition to these four books of scripture, the inspired words of our living prophets become scripture to us. Their words come to us through conferences, Church publications, and instructions to local priesthood leaders. "We believe all that God has revealed, all that he does now reveal, and we believe that he will yet reveal many great and important things pertaining to the Kingdom of God" (Articles of Faith 1:9).

Discussion

- Read D&C 68:4. What is scripture?
- Name the standard works of the Church. Have four people each tell about what is in one of the standard works and how we received it.
- Ask a class member to read or quote the ninth article of faith.
- Show a copy of a Church publication. Have someone read some inspired words of the prophet found there.

Studying the Scriptures

We should each study the scriptures every day. We should share these truths with our children. Our standard works should be placed where our children will see them and learn to love them and use them for the truths they contain.

If we desire to avoid the evils of this world, we must feed our minds with the truth and righteousness found in the scriptures. We will grow closer to God and to each other as we read and ponder the scriptures together.

As we read, ponder, and pray about the scriptures and ask God for understanding, the Holy Ghost will bear witness to us of the truth of these things. We will each know for ourselves that these things are true. We will not be deceived (see Joseph Smith—Matthew 1:37). We can receive the same feelings Nephi expressed when he said, "My soul delighteth in the things of the Lord; and my heart pondereth continually upon the things which I have seen and heard" (2 Nephi 4:16).

Discussion

• Plan the time and place for your scripture study, and set a goal to study each day. Discuss how to keep the commitment to study the scriptures each day.

Additional Scriptures

• 1 Nephi 19:1–3; 1 Nephi 14:20–26 (prophets commanded to write)
• 1 Nephi 19:1–3, 6–7; Alma 37:1–8 (great worth of scriptures)
• 2 Nephi 33:10 (scriptures testify of Christ)
• Alma 29:8 (Lord speaks to all nations through scriptures)
• 2 Timothy 3:16–17; 1 Nephi 19:21–24 (why and how scriptures are given)
• 2 Peter 1:20; Alma 13:20; D&C 10:62 (scriptures are clear and do not distort)
• D&C 128:18; 1 Nephi 14:25–26 (scriptures yet to come)
• 2 Nephi 29:3–10 (scriptures to Jews and to Gentiles)

VISUAL AIDS

Support Materials

Key to Visual Aids 1–16

1. Isaiah, one of the prophets of the Old Testament, foretold the coming of Jesus Christ.
2. John the Baptist baptized Jesus in the Jordan River.
3. Jesus called Peter and others to follow him.
4. Jesus ordained Twelve Apostles.
5. Jesus loved and blessed the children.
6. Jesus taught the people the gospel. (*The Sermon on the Mount,* by Carl Bloch. Original at the Chapel of Frederiksborg Castle, Denmark. Used by permission of the Frederiksborgmuseum.)
7. In the Garden of Gethsemane, the Savior took upon himself the sins of all mankind.
8. Jesus died for our sins on the cross at Calvary.
9. On the third day, the Savior rose from the grave.
10. The resurrected Savior showed his wounds to his Apostles.
11. The resurrected Savior visited his people in the Americas.
12. Joseph Smith was inspired by James 1:5–6 to ask God which was the true Church of Jesus Christ.
13. In answer to Joseph Smith's prayer, Heavenly Father and Jesus Christ visited him.
14. The angel Moroni delivered to Joseph Smith the golden plates that contained the Book of Mormon.
15. John the Baptist visited Joseph Smith and Oliver Cowdery and conferred upon them the Aaronic Priesthood.
16. Peter, James, and John conferred the Melchizedek Priesthood upon Joseph Smith and Oliver Cowdery.

JESUS CHRIST AS OUR SAVIOR

Unit Four

The Savior Jesus Christ, known as Jehovah in the premortal existence, was born in a humble stable.

THE LIFE OF CHRIST

Chapter 11

Every person who comes to earth depends on Jesus Christ to fulfill the promise He made in heaven to be our Savior. Without him, the plan of salvation would have failed. Because his mission was necessary, all of the prophets from Adam to Christ testified that he would come (see Acts 10:43). All of the prophets since Christ have testified that he did come. Each of us needs to study the life of the Savior and follow him faithfully throughout our lives. We need to have a personal relationship with him.

The Life of Christ Was Predicted Long before His Birth

An angel told Adam that the Savior's name would be Jesus Christ (see Moses 6:51–52). Enoch saw that Jesus would die upon the cross and be resurrected (see Moses 7:55–56). Noah and Moses also testified of him (see Moses 8:23–24). About eight hundred years before the Savior was born on the earth, Isaiah foresaw his life. When Isaiah saw the grief and sorrow that the Savior would suffer to pay the price for our sins, he exclaimed:

"He is despised and rejected of men; a man of sorrows, and acquainted with grief. . . .

"Surely he hath borne our griefs, and carried our sorrows. . . .

"He was wounded for our transgressions, he was bruised for our iniquities. . . .

"He was oppressed, and he was afflicted, yet he opened not

While yet a boy, the Savior taught the learned men in the temple.

By Carl Bloch. Original at the Chapel of Frederiksborg Castle, Denmark.
Used by permission of the Frederiksborgmuseum.

his mouth: he is brought as a lamb to the slaughter" (Isaiah 53:3–7).

Nephi also saw a vision of the Savior's future birth and mission. He saw a beautiful virgin, and an angel explained, "Behold, the virgin whom thou seest is the mother of the Son of God, after the manner of the flesh" (1 Nephi 11:18). Then Nephi saw the virgin holding a child in her arms. The angel declared, "Behold the lamb of God, yea, even the Son of the Eternal Father!" (1 Nephi 11:21).

About 124 years before Jesus was born, King Benjamin, another Nephite prophet and king, also foresaw the Savior's life:

"For behold, the time cometh, and is not far distant, that with power, the Lord Omnipotent who reigneth, who was, and is from all eternity to all eternity, shall come down from heaven among the children of men, and shall dwell in a tabernacle of clay, and shall go forth amongst men, working mighty miracles, such as healing the sick, raising the dead, causing the lame to walk, the blind to receive their sight, and the deaf to hear, and curing all manner of diseases.

"And he shall cast out devils, or the evil spirits which dwell in the hearts of the children of men.

"And lo, he shall suffer temptations, and pain of body, hunger, thirst, and fatigue, even more than man can suffer, except it be unto death; for behold, blood cometh from every pore, so great shall be his anguish for the wickedness and the abominations of his people.

"And he shall be called Jesus Christ, the Son of God, the Father of heaven and earth, the Creator of all things from the beginning; and his mother shall be called Mary" (Mosiah 3:5–8).

He Was the Only Begotten of the Father
The story of the birth and life of the Savior is found in the New Testament in the books of Matthew, Mark, Luke, and John. From their accounts we learn that Jesus was born of a virgin named Mary. She was engaged to marry Joseph when an angel of the Lord appeared to her. The angel told her that

she was to be the mother of the Son of God. She asked him how this was possible (see Luke 1:34). He told her, "The Holy Ghost shall come upon thee, and the power of the Highest shall overshadow thee: therefore also that holy thing which shall be born of thee shall be called the Son of God" (Luke 1:35). Thus, God the Father became the literal father of Jesus Christ.

Jesus is the only person on earth to be born of a mortal mother and an immortal father. That is why he is called the Only Begotten Son. From his mother he inherited mortality and was subject to hunger, thirst, fatigue, pain, and death. He inherited divine powers from his Father. No one could take the Savior's life from him unless He willed it. He had power to lay it down and power to take up his body again after dying. (See John 10:17–18.)

Discussion
• Read Luke 1:34–35. Why was Jesus Christ known as the Only Begotten of the Father?
• What did he inherit from his Father?
• What did he inherit from his mother?

He Led a Perfect Life
From his youth, Jesus obeyed all that was required of him by our Heavenly Father. Under the guidance of Mary and Joseph, Jesus grew much as other children grow. He loved and obeyed the truth. Luke tells us, "And the child grew, and waxed strong in spirit, filled with wisdom: and the grace of God was upon him" (Luke 2:40).

By the time he was twelve years old, Jesus knew he had been sent to do the will of his Father. He went with his parents to Jerusalem. When his parents were returning home, they discovered that he was not with their group. They went back to Jerusalem to look for him. "After three days they found him in the temple, sitting in the midst of the doctors, both hearing them, and asking them questions. And all that heard him were astonished at his understanding and answers" (Luke 2:46–47).

Joseph and Mary were relieved to find him but unhappy that he had treated them so. Mary said: *"Son, why hast thou thus dealt with us? Behold, thy father [Joseph] and I have sought thee sorrowing."* Jesus answered her gently, reminding her that Joseph was only a stepfather: *"Wist ye not that I must be about my [Heavenly] Father's business?"* (Luke 2:48–49).

In order to fulfill his mission, Jesus was to do the will of his Father in Heaven. *"I do nothing of myself,"* he declared, "but as my Father hath taught me, I speak these things. . . . I do always those things that please him"* (John 8:28–29).

When Jesus was thirty years old, he came to his cousin John to be baptized in the Jordan River. John was reluctant to baptize Jesus because he knew that Jesus had never sinned. Jesus asked John to baptize him in order *"to fulfil all righteousness."* John did baptize the Savior, immersing him completely in the water. When Jesus was baptized, his Father spoke from heaven, saying, *"This is my beloved Son, in whom I am well pleased."* The Holy Ghost descended, as shown by the sign of the dove. (See Matthew 3:13–17.)

Soon after Jesus' baptism, Satan came to him to tempt him. He wanted Jesus to fail his mission. If Satan could get him to commit just one sin, then Jesus would not be worthy to be our Savior, and the plan would fail. In this way Satan could make us as miserable as he is. We would never be able to return to our Heavenly Father.

Satan's temptations came after Jesus had been fasting for forty days. Jesus firmly resisted all these temptations, then commanded Satan to leave. When Satan was gone, angels came and ministered to Jesus. (See Matthew 4:1–11.)

He Taught Us How to Love and Serve One Another

After being tempted by Satan, Jesus began his public ministry. He came to earth not only to die for us but also to teach us how to live. He taught that there are two great commandments: first, to love God with all our heart, mind, and strength; and second, to love others as we love ourselves (see Matthew 22:36–39). His life is an example of how we should obey these two commandments. If we love God, we will trust and obey him, as Jesus did. If we love others, we will help them meet their physical and spiritual needs.

Jesus spent his life serving others. He cured them of diseases. He made the blind see, the deaf hear, and the lame walk. Once when he was healing the sick, it became late and the people were hungry. Instead of sending them away, he blessed five loaves of bread and two fish and miraculously was able to feed a multitude of five thousand people. (See Matthew 14:14–21.) He taught that whenever we find people hungry, cold, naked, or lonely, we should help them all we can. When we help others, we are serving the Lord. (See Matthew 25:35–46.)

Jesus loved others with all his heart. Often his heart was so full of compassion that he wept. He loved little children, the elderly, and the humble, simple people who had faith in him. He loved those who had sinned, and with great compassion he taught them to repent and be baptized. He taught, "I am the way, the truth, and the life" (John 14:6).

Jesus even loved those who sinned against him and were unrepentant. At the end of his life, as he hung on the cross, he prayed to the Father for the soldiers who had crucified him, pleading, "Father, forgive them; for they know not what they do" (Luke 23:34). He taught, "This is my commandment, That ye love one another, as I have loved you" (John 15:12).

Discussion
- Read Matthew 22:36–40. What are some ways we can show the Lord that we love him?
- Read Matthew 5:48. Is it possible to become perfect in aspects of our own daily lives (such as paying debts, keeping the Sabbath day holy, fasting, keeping the Word of Wisdom)?

He Organized the Only True Church

Jesus wanted his gospel taught to people all over the earth, so he chose Twelve Apostles to testify of him. They were the original leaders of his church. They received the authority to act in his name and do the works they had seen him do. Those who received authority from them were also able to teach, baptize, and perform other ordinances in his name. After his death, they continued to do his work until the people became so wicked that they killed the Apostles.

Discussion
• Why did Jesus choose the Twelve Apostles?
• Read Mark 3:14–15. For what purpose were the Apostles ordained?

He Redeemed Us from Our Sins and Saved Us from Death

When his work of teaching and blessing the people was finished, Jesus prepared to make the ultimate sacrifice for all the sins of mankind. He had been condemned to die because he had testified to the people that he was the Son of God.

The night before his crucifixion, he went to a garden called Gethsemane. There he knelt and prayed. Soon he was weighed down by deep sorrow and wept as he prayed. Latter-day Apostle Orson F. Whitney was permitted to see the Savior's suffering in a vision. Seeing the Savior weep, he said: "I was so moved at the sight that I also wept, out of pure sympathy. My whole heart went out to Him; I loved Him with all my soul, and longed to be with Him as I longed for nothing else" (in Bryant Hinckley, *The Faith of Our Pioneer Fathers,* p. 211). Jesus "went a little further, and fell on his face, and prayed, saying, O my Father, if it be possible, let this cup pass from me: nevertheless not as I will, but as thou wilt" (Matthew 26:39).

In a modern revelation the Savior described how great his suffering was, saying it caused him "to tremble because of pain, and to bleed at every pore, and to suffer both body and spirit" (D&C 19:18). The awful anguish of taking upon himself every sin that any human being has ever committed went through the Savior's body. No mortal person can comprehend just how great this burden was. No other person could have endured such agony of body and spirit. "He descended below all things . . . that he might be in all things and through all things, the light of truth" (D&C 88:6).

But his suffering was not yet complete. The following day, Jesus was beaten, humiliated, and spit upon. He was required to carry his own cross up the hill; then he was lifted up and nailed to it. He was tortured in one of the cruelest ways men have ever devised. After nine hours on the cross, he cried out in agony, "My God, my God, why hast thou forsaken me?" (Mark 15:34). In Jesus' bitterest hour, the Father had withdrawn his spirit from him so Jesus could finish suffering the penalty for the sins of all mankind that Jesus might have complete victory over the forces of sin and death.

When the Savior knew that his sacrifice had been accepted by the Father, he exclaimed in a loud voice, "It is finished" (John 19:30). "Father, into thy hands I commend my spirit" (Luke 23:46). He bowed his head and voluntarily gave up his spirit. The Savior was dead. A violent earthquake shook the earth.

Some friends took the Savior's body to a tomb, where it lay for three days. During this time his spirit went and organized the missionary work to other spirits who needed to receive his gospel (see 1 Peter 3:18–20; D&C 138). On the third day, a Sunday, he returned to his body and took it up again. He was the first to overcome death. The prophecy had been fulfilled "that he must rise again from the dead" (John 20:9).

Shortly after his resurrection, the Savior appeared to the Nephites and established his Church in the Americas. He taught the people and blessed them. This moving account is found in 3 Nephi 11 through 28.

Discussion
• How do you feel as you ponder the Savior's sacrifice for us?

What Does the Savior's Life Mean for Us?

Jesus taught: "Greater love hath no man than this, that a man lay down his life for his friends. Ye are my friends, if ye do whatsoever I command you" (John 15:13–14). He willingly and humbly went through the sorrow in Gethsemane and the suffering on the cross.

The Savior will have died in vain for our sins if we do not come unto him, repent of our sins, and love him with all our hearts. He said:

"And this is the gospel which I have given unto you—that I came into the world to do the will of my Father, because my Father sent me.

"And my Father sent me that I might be lifted up upon the cross; and after that I had been lifted up upon the cross, that I might draw all men unto me . . . that they may be judged according to their works. . . .

"For the works which ye have seen me do that shall ye also do; . . .

"Therefore, what manner of men ought ye to be? Verily I say unto you, *even as I am*" (3 Nephi 27:13–15, 21, 27; italics added).

Discussion
• Imagine that you had a large debt but could not pay it. How would you feel about a person who offered to pay the debt for you? Compare this to the sacrifice of Jesus.

Additional Scriptures
• 2 Nephi 25:12 (the Only Begotten of the Father in the flesh)
• Moses 6:57 (Jesus Christ named as the Only Begotten)
• Matthew, Mark, Luke, John (life and teachings of Jesus Christ)
• Matthew 10:1–8; Luke 9:1–2 (Apostles ordained with power and authority)
• Matthew 26–28; Mark 14–16; Luke 22–24 (Jesus in the Garden; betrayed, crucified, and resurrected)

In the Garden of Gethsemane,
Christ took upon himself the sins of all mankind.

THE ATONEMENT

Jesus Christ[@]came into the world . . . to be crucified for the world, and to bear the sins of the world, and to sanctify the world, and to cleanse it from all unrighteousness; that through him all might be saved[@] (D&C 76:41–42). The great sacrifice he made to pay for our sins and overcome death is called the *Atonement.* It is the most important event that has ever occurred in the history of mankind: [@]For it is expedient that an atonement should be made; for according to the great plan of the Eternal God there must be an atonement made, or else all mankind must unavoidably perish; . . . yea, all are fallen and are lost, and must perish except it be through the atonement[@] (Alma 34:9).

Discussion

• Why did Jesus come to the earth?

The Atonement Was Necessary for Our Salvation
The fall of Adam brought two kinds of death into the world: physical death and spiritual death. Physical death is separation of the body and spirit. Spiritual death is separation from God. If these two kinds of death had not been overcome by Jesus' atonement, two consequences would have resulted: our bodies and our spirits would have been separated forever, and we could not have lived again with our Heavenly Father.

Christ died on the cross for the sins of all mankind.

But our wise Heavenly Father prepared a wonderful, merciful plan to save us from physical and spiritual death. He planned for a Savior to come to earth to ransom (redeem) us from our sins and from death. Because of our sins and the weakness of our mortal bodies, we could not ransom ourselves (see Alma 34:10–12). The one who would be our Savior would need to be sinless and to have power over death.

Discussion
• Compare our earthly bodies to a hand with a glove on it. Take off the glove. Explain that this is like physical death — the spirit (the hand) and the body (the glove) are separated.

Christ Was the Only One Who Could Atone for Our Sins
There are several reasons why Jesus Christ was the only person who could be our Savior. One reason is that Heavenly Father chose him to be the Savior. He was the Only Begotten Son of God and thus had power over death. Jesus explained: "I lay down my life, that I might take it again. No man taketh it from me, but I lay it down of myself. I have power to lay it down, and I have power to take it again" (John 10:17–18).

Jesus also qualified to be our Savior because he is the only person who has ever lived on the earth who did not sin. This made him a worthy sacrifice to pay for the sins of others.

Discussion
• Have class members discuss the reasons why Jesus was the only one who could atone for our sins.

Christ Suffered and Died to Atone for Our Sins
The Savior atoned for our sins by suffering in Gethsemane and by giving his life on the cross. It is impossible for us to fully understand how he suffered for all of our sins. In the Garden of Gethsemane, the weight of our sins caused him to feel such agony and heartbreak that he bled from every pore (see D&C 19:18–19). Later, as he hung upon the cross, Jesus suffered painful death by one of the most cruel methods known to man.

How Jesus loves us, to suffer such spiritual and physical agony for our sake! How great the love of Heavenly Father that he would send his Only Begotten Son to suffer and die for the rest of his children. *"For God so loved the world, that he gave his only begotten Son, that whosoever believeth in him should not perish, but have everlasting life"* (John 3:16).

• Ask class members to imagine themselves in the Garden of Gethsemane as witnesses of the suffering of Jesus Christ. Have someone read the account in Luke 22:39–44.

The Atonement and Resurrection Bring Resurrection to All
On the third day after his crucifixion, Christ took up his body again and became the first person to be resurrected. When his friends went to seek him, the angels who guarded his tomb told them, *"He is not here: for he is risen, as he said"* (Matthew 28:6). His spirit had reentered his body, never to be separated again.

Christ thus overcame physical death. Because of his atonement, everyone born on this earth will be resurrected (see 1 Corinthians 15:21–22). Just as Jesus was resurrected, our spirits will be reunited with our bodies, *"that they can die no more . . . , never to be divided"* (Alma 11:45). This condition is called *immortality*. All people who have ever lived will be resurrected, *"both old and young, both bond and free, both male and female, both the wicked and the righteous"* (Alma 11:44).

Discussion
• Refer again to the hand and glove. Explain that because Jesus Christ atoned for our sins, all people will someday be resurrected. (Put the glove on your hand.) Our bodies and our spirits will reunite.

The Atonement Makes It Possible for Those Who Have Faith in Christ to Be Saved from Their Sins
The Savior's atonement makes it possible for us to overcome spiritual death. Although all people will be resurrected with a body of flesh and bone, only those who accept the Atonement will be saved from spiritual death.

We accept Christ's atonement by placing our faith in him. Through this faith, we repent of our sins, are baptized, receive the Holy Ghost, and obey his commandments. We become faithful disciples of Jesus Christ. We are forgiven and cleansed from sin and prepared to return and live forever with our Heavenly Father.

The Savior tells us, "For behold, I, God, have suffered these things for all, that they might not suffer . . . even as I" (D&C 19:16–17). Christ did his part to atone for our sins. To make his atonement fully effective in our lives, we must strive to obey him and repent of our sins.

Elder Boyd K. Packer of the Council of the Twelve gave the following illustration to show how Christ's atonement makes it possible to be saved from sin *if* we do our part.

"Let me tell you a story—a parable.

"There once was a man who wanted something very much. It seemed more important than anything else in his life. In order for him to have his desire, he incurred a great debt.

"He had been warned about going into that much debt, and particularly about his creditor. But it seemed so important for him to do what he wanted to and to have what he wanted right now. He was sure he could pay for it later.

"So he signed a contract. He would pay it off some time along the way. He didn't worry too much about it, for the due date seemed such a long time away. He had what he wanted now, and that was what seemed important.

"The creditor was always somewhere in the back of his mind, and he made token payments now and again, thinking somehow that the day of reckoning really would never come.

"But as it always does, the day came, and the contract fell due. The debt had not been fully paid. His creditor appeared and demanded payment in full.

"Only then did he realize that his creditor not only had the power to repossess all that he owned, but the power to cast him into prison as well.

" 'I cannot pay you, for I have not the power to do so,' he confessed.

" 'Then,' said the creditor, 'we will exercise the contract, take your possessions and you shall go to prison. You agreed to that. It was your choice. You signed the contract, and now it must be enforced.'

" 'Can you not extend the time or forgive the debt?' the debtor begged. 'Arrange some way for me to keep what I have and not go to prison. Surely you believe in mercy? Will you not show mercy?'

"The creditor replied, 'Mercy is always so one-sided. It would serve only you. If I show mercy to you, it will leave me unpaid. It is justice I demand. Do you believe in justice?'

" 'I believed in justice when I signed the contract,' the debtor said. 'It was on my side then, for I thought it would protect me. I did not need mercy then, nor think I should need it ever. Justice, I thought, would serve both of us equally as well.'

" 'It is justice that demands that you pay the contract or suffer the penalty,' the creditor replied. 'That is the law. You have agreed to it and that is the way it must be. Mercy cannot rob justice.'

"There they were: One meting out justice, the other pleading for mercy. Neither could prevail except at the expense of the other.

" 'If you do not forgive the debt there will be no mercy,' the debtor pleaded.

" 'If I do, there will be no justice,' was the reply.

"Both laws, it seemed, could not be served. They are two

eternal ideals that appear to contradict one another. Is there no way for justice to be fully served, and mercy also?

"There is a way! The law of justice *can* be fully satisfied and mercy *can* be fully extended—but it takes someone else. And so it happened this time.

"The debtor had a friend. He came to help. He knew the debtor well. He knew him to be shortsighted. He thought him foolish to have gotten himself into such a predicament. Nevertheless, he wanted to help because he loved him. He stepped between them, faced the creditor, and made this offer.

" 'I will pay the debt if you will free the debtor from his contract so that he may keep his possessions and not go to prison.'

"As the creditor was pondering the offer, the mediator added, 'You demanded justice. Though he cannot pay you, I will do so. You will have been justly dealt with and can ask no more. It would not be just.'

"And so the creditor agreed.

"The mediator turned then to the debtor. 'If I pay your debt, will you accept me as your creditor?'

" 'Oh yes, yes,' cried the debtor. 'You saved me from prison and show mercy to me.'

" 'Then,' said the benefactor, 'you will pay the debt to me and I will set the terms. It will not be easy, but it will be possible. I will provide a way. You need not go to prison.'

"And so it was that the creditor was paid in full. He had been justly dealt with. No contract had been broken.

"The debtor, in turn, had been extended mercy. Both laws stood fulfilled. Because there was a mediator, justice had claimed its full share, and mercy was satisfied" (in Conference Report, Apr. 1977, pp. 79–80; or *Ensign,* May 1977, pp. 54–55).

Our sins are our spiritual debts. Without Jesus Christ, who is our Savior and Mediator, we would all pay for our sins by suffering spiritual death. But because of him, if we will keep his terms, which are to repent and keep his commandments, we may return to live with our Heavenly Father.

It is wonderful that Christ has provided us a way to be healed from our sins. He said:

"Behold, I have come unto the world . . . to save the world from sin.

"Therefore, whoso repenteth and cometh unto me as a little child, him will I receive, for of such is the kingdom of God. Behold, for such I have laid down my life, and have taken it up again; therefore repent, and come unto me ye ends of the earth, and be saved" (3 Nephi 9:21–22).

Discussion
- Read Acts 2:38. What must we do to show that we accept the Atonement?
- Read D&C 19:16–17. What is the penalty for those who do not accept the atonement of the Savior?

Additional Scriptures
- Alma 34:9–16 (Atonement necessary; sacrifice of God)
- Romans 5:12–17 (by one came death, by one came life)
- Helaman 14:15–18 (purpose of Jesus' death)
- Articles of Faith 1:3 (all may be saved)
- 1 Peter 1:18–20 (Jesus was foreordained)
- Matthew 16:21 (Jesus' sacrifice was necessary)
- Luke 22:39–46 (Jesus' suffering in the Garden)
- 1 John 1:7 (Jesus cleanses from sin)
- 2 Nephi 9:21–22 (the Savior suffered for all people)
- Mosiah 16:6–8 (resurrection possible only through Jesus)
- Alma 11:40–45; Mormon 9:12–14 (all to be resurrected)
- Isaiah 1:18 (sins shall be made white)
- 1 Corinthians 15:40–44 (description of the Resurrection)

THE CHURCH OF JESUS CHRIST

Unit Five

Moses conferred the priesthood on Aaron by the laying on of hands.

THE PRIESTHOOD

Chapter 13

What Is the Priesthood?

The priesthood is the power and authority of God. By his priesthood power the heavens and the earth were created. By this power the universe is kept in perfect order. Through this power he accomplishes his work and glory, which is "to bring to pass the immortality and eternal life of man" (Moses 1:39).

Our Heavenly Father shares his priesthood power with worthy male members of the Church. The priesthood enables them to act in God's name for the salvation of the human family. Through it they can be authorized to preach the gospel, administer the ordinances of salvation, and govern God's kingdom on earth.

Why Do We Need the Priesthood on the Earth?

We must have priesthood authority to act in the name of God when performing the sacred ordinances of the gospel, such as baptism, confirmation, administration of the sacrament, and temple marriage. If a man does not have the priesthood, even though he may be sincere, the Lord will not recognize ordinances he performs (see Matthew 7:21–23). These important ordinances must be performed on the earth by men holding the priesthood.

Men need the priesthood to preside in The Church of Jesus Christ of Latter-day Saints and to direct the work of the Church in all parts of the world. When Christ lived on the earth, he chose his Apostles and ordained them so that they could lead his Church. He gave them the power and authority of the priesthood to act in his name. (See Mark 3:13–15; John 15:16.)

Another reason the priesthood is needed on the earth is so we can understand the will of the Lord and carry out his purposes. God reveals his will to his authorized priesthood representative on the earth, the prophet. The prophet, who is President of the Church, serves as the spokesman for God to all members of the Church and all people on the earth.

Discussion
• Name some things that can be done only by men who hold the priesthood. Discuss the need for priesthood authority.

How Do Men Receive the Priesthood?

The Lord has prepared an orderly way for his priesthood to be given to his sons on the earth. A worthy male member of the Church receives the priesthood "by the laying on of hands by those who are in authority, to preach the Gospel and administer in the ordinances thereof" (Articles of Faith 1:5).

This is the same way men received the priesthood long ago, even in the days of Moses: "And no man taketh this honour unto himself, but he that is called of God, as was Aaron" (Hebrews 5:4). Aaron received the priesthood from Moses, his priesthood leader (see Exodus 28:1). Only those who hold the priesthood can ordain others.

Men cannot buy and sell the power and authority of the priesthood. Nor can they take this authority upon themselves. In the New Testament we read of a man named Simon who lived when Christ's Apostles presided over the Church. Simon became converted and was baptized into the Church. Because he was a skillful magician, the people believed he had the power of God. But Simon did not have the priesthood, and he knew it.

Simon knew that the Apostles and the other priesthood leaders of the Church had the true power of God. He saw them use their priesthood to do the Lord's work, and he wanted this power for himself. He offered to buy the priesthood. (See Acts 8:9–19.) But Peter, the chief Apostle, said, *"Thy money perish with thee, because thou hast thought that the gift of God may be purchased with money"* (Acts 8:20).

Discussion
• Have someone read or quote the fifth article of faith.
• Who is given the priesthood? How is it given?
• Who may ordain a male member to the priesthood?

How Do Men Properly Use the Priesthood?
The priesthood should be used to bless the lives of our Heavenly Father's children here on earth. Priesthood holders should preside in love and kindness. They should not force their families and others to obey them. The Lord has told us that the power of the priesthood cannot be controlled except in righteousness (see D&C 121:36). When we try to use the priesthood to gain wealth or fame or for any other selfish purpose, *"behold, the heavens withdraw themselves; the Spirit of the Lord is grieved; and when it is withdrawn, Amen to the priesthood or the authority of that man"* (D&C 121:37).

When a man uses the priesthood *"by persuasion, by long-suffering, by gentleness and meekness, and by love unfeigned"* (D&C 121:41), he can do many wonderful things for his family and others. He can baptize and confirm, administer the sacrament, and bless the sick. He can give priesthood blessings to his family members to encourage and protect them when they have special needs. He can also help other families with these ordinances and blessings when asked to do so.

Men use priesthood authority to preside in the Church in such callings as branch president, bishop, quorum president, or stake and mission leader. Women who hold positions in the Church as officers and teachers work under the direction of the priesthood.

Discussion
- Read D&C 121:34–40. How should the priesthood not be used?
- Read D&C 121:41–44. How should the priesthood be used?

What Blessings Come When We Use the Priesthood Properly?

The Lord has promised great blessings to righteous priesthood holders who use the priesthood to bless others:

ʷThen shall thy confidence wax strong in the presence of God; and the doctrine of the priesthood shall distil upon thy soul as the dews from heaven.

"The Holy Ghost shall be thy constant companion, and thy scepter an unchanging scepter of righteousness and truth; and thy dominion shall be an everlasting dominion, and without compulsory means it shall flow unto thee forever and everᵂ (D&C 121:45–46).

A great latter-day prophet, David O. McKay, promised every man who uses the priesthood in righteousness that heʷwill find his life sweetened, his discernment sharpened to decide quickly between right and wrong, his feelings tender and compassionate, yet his spirit strong and valiant in defense of right; he will find the priesthood a neverfailing source of happiness—a well of living water springing up unto eternal lifeᵂ ("Priesthood," *Instructor,* Oct. 1968, p. 378).

Discussion
- What are some of the blessings you have received through the priesthood?
- What are some of the blessings you can receive through the priesthood?

Additional Scriptures
- D&C 107:1–100 (revelation on priesthood)
- D&C 20:38–67 (duties of the priesthood explained)

PRIESTHOOD ORGANIZATION

Chapter 14

The Church of Jesus Christ of Latter-day Saints is governed by the priesthood. The priesthood, which is always associated with God's work, *"continueth in the church of God in all generations, and is without beginning of days or end of years"* (D&C 84:17). It is upon the earth today. Men young and old are baptized into the Church, and when they are judged worthy they are ordained to the priesthood. They are given the authority to act for the Lord and do his work on the earth.

Two Divisions of Priesthood

The priesthood is divided into two parts: the Melchizedek Priesthood and the Aaronic Priesthood (see D&C 107:1). The greater priesthood is the Melchizedek Priesthood. Long ago it was called *"the Holy Priesthood, after the Order of the Son of God."* But the name was changed so the name of the Lord would not be used so often. The Church in ancient days called the priesthood *"the Melchizedek Priesthood"* after a great high priest who lived during the time of Abraham. (See D&C 107:2–4.)

The lesser priesthood is an appendage to the Melchizedek Priesthood. It is called the Aaronic Priesthood because it was conferred on Aaron and his sons throughout all their generations. Those who hold the Aaronic Priesthood have authority

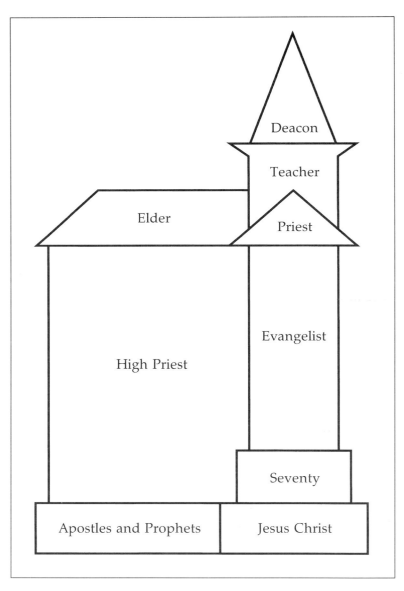

The Church of Jesus Christ can be compared to a building with Christ as the chief cornerstone and the Apostles and prophets as the foundation.

to administer the outward ordinances of repentance and baptism. (See D&C 107:13–14, 20.)

Those holding the Melchizedek Priesthood have the power and authority to lead the Church and direct the preaching of the gospel in all parts of the world. They are in charge of all the spiritual work of the Church (see D&C 84:19–22). They direct the work done in the temples; they preside over wards, branches, stakes, and missions; they heal the sick, bless babies, and give special blessings to Church members. The Lord's chosen prophet, the President of the Church, is the presiding high priest over the Melchizedek Priesthood (see D&C 107:65–67).

Discussion
• Read D&C 107:1–4. What are the two divisions of the priest-hood? How did the Melchizedek Priesthood get its name?

Keys of the Priesthood
"There is a difference between priesthood and the 'keys' of the priesthood. A priest in a ward has power sufficient to baptize, yet he has not the right to perform this ordinance until he has been authorized by the bishop. The bishop has the 'keys' to administer to the affairs belonging under his ecclesiastical jurisdiction. Therefore, he is the person who can tell a priest to baptize.

"The president and prophet of the Church has the 'keys' of the priesthood to administer in all spiritual and temporal affairs of the Church. It is his right to delegate stake presidents, bishops, patriarchs and others, as holders of the 'keys' pertaining to specific offices in certain geographical areas.

"President Joseph F. Smith taught on this subject:

" 'Every man ordained to any degree of the priesthood has this authority delegated to him. But it is necessary that every act performed under this authority shall be done at the proper time and place, in the proper way, and after the proper order.

The power of directing these labors constitutes the keys of the priesthood' (*Gospel Doctrine,* p. 136)" (Melvin R. Brooks, *L.D.S. Reference Encyclopedia,* p. 393).

Discussion
• What is the difference between the priesthood and the keys of the priesthood?

The Offices and Duties of the Aaronic Priesthood
When the Aaronic Priesthood is conferred on a man or boy, he is ordained to an office in that priesthood. The offices in the Aaronic Priesthood are deacon, teacher, priest, and bishop. Each office carries duties and responsibilities. Each group or quorum is presided over by a group leader or quorum president who teaches the members their duties and asks them to fill assignments.

Some men join the Church or become active after they have passed the usual age to receive the offices of this priesthood. They are usually ordained to an office in the Aaronic Priesthood and can soon be advanced to higher offices if they are worthy.

Deacon
A boy who has been baptized and confirmed a member of the Church and is worthy may be ordained to the office of deacon when he is twelve years old. The deacons are usually assigned to pass the sacrament to members of the Church, act as ushers, keep Church buildings and grounds in good order, act as messengers for priesthood leaders, and fulfill special assignments such as collecting fast offerings.

Teacher
A worthy boy may be ordained a teacher when he is fourteen years old or older. Teachers have all the duties, rights, and powers of the office of deacon plus additional ones. Teachers in the Aaronic Priesthood are to help Church members live the commandments (see D&C 20:53–59). To help fulfill this

responsibility, they are usually called as home teachers. They visit the homes of Church members and encourage them to live the principles of the gospel. They have been commanded to teach the truths of the gospel from the scriptures (see D&C 42:12). Teachers also prepare the bread and water for the sacrament service.

Priest

A worthy boy may be ordained a priest when he is sixteen years old or older. Priests have all the duties, rights, and powers of the offices of deacon and teacher plus some additional ones (see D&C 20:46–51). A priest may baptize. He may also administer the sacrament. He may ordain other priests, teachers, and deacons. A priest may take charge of meetings when there is no Melchizedek Priesthood holder present. He is to preach the gospel to those around him.

Bishop

A bishop is ordained and set apart to preside over the Aaronic Priesthood in a ward. He is the president of the priests quorum (see D&C 107:87–88). When he is acting in his Aaronic Priesthood office, a bishop deals primarily with temporal matters, such as administering finances and records and directing care for the poor and needy (see D&C 107:68).

A bishop is also ordained a high priest so he can preside over all members in the ward (see D&C 107:71–73; 68:15). A bishop is a judge in Israel (see D&C 107:74) and interviews members for temple recommends, priesthood ordinations, and other needs. It is his right to have the gift of discernment.

Discussion

• Discuss the duties of the deacon, teacher, priest, and bishop.

The Offices and Duties of the Melchizedek Priesthood

The offices of the Melchizedek Priesthood are elder, high priest, patriarch, seventy, and Apostle.

Elder

Elders are called to teach, expound, exhort, baptize, and watch over the Church (see D&C 20:42). All Melchizedek Priesthood holders are elders. They have the authority to bestow the gift of the Holy Ghost by the laying on of hands (see D&C 20:43). Elders should conduct meetings of the Church as they are led by the Holy Ghost (see D&C 20:45; 46:2). Elders may administer to the sick (see D&C 42:44). They are commanded to bless little children (see D&C 20:70). Elders may preside over Church meetings when there is no high priest present (D&C 107:11).

High Priest

A high priest may be given the authority to officiate in the Church and be in charge of spiritual things (see D&C 107:10, 12). He may also officiate in all lesser offices (see D&C 68:19). Stake presidents, mission presidents, high councilors, bishoprics, and other leaders of the Church are ordained high priests.

Patriarch

Patriarchs are ordained by General Authorities, or by stake presidents when they are authorized by the Council of the Twelve, to give special patriarchal blessings to members of the Church. These blessings give us some understanding of our callings on earth. They are the word of the Lord personally to us. Patriarchs are also ordained high priests (see D&C 107:39–56).

Seventy

Seventies are special witnesses of Jesus Christ to the world and assist in building up and regulating the Church (see D&C 107:25, 34, 38, 93–97).

Apostle

An Apostle is a special witness of Jesus Christ in all the world (see D&C 107:23). The Apostles administer the affairs of the

Church throughout the world. Those who are ordained to the office of Apostle in the Melchizedek Priesthood are usually set apart as members of the Council of Twelve Apostles. Each one is given all the keys of the kingdom of God on earth, but only the senior Apostle, who is President of the Church, actively exercises all of the keys. The others act under his direction.

Discussion
• Discuss the duties of elder, high priest, patriarch, seventy, and Apostle.

The Quorums of the Aaronic Priesthood
The Lord has instructed that the holders of the priesthood be organized into quorums. A quorum is a body of brethren holding the same priesthood office.

There are three quorums of the Aaronic Priesthood:

1. The deacons quorum, which consists of up to twelve deacons (see D&C 107:85). The presidency of the deacons quorum is called by the bishop from among the quorum members.
2. The teachers quorum, which consists of up to twenty-four teachers (see D&C 107:86). The presidency of the teachers quorum is called by the bishop from among the quorum members.
3. The priests quorum, which consists of up to forty-eight priests (see D&C 107:87–88). It is presided over by the bishop of the ward to which the quorum belongs. The bishop is a high priest and thus also belongs to the high priests quorum.

Whenever the number specified for a quorum is exceeded, the quorum may be divided.

The Quorums of the Melchizedek Priesthood
There are in the stakes of Zion the following Melchizedek Priesthood quorums:

Elders Quorum

Each elders quorum *"*is instituted for standing ministers; nevertheless they may travel, yet they are ordained to be standing ministers*"* (D&C 124:137). They do most of their work near their homes. The quorum is to consist of up to ninety-six elders, presided over by a quorum presidency that is called by the stake president.

High Priests Quorum

Each quorum includes all high priests residing within the boundaries of a stake, including patriarchs and bishops. The stake president and his counselors are the presidency of this quorum. The high priests in each ward are organized into a group with a group leader.

Importance of Priesthood Quorums

When ordained to the priesthood, a man or boy automatically becomes a member of a priesthood quorum. From then on through life, it is expected that he will hold membership in a quorum of the priesthood according to his office. (See Boyd K. Packer, "The Quorum," in *Strengthen Your Brethren* [Melchizedek Priesthood Personal Study Guide 4, 1991], pp. 142–48.)

If a priesthood quorum functions properly, the members of the quorum are encouraged, blessed, fellowshipped, and taught the gospel by their leaders. Even though a man may be called and released from Church assignments such as teacher, officer, bishop, high councilor, or stake president, his membership in his quorum does not change. Membership in a quorum of the priesthood should be regarded as a sacred privilege.

Discussion

- What is a quorum? How does a quorum help strengthen individual members?
- How many members make up a quorum of elders, high priests, deacons, teachers, priests?

Additional Scriptures

- Alma 13:1–19 (manner in which men were ordained to the priesthood)
- Hebrews 7:11–13 (Melchizedek Priesthood restored at the coming of Christ)
- Matthew 16:19; D&C 68:12 (Apostles given power; what they seal on earth is sealed in heaven)
- D&C 20:38–67 (duties of elders, priests, teachers, deacons)
- D&C 84; 107 (revelations on the priesthood)
- 1 Corinthians 12:14–31 (all offices of the priesthood are important)

Abraham made a covenant with the Lord.

THE LORD'S COVENANT PEOPLE

From the beginning the Lord has made covenants with his children on earth. When his people make covenants (or promises) with him, they know what he expects of them and what blessings they may expect from him. They can better carry out his work on earth. The people who covenant with the Lord and with whom the Lord makes covenants is known as *the Lord's covenant people*. Members of the Church are part of the Lord's covenant people.

Discussion
• Read Deuteronomy 26:18. What does the Lord mean when he calls his people a *peculiar people?*
• Why are Latter-day Saints called a covenant people?

What Is a Covenant?
Within the gospel, a covenant means a sacred agreement or mutual promise between God and a person or a group of people. In making a covenant, God promises a blessing for obedience to particular commandments. He sets the terms of his covenants, and he reveals these terms to his prophets. If we choose to obey the terms of the covenant, we receive promised blessings. If we choose not to obey, he withholds the blessings, and in some instances a penalty also is given.

For example, when we join the Church we make several covenants with God (see chapter 20, "Baptism"). We covenant with the Savior at baptism to take upon ourselves his name. He promises that *"* as many as . . . are baptized in my name, which is Jesus Christ, and endure to the end, the same shall be saved*"* (D&C 18:22). We covenant with the Lord as we partake of the sacrament. We promise to remember him and to obey his commandments. We are promised that the Holy Spirit will be with us. (See D&C 20:77–79.) As members of the Church, we also covenant to obey the law of chastity, to keep the Sabbath day holy, and to be honest. When we enter into the eternal marriage covenant, we make other sacred promises and are promised exaltation for faithful obedience (see D&C 132; see also chapter 47 in this manual).

God has also made special covenants with particular persons or groups. He made special covenants with Adam, Enoch, Noah, the children of Israel, and Lehi (see Moses 6:52; Moses 6:31–36; Genesis 9:9–17; Exodus 19:5–6; 2 Nephi 1). He made a special covenant with Abraham and his descendants that blesses members of the Church today.

Discussion
• What is a covenant?
• What kinds of covenants have we made with God?
• What blessings has he promised us for keeping certain covenants?

God's Covenant with Abraham and His Descendants
Abraham, an Old Testament prophet, was a very righteous man. He refused to worship his father's idols. He kept all of the Lord's commandments. Because of Abraham's righteousness, the Lord made a covenant with him and his descendants.

The Lord promised Abraham that he would have numberless descendants. He promised that all of them would be entitled to receive the gospel, the blessings of the priesthood, and all of the ordinances of exaltation. These descendants, through the power of the priesthood, would carry the gospel to all nations. Through them, all the families of the earth would be blessed (see Abraham 2:11). God further promised that if they were righteous he would establish his covenant with all generations of Abraham's children (see Genesis 17:4–8).

God made the same covenant with Abraham's son Isaac and again with Isaac's son Jacob. God changed Jacob's name to Israel. Since that time, the descendants of Jacob, called Israelites, have been known as God's covenant people.

Discussion
• Read Abraham 2:9–11. List the promises that God has made to his covenant people.

Members of the Church Are a Covenant People
The blood descendants of Abraham are not the only people whom God calls his covenant people. In speaking to Abraham, God said, "As many as receive this Gospel shall be called after thy name, and shall be accounted thy seed [lineage], and shall rise up and bless thee, as their father" (Abraham 2:10). Thus, two groups of people are included in the covenant made with Abraham: (1) Abraham's righteous blood descendants and (2) those adopted into his lineage by accepting and living the gospel of Jesus Christ.

When we are baptized into the Church, we are adopted into Abraham's family and have part in the covenant the Lord made with Abraham, Isaac, and Jacob (see Galatians 3:26–29). If we are obedient, we inherit the blessings of that covenant. We have the right to receive help and guidance from the Holy Ghost. We have the right to hold the priesthood. We can gain eternal life in the celestial kingdom. There are no greater blessings than these.

Along with the blessings we receive as the Lord's covenant people, we have great responsibilities. The Lord promised Abraham that through his descendants the gospel would be taken to all the earth. We are fulfilling this responsibility through the full-time missionary program of the Church and the missionary work done by the members. This opportunity to preach the gospel to all the world belongs only to the Lord's Church and his covenant people.

As the Lord's covenant people, we must keep his commandments. The Lord said, *"I, the Lord, am bound when ye do what I say; but when ye do not what I say, ye have no promise"* (D&C 82:10). If we reject our covenant after accepting the gospel, the covenant becomes void and we will stand condemned before God (see D&C 132:4). He has said: *"Refrain from sin, lest sore judgments fall upon your heads. For of him unto whom much is given much is required; and he who sins against the greater light shall receive the greater condemnation"* (D&C 82:2–3).

Discussion
- Read the words of the Savior in Matthew 5:14–16. What responsibility do we have as members of the Church to be a light (example) unto the world?
- What does this have to do with how we dress, act, and keep the commandments of God?
- What happens when we break a covenant we have made?

The New and Everlasting Covenant
The fulness of the gospel is called *the new and everlasting covenant.* It includes the covenants made at baptism, during the sacrament, in the temple, and at any other time. The Lord calls it "everlasting" because it is ordained by an everlasting God and because the covenant will never be changed. He gave this same covenant to Adam, Enoch, Noah, Abraham, and other prophets. In this sense it is not new. But the Lord calls it "new" because each time the gospel is restored after being taken from the earth, it is new to the people who receive it (see Jeremiah 31:31–34; Ezekiel 37:26).

When we accept the new and everlasting covenant, we agree to repent, be baptized, receive the Holy Ghost, receive our endowments, receive the covenant of marriage in the temple, and follow and obey Christ to the end of our lives. As we keep our covenants, our Heavenly Father promises us that we will receive exaltation in the celestial kingdom (see D&C 132:20–24; see also chapter 47 in this manual).

How blessed we are to be God's covenant people. To the faithful Saint, the Lord has promised, "All that my Father hath shall be given unto him" (D&C 84:38). The greatness of that promise is hard for mortals to understand. The commandments he gives are for our benefit, and as we are faithful we may forever share the blessings and beauties of heaven and earth. We may live in his presence and partake of his love, compassion, power, greatness, knowledge, wisdom, glory, and dominions.

• What do we agree to do when we enter the new and everlasting covenant?

Additional Scriptures
• 1 Nephi 13:23–26 (covenants recorded in the Bible)
• 1 Peter 2:9–10 (peculiar people)
• D&C 54:4–6 (effects of covenants kept and broken)
• D&C 132:7 (covenants made by proper authority)
• D&C 133:57–60 (purpose of covenants)
• D&C 35:24 (promises for obedience to covenants)

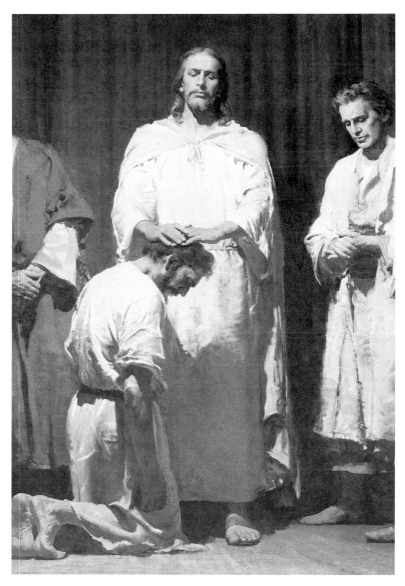

Jesus Christ ordained Apostles.

THE CHURCH OF JESUS CHRIST IN FORMER TIMES

Chapter 16

---

*"*We believe in the same organization that existed in the Primitive Church, namely, apostles, prophets, pastors, teachers, evangelists, and so forth*"* (Articles of Faith 1:6).

Jesus established his Church when he was on the earth. It was called the *Church of Jesus Christ* (see 3 Nephi 27:8), and the members were called Saints. Through the persecution and martyrdom of Church leaders and the general wickedness of the people, the Church of Jesus Christ was taken from the earth.

Today the Church of Jesus Christ has been restored and is called *The Church of Jesus Christ of Latter-day Saints.* All of the offices and functions of the Church in the days of Jesus are present in the Church today.

Discussion

• Have someone read or quote the sixth article of faith. Read Ephesians 4:11. Discuss the similarity of this scripture and the article of faith.

Some Features That Identify the Church of Jesus Christ

Revelation

When Jesus established his church, he personally instructed and directed its leaders. He, in turn, received his instructions from his Father in Heaven. Thus the Church of Jesus Christ was directed by God and not by men (see Hebrews 1:1–2).

Jesus taught his followers that revelation was the "rock" upon which he would build his Church (see Matthew 16:16–18).

Before Jesus ascended into heaven after his resurrection, he told his Apostles, "I am with you alway, even unto the end of the world" (Matthew 28:20). True to his word, he continued to guide them from heaven. He sent the Holy Ghost to be a comforter and a revelator to them (see Luke 12:12; John 14:26). He spoke to Saul in a vision (see Acts 9:3–6). He revealed to Peter that the gospel should be taught not only to the Jews but to the whole world (see Acts 10). He revealed many glorious truths to John, which are written in the Book of Revelation. The New Testament records many other ways in which Jesus revealed his will to guide his church and enlighten his disciples.

Authority from God
The ordinances and principles of the gospel cannot be administered and taught without the priesthood. The Father gave this authority to Jesus Christ (see Hebrews 5:4–6), who in turn ordained his Apostles and gave them the power and authority of the priesthood (see Luke 9:1–2; Mark 3:14). He reminded them, "Ye have not chosen me, but I have chosen you, and ordained you" (John 15:16).

That there might be order in his church, Jesus gave the greatest responsibility and authority to the Twelve Apostles. He appointed Peter chief Apostle and gave him the keys to seal blessings both on earth and in heaven (see Matthew 16:19). Jesus also ordained other officers with specific duties to perform. After he ascended into heaven, the pattern of appointment and ordination was continued. Others were ordained to the priesthood by those who had already received that authority. Jesus made it known through the Holy Ghost that he approved of those ordinations (see Acts 1:24).

The Church Organization
The Church of Jesus Christ was a carefully organized unit. It was compared to a perfectly formed building that was "built

upon the foundation of the apostles and prophets, Jesus Christ himself being the chief corner stone" (Ephesians 2:20).

Jesus appointed other priesthood leaders to assist the Apostles in the work of the ministry. He sent officers called *seventies* in pairs to preach the gospel (see Luke 10:1). Other officers in the Church were evangelists (patriarchs), pastors (presiding leaders), high priests, elders, bishops, priests, teachers, and deacons (see chapter 14, "Priesthood Organization"). These officers were all necessary to do missionary work, perform ordinances, and instruct and inspire Church members. These officers helped the members come to a "unity of the faith, and of the knowledge of the Son of God" (Ephesians 4:13).

The Bible does not tell us everything about the priesthood or the organization and government of the Church. However, enough of the Bible has been preserved to show the beauty and perfection of the Church organization. The Apostles were commanded to go into all the world and preach. They could not stay in any one city to supervise new converts. Therefore, local priesthood leaders were called and ordained, and the Apostles presided over them. The Apostles visited and wrote letters to the leaders in the various branches. Thus, our New Testament contains letters written by the Apostles Paul, Peter, James, John, and Jude, giving counsel and instruction to the local priesthood leaders.

The New Testament shows that this Church organization was intended to continue. For example, the death of Judas left only eleven Apostles. Soon after Jesus had ascended into heaven, the eleven Apostles met together to choose someone to take the place of Judas. Through revelation from the Holy Ghost, they chose Matthias. (See Acts 1:23–26.) Later, other Apostles died or were killed. Paul, Barnabas, and James, the brother of the Lord, were all ordained in their places. Jesus had set a pattern for twelve Apostles to govern the Church. It seemed clear that the organization was to continue as he had established it.

First Principles and Ordinances

The Apostles taught two basic principles: faith in the Lord Jesus Christ and repentance. After new converts had faith in Jesus Christ as the Son of God and their Redeemer and had repented of their sins, they received two ordinances: baptism by immersion and the laying on of hands for the gift of the Holy Ghost. These were the first principles and ordinances of the gospel. Jesus had taught, "Except a man be born of water and of the Spirit, he cannot enter into the kingdom of God" (John 3:5). Everyone needed these saving ordinances of baptism and the gift of the Holy Ghost.

Ordinances Performed for the Dead

Jesus has provided for everyone to hear the gospel, whether on earth or after death. Between his death and resurrection, Jesus went among the spirits of those who had died. He organized missionary work among those who were dead. He appointed righteous messengers and gave them power to teach the gospel to all the spirits of people who had died. This gave them an opportunity to accept the gospel. (See 1 Peter 3:18–20; 4:6; D&C 138.) Living members of his Church then performed ordinances in behalf of the dead (see 1 Corinthians 15:29). Ordinances such as baptism and confirmation must be done on earth.

Spiritual Gifts

All faithful members of the Church were entitled to receive gifts of the Spirit. These were given to them according to their individual needs, capacities, and assignments. Some of these gifts were faith, including the power to heal and to be healed; prophecy; and visions. (The gifts of the Spirit are discussed in more detail in chapter 22.) Spiritual gifts always exist in the true Church of Jesus Christ (see 1 Corinthians 12:4–11). Jesus told his disciples that these signs or spiritual gifts always follow them that believe (see Mark 16:17–18). Many of his disciples performed miracles, prophesied, or beheld visions through the power of the Holy Ghost.

The Church of Jesus Christ in the Americas

After Jesus was resurrected, he visited the people in America and organized his Church among them (see 3 Nephi 11–28). Then he left them and ascended into heaven. For over two hundred years they lived righteously and were among the happiest people whom God had created (see 4 Nephi 1:16).

Discussion

• List the features that identify the Church of Jesus Christ. Are all of these features found in any other church?

Apostasy from the True Church

Throughout history, evil people have tried to destroy the work of God. This happened while the Apostles were still alive and supervising the young, growing Church. Some members taught ideas from their old pagan or Jewish beliefs instead of the simple truths taught by Jesus. In addition, there was persecution from outside the Church. Church members were tortured and killed for their beliefs. One by one, the Apostles were killed. Because of the persecution, surviving Apostles could not meet to choose and ordain men to replace those who were dead. Eventually, local priesthood leaders were the only ones who had authority to direct the scattered branches of the Church. The perfect organization of the Church no longer existed, and confusion resulted. More and more error crept into Church doctrine, and soon the destruction of the Church was complete. The period of time when the true Church no longer existed on earth is called the *Great Apostasy.*

Soon pagan beliefs dominated the thinking of those called Christians. The Roman emperor adopted this false Christianity as the state religion. This church was very different from the church Jesus organized. Members of this church believed that God was a being without form or substance.

These people lost the understanding of God's love for us. They did not know that we are his children. They did not understand the purpose of life. Many of the ordinances were changed because the priesthood and revelation were no longer on the earth.

The emperor chose his own leaders and called them by the same titles used by priesthood leaders in the true Church of Christ. Church officers were given honor and wealth. Bishops and archbishops fought among themselves to gain more power. There were no Apostles or other priesthood leaders with power from God, and there were no spiritual gifts. The prophet Isaiah had foreseen this condition, prophesying, "The earth also is defiled under the inhabitants thereof; because they have transgressed the laws, changed the ordinance, broken the everlasting covenant" (Isaiah 24:5). It was the Church of Jesus Christ no longer; it was a church of men. Even the name had been changed. In the Americas, apostasy also occurred (see 4 Nephi).

Discussion
• What does the term *apostasy* mean?
• Have someone review the story of the Apostasy.
• What were some of the signs of the Apostasy?

A Restoration Foretold
God had foreseen the Apostasy and prepared for the gospel to be restored. The Apostle Peter spoke of this to the Jews: "He shall send Jesus Christ, which before was preached unto you: whom the heaven must receive until the times of restitution of all things, which God hath spoken by the mouth of all his holy prophets since the world began" (Acts 3:20–21).

John the Revelator had also foreseen the time when the gospel would be restored. He said, "I saw another angel fly in the midst of heaven, having the everlasting gospel to preach unto them that dwell on the earth, and to every nation, and kindred, and tongue, and people" (Revelation 14:6).

Discussion
- Read Daniel 2:44–45. What did Daniel see? Explain that the Church is the "stone" mentioned in this scripture.

Additional Scriptures
- Ephesians 2:19 (members called Saints)
- 1 Corinthians 12:12–31 (Church likened to a perfect body)
- Luke 10:1; Acts 14:23; Titus 1:7; 1 Timothy 2:7 (officers of the Church identified)
- John 8:26–29 (the Father directs Jesus)
- Luke 9:1; James 1:17; 5:14–15 (spiritual gifts)
- 2 Peter 2:1; Matthew 24:9–12; John 16:1–3; Amos 8:11; 2 Thessalonians 2:3–4 (Apostasy predicted)
- Daniel 2:44–45; Matthew 24:14; Micah 4:1; Isaiah 2:2–4 (Restoration predicted)

The Father and the Son visited Joseph Smith.

THE CHURCH OF JESUS CHRIST TODAY

Chapter 17

When Jesus lived on the earth, he established his Church, the only true Church. He organized his Church so the truths of the gospel could be taught to all people and the ordinances of the gospel could be administered correctly with authority. Through this organization, Christ could bring the blessings of salvation to mankind.

After the Savior ascended into heaven, men changed the ordinances and doctrines that he and his Apostles had established. Because of apostasy, there was no direct revelation from God. The true church was no longer on the earth. Men organized different churches that claimed to be true but taught conflicting doctrines. There was much confusion and contention over religion. The Lord had foreseen these conditions, saying there would be "a famine in the land, not a famine of bread, nor a thirst for water, but of hearing the words of the Lord. . . . They shall . . . seek the word of the Lord, and shall not find it" (Amos 8:11–12).

Discussion
• What does it feel like to go without food or water?
• Read Amos 8:11–12. What kind of famine is spoken of in this scripture? Compare the famine to the period of time before the Restoration.

The Lord Promised to Restore His True Church

The Savior promised to restore his church in the latter days. He said, ❝I will proceed to do a marvellous work among this people, even a marvellous work and a wonder❞ (Isaiah 29:14).

For many years people lived in spiritual darkness. About 1700 years after Christ, people were becoming more and more interested in knowing the truth about God and religion. Some of them could see that the gospel Jesus taught was no longer on the earth. Some recognized that there was no revelation and no true authority and that the church that Christ organized did not exist on the earth. The time had arrived for the Church of Jesus Christ to be restored to the earth.

Discussion
• Read Isaiah 29:14. What is the ❝marvellous work❞ spoken of in Isaiah?

New Revelation from God

In the spring of 1820, one of the most important events in the history of the world occurred. The time had come for the marvelous work and wonder of which the Lord had spoken. As a young boy, Joseph Smith wanted to know which of all the churches was the true Church of Christ. He went into the woods near his home and prayed humbly and intently to his Heavenly Father, asking which church he should join. On that morning a miraculous thing happened. Heavenly Father and Jesus Christ appeared to Joseph Smith. The Savior told him not to join any church because the true church was not on the earth. He also said that the teachings of present churches were ❝an abomination in his sight❞ (Joseph Smith—History 1:19; see also 1:7–20). Beginning with this event, there was again direct revelation from the heavens. The Lord had chosen a new prophet. Since that time the heavens have not been closed. Revelation continues to this day through each of his chosen prophets. Joseph was to be the one to help restore the true gospel of Jesus Christ.

Discussion
• Have a class member read Joseph Smith—History 1:7–21 or tell the Joseph Smith story.

Authority from God Was Restored
In restoring the gospel, God again gave the priesthood to men. John the Baptist came in 1829 to ordain Joseph Smith and Oliver Cowdery to the Aaronic Priesthood (see D&C 13; 27:8). Then Peter, James, and John, the presidency of the Church in ancient times, came and gave Joseph and Oliver the Melchizedek Priesthood and the keys of the kingdom of God (see D&C 27:12–13). Later, additional keys of the priesthood were restored by heavenly messengers such as Moses, Elias, and Elijah (see D&C 110:11–16). Through the Restoration the priesthood was returned to the earth. Those who hold this priesthood today have the authority to perform ordinances such as baptism. They also have the authority to direct the Lord's kingdom on earth.

Discussion
• Have a class member tell about the restoration of the priesthood. Include the following: the restoration of the Aaronic Priesthood, the restoration of the Melchizedek Priesthood, and the effect of these restorations on the Lord's work.

Christ's Church Was Organized Again
On 6 April 1830, the Savior again directed the organization of his Church on the earth (see D&C 20:1). His Church is called The Church of Jesus Christ of Latter-day Saints (see D&C 115:4). Christ is the head of his Church today, just as he was in ancient times. The Lord has said that it is "the only true and living church upon the face of the whole earth, with which I, the Lord, am well pleased" (D&C 1:30).

Joseph Smith was sustained as prophet and "first elder" of the Church (see D&C 20:2–4). Later the First Presidency was organized, and he was sustained as President. When the Church was first organized, only the framework was set up. The organization was completed during the next several years.

The Church was organized with the same offices as were in the ancient Church. That organization included Apostles, prophets, seventies, evangelists (patriarchs), pastors (presiding officers), high priests, elders, bishops, priests, teachers, and deacons. These same offices are in his church today (see Articles of Faith 1:6).

A prophet, acting under the direction of the Lord, leads the Church. This prophet is also the President of the Church. He holds all the authority necessary to direct the Lord's work on earth (see D&C 107:65, 91). Two counselors assist the President. Twelve Apostles, who are special witnesses of Jesus Christ, teach the gospel in all parts of the world. Other general officers of the Church with special assignments include the Presiding Bishopric and the Quorums of the Seventy.

The offices of the priesthood include Apostles, seventies, patriarchs, high priests, elders, priests, teachers, and deacons. These are the same offices that existed in the original Church.

The Church has grown much larger than it was in the days of Jesus. As it has grown, the Lord has revealed additional units of organization within the Church. When the Church is fully organized in an area, it has local divisions called *stakes.* A stake president and his two counselors preside over each stake. The stake has twelve high councilors who help do the Lord's work in the stake. Melchizedek Priesthood quorums are organized in the stake under the direction of the stake president (see chapter 14, "Priesthood Organization").

Each stake is divided into smaller areas called *wards.* A bishop and his two counselors preside over each ward. In areas of the world where the Church is developing, there are missions, which are divided into the smaller units of districts, branches, small branches, groups, and families.

Discussion
• Read the testimony of Joseph Smith contained in the preface to Doctrine and Covenants 20.

First Principles and Ordinances Were Restored

The Church today teaches the same principles and performs the same ordinances as were performed in the days of Jesus. The first principles and ordinances of the gospel are faith in the Lord Jesus Christ, repentance, baptism by immersion, and the laying on of hands for the gift of the Holy Ghost (see Articles of Faith 1:4). These precious truths were returned in their fulness when the Church was restored.

Through the gift and power of God, Joseph Smith translated the Book of Mormon, which contains the plain and precious truths of the gospel. Many other revelations followed and have been recorded as scripture in the Doctrine and Covenants and the Pearl of Great Price (see chapter 10, "Scriptures").

Discussion

• Read the fourth article of faith and discuss what it means to Church members.

Other Important Truths Were Restored

Other important truths that the Lord restored include the following:

1. Our Heavenly Father is a real person with a tangible, perfected body of flesh and bones.
2. We existed in premortal life as spirit children of God.
3. The priesthood is necessary to administer the ordinances of the gospel.
4. Men will be punished for their own sins and not for Adam's transgression.
5. Children do not need to be baptized until they are accountable (eight years old).
6. There are three degrees of glory in the heavens, and people will be rewarded according to their actions on earth.
7. Family relationships can be eternal through the sealing power of the priesthood.
8. The temple endowment and sealings are available for both the living and the dead.

The Church of Jesus Christ Will Never Be Destroyed

Since its restoration in 1830, The Church of Jesus Christ of Latter-day Saints has grown rapidly in membership. There are members in nearly every country in the world. The Church will continue to grow. As Christ said, "This Gospel of the Kingdom shall be preached in all the world, for a witness unto all nations" (Joseph Smith—Matthew 1:31). The Church will never again be taken from the earth. Its mission is to take the truth to every person. Thousands of years ago, the Lord said he would "set up a kingdom, which shall never be destroyed: and the kingdom shall not be left to other people, . . . and it shall stand for ever" (Daniel 2:44).

Discussion

• Read D&C 84:76. What can you do to help spread the kingdom of God?

Additional Scriptures

• Revelation 14:6; Daniel 2:44–45; Isaiah 2:2–4; 2 Nephi 3:6–15 (Restoration foretold)
• D&C 110; 128:19–21; 133:36–39, 57–58 (restoration of the gospel)
• Ephesians 2:20 (Jesus Christ the cornerstone of the Church)
• D&C 20:38–67 (duties of officers of the Church)
• Matthew 24:14 (gospel to be preached to all nations)

THE GOSPEL OF JESUS CHRIST

Unit Six

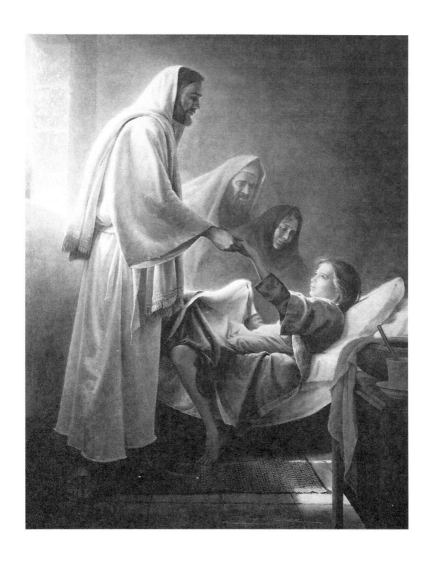

To return to Heavenly Father, we must have faith in Jesus Christ.

FAITH IN JESUS CHRIST

Chapter 18

Faith in the Lord Jesus Christ is the first principle of the gospel. It is necessary to our salvation. King Benjamin declared, "Salvation cometh to none . . . except it be through repentance and faith on the Lord Jesus Christ" (Mosiah 3:12).

What Is Faith?

Faith is confidence in things that are not seen but that are true (see Hebrews 11:1; Alma 32:21). The Prophet Joseph Smith taught that faith motivates our day-to-day activities. He said that faith is a principle of power and the moving cause of action within us.

Would we study and learn if we did not believe we could obtain wisdom and knowledge? Would we work each day if we did not hope that by doing so we could accomplish something? Would a farmer plant if he did not expect to harvest? Each day we act upon things we hope for when we cannot see the end result. This is faith. (See Hebrews 11:3.)

Many scriptural stories tell how great things were accomplished through faith.

By faith Noah built an ark and saved his family from the flood (see Hebrews 11:7). Moses parted the waters of the Red Sea (see Hebrews 11:29). Elijah called down fire from heaven (see 1 Kings 18:17–40). Nephi called for a famine (see Helaman

11:3–5). He also asked the Lord to end the famine (see Helaman 11:9–17). Seas have been calmed, visions opened, and prayers answered, all through the power of faith.

As we carefully study the scriptures, we learn that faith is a strong belief of truth within our souls that motivates us to do good. This causes us to ask: In whom should we have faith?

Discussion
• Ask the group to think about their everyday activities. How does faith move you to action?

Why Should We Have Faith in Jesus Christ?
We must center our faith in the Lord Jesus Christ.

To have faith in Jesus Christ means to have such trust in him that we obey whatever he commands. There is no faith where there is no obedience. Likewise, there is true obedience only where there is faith. As we place our faith in Jesus Christ, becoming his obedient disciples, Heavenly Father will forgive our sins and prepare us to return to him.

The Apostle Peter preached that *"there is none other name under heaven given among men, whereby we must be saved"* (Acts 4:12). Jacob taught that men must have *"perfect faith in the Holy One of Israel [Jesus Christ], or they cannot be saved in the kingdom of God"* (2 Nephi 9:23). Through faith in the Savior and through repentance, we make his atonement fully effective in our lives. Through faith we can also receive strength to overcome temptations (see Alma 37:33).

We cannot have faith in Jesus Christ without also having faith in our Heavenly Father. If we have faith in them, we will also have faith that the Holy Ghost, whom they send, will teach us all truth and will comfort us.

Discussion
• Read Acts 4:10–12 and Alma 37:33. Why do we need to have faith in Jesus Christ?

How Can We Increase Our Faith in Jesus Christ?

Knowing of the many blessings that come through exercising faith in Jesus Christ, we should seek to increase our faith in him. The Savior said, "If ye have faith as a grain of mustard seed, . . . nothing shall be impossible unto you" (Matthew 17:20). A mustard seed is very small, but it grows into a large tree.

How can we increase our faith? The same way we increase or develop any other skill. How do we develop skills in wood-carving, weaving, painting, cooking, making pottery, or playing a musical instrument? We study and practice and work at it. As we do so, we improve. So it is with faith. If we want to increase our faith in Jesus Christ, we must work at it. The Prophet Alma compared increasing our faith to planting a seed:

"But behold, if ye will awake and arouse your faculties, even to an experiment upon my words, and exercise a particle of faith, yea, even if ye can no more than desire to believe, let this desire work in you, even until ye believe in a manner that ye can give place for a portion of my words.

"Now, we will compare the word unto a seed. Now, if ye give place, that a seed may be planted in your heart, behold, if it be a true seed, or a good seed, if ye do not cast it out by your unbelief, that ye will resist the Spirit of the Lord, behold, it will begin to swell within your breasts; and when you feel these swelling motions, ye will begin to say within your-selves—It must needs be that this is a good seed, or that the word is good, for it beginneth to enlarge my soul; yea, it beginneth to enlighten my understanding. . . .

"Now behold, would not this increase your faith?" (Alma 32:27–29).

So we can increase our faith in God by acting on our *desire* to have faith in him.

We can also increase our faith by praying to Heavenly Father about our hopes, desires, and needs (see Alma 34:17–25). But we must not suppose that all we have to do is ask. We are told in the scriptures that "faith, if it hath not works, is dead, being alone" (James 2:17). The following story is about a man whose faith was shown by his works.

This man wanted to study the scriptures, but he could not read. He prayed for Heavenly Father to help him learn to read. In time a teacher came to his village, and he asked the teacher to help him. He learned the alphabet. He studied sounds and learned to put the letters together to make words. Soon he was reading simple words. The more he practiced, the more he learned. He thanked the Lord for sending the teacher and for helping him learn to read. This man has increased his faith, humility, and knowledge to such a degree that he has served as a branch president in the Church.

President Spencer W. Kimball explained: "There must be works with faith. How foolish it would be to ask the Lord to *give* us knowledge, but how wise to ask the Lord's help to acquire knowledge, to study constructively, to think clearly, and to retain things that we have learned" (*Faith Precedes the Miracle*, p. 205).

Faith involves doing all we can to bring about the things we hope and pray for. President Kimball said: "In faith we plant the seed, and soon we see the miracle of the blossoming. Men have often misunderstood and have reversed the process." He continued by explaining that many of us want to have health and strength without keeping the health laws. We want to have prosperity without paying our tithes. We want to be close to the Lord but don't want to fast and pray. We want to have rain in due season and to have peace in the land without observing the Sabbath as a holy day and without keeping the other commandments of the Lord. (See *Faith Precedes the Miracle*, p. 4.)

An important way to increase our faith is to hear and study the word of the Lord. We hear the word of the Lord at our Church meetings. We can study his word in the scriptures.

*"*And as all have not faith, seek ye diligently and teach one another words of wisdom; yea, seek ye out of the best books words of wisdom; seek learning, even by study and also by faith*"* (D&C 88:118).

Discussion

• Read James 2:17. Why do you think President Kimball said *"*faith involves doing everything we can*"*? How can we strengthen our faith? (Pray, fast, study the scriptures, obey commandments.)

• Challenge class members to strengthen their faith in these ways.

What Are Some Blessings That Follow Faith?

By faith, miracles are wrought, angels appear, the gifts of the Spirit are given, prayers are answered, and men become the sons of God (see Moroni 7:25–26, 36–37). The Prophet Joseph Smith taught:

*"*When faith comes it brings . . . apostles, prophets, evangelists, pastors, teachers, gifts, wisdom, knowledge, miracles, healings, tongues, interpretation of tongues, etc. All these appear when faith appears on the earth, and disappear when it disappears from the earth; for these are the effects of faith. . . . And he who possesses it will, through it, obtain all necessary knowledge and wisdom, until he shall know God, and the Lord Jesus Christ, whom he has sent — whom to know is eternal life. Amen*"* (*Lectures on Faith,* p. 69).

Discussion

• Tell a story about how showing faith made a person stronger, or tell a story about faith from the list of additional scriptures.

Additional Scriptures

• Hebrews 11; Alma 32 (nature of faith explained)
• Exodus 14:19–22 (parting the waters of the Red Sea)
• Genesis 6–8 (Noah and the flood)
• Matthew 8:5–33 (sick healed, tempest, miracles of faith)
• Mark 5:25–34 (healed by faith)

REPENTANCE

Chapter 19

Faith in Jesus Christ naturally leads to repentance. There has been the need for repentance in the world from the time of Adam to the present day. The Lord instructed Adam, "Wherefore teach it unto your children, that all men, everywhere, must repent, or they can in nowise inherit the kingdom of God, for no unclean thing can dwell there, or dwell in his presence" (Moses 6:57).

We All Need to Repent
We come to earth for the purpose of growing and progressing. This is a lifelong process. During this time we all sin. We all have need to repent. Sometimes we sin because of ignorance, sometimes because of our weaknesses, and sometimes because of willful disobedience. In the Bible we read that "there is not a just man upon earth, that doeth good, and sinneth not" (Ecclesiastes 7:20) and that "if we say that we have no sin, we deceive ourselves, and the truth is not in us" (1 John 1:8).

What is sin? The Apostle James said, "To him that knoweth to do good, and doeth it not, to him it is sin" (James 4:17). Another Apostle described sin as "all unrighteousness" (1 John 5:17).

That is why the Lord said "all men, everywhere, must repent" (Moses 6:57). Except for Jesus Christ, who lived a perfect life, everyone who has lived upon the earth has sinned. Our

Heavenly Father in his great love has provided us this opportunity to repent of our sins.

Discussion
• Why do all people need to repent?

What Is Repentance?

Repentance is the way provided for us to become free from
our sins and receive forgiveness for them. Sins slow our spiritual progression and can even stop it. Repentance makes it
possible for us to grow and develop spiritually again.

The privilege of repenting is made possible through the
atonement of Jesus Christ. In a way we do not fully understand, Jesus paid for our sins. President Joseph Fielding Smith
said of this:

"I have suffered pain, you have suffered pain, and sometimes
it has been quite severe; but I cannot comprehend pain . . .
that would cause the blood, like sweat, to come out upon the
body. It was something terrible, something terrific. . . .

"There was *no man ever born into this world that could have stood
under the weight of the load that was upon the Son of God, when he
was carrying my sins and yours* and making it possible that we
might escape from our sins" (*Doctrines of Salvation*, 1:130–31).

Repentance sometimes requires great courage, much
strength, many tears, unceasing prayers, and untiring efforts
to live the commandments of the Lord.

Discussion
• What does the word *repentance* mean to you?

How Do We Repent?

Elder Spencer W. Kimball declared: "There is *no royal road to
repentance,* no privileged path to forgiveness. Every man must
follow the same course whether he be rich or poor, educated or untrained, tall or short, prince or pauper, king or
commoner. . . . There is only one way. It is a long road spiked
with thorns and briars and pitfalls and problems" (*The Miracle
of Forgiveness*, p. 149).

Discussion

• Why must we repent of our sins?

We Must Recognize Our Sins

The first step of repentance is to admit to ourselves that we have sinned. If we do not admit this, we cannot repent.

Alma counseled his son Corianton, who had been unfaithful in his missionary calling and had committed serious sins: "Let your sins trouble you, with that trouble which shall bring you down unto repentance. . . . Do not endeavor to excuse yourself in the least point" (Alma 42:29–30). The scriptures advise us further not to justify our sinful practices (see Luke 16:15–16).

We cannot hide any act of our lives from ourselves or from the Lord.

We Must Feel Sorrow for Our Sins

In addition to recognizing our sins, we must feel sincere sorrow for what we have done. We must feel that our sins are terrible. We must want to unload and abandon them. The scriptures tell us, "All those who humble themselves before God, and desire to be baptized, and come forth with broken hearts and contrite spirits, and . . . have truly repented of all their sins . . . shall be received by baptism into his church" (D&C 20:37).

We Must Forsake Our Sins

Our sincere sorrow should lead us to forsake (stop) our sins. If we have stolen something, we will steal no more. If we have lied, we will lie no more. If we have committed adultery, we will stop. The Lord revealed to the Prophet Joseph Smith, "By this ye may know if a man repenteth of his sins—behold, he will confess them and forsake them" (D&C 58:43).

We Must Confess Our Sins

Confessing our sins is very important. The Lord has commanded us to confess our sins. Confession relieves a heavy burden from the sinner. The Lord has promised, "I, the Lord, forgive sins, and am merciful unto those who confess their sins with humble hearts" (D&C 61:2).

We must confess all our sins to the Lord. In addition, we must confess serious sins, such as adultery, fornication, and robbery, which might affect our standing in the Church, to the proper priesthood authority. If we have sinned against another person, we should confess to the person we have injured. Some less serious sins involve no one but ourselves and the Lord. These may be confessed privately to the Lord.

We Must Make Restitution

Part of repentance is to make restitution. This means that as much as possible we must make right any wrong that we have done. For example, a thief should give back what he has stolen. A liar should make the truth known. A gossip who has slandered the character of a person should work to restore the good name of the person he has harmed. As we do these things, God will not mention our sins to us when we are judged (see Ezekiel 33:15–16).

We Must Forgive Others

A vital part of repentance is to forgive those who have sinned against us. The Lord will not forgive us unless our hearts are fully cleansed of all hate, bitterness, and bad feelings against other people (see 3 Nephi 13:14–15). "Wherefore, I say unto you, that ye ought to forgive one another; for he that forgiveth not his brother his trespasses standeth condemned before the Lord; for there remaineth in him the greater sin" (D&C 64:9).

We Must Keep the Commandments of God

To make our repentance complete we must keep the commandments of the Lord (see D&C 1:32). We are not fully repentant if we do not pay tithes or keep the Sabbath day holy or obey the Word of Wisdom. We are not repentant if we do not sustain the authorities of the Church and do not love the

Lord and our fellowmen. If we do not pray and are unkind to others, we are surely not repentant. When we repent, our life changes.

Elder Kimball said: "Repentance means not only to convict yourselves of the horror of the sin, but to confess it, abandon it, and restore to all who have been damaged to the total extent possible; then spend the balance of your lives trying to live the commandments of the Lord so he can eventually pardon you and cleanse you" (*The Miracle of Forgiveness*, p. 200).

Discussion
• Discuss the steps of repentance.

How Repentance Helps Us
As we repent, the atonement of Jesus Christ becomes fully effective in our lives, and the Lord forgives our sins. We become free from the bondage of our sins, and we find joy.

Alma recounted his experience of repenting from his sinful past:

"My soul was harrowed up [troubled] to the greatest degree and racked with all my sins.

"Yea, I did remember all my sins and iniquities, for which I was tormented with the pains of hell; yea, I saw that I had rebelled against my God, and that I had not kept his holy commandments.

" . . . So great had been my iniquities, that the very thought of coming into the presence of my God did rack my soul with inexpressible horror.

" . . . It came to pass that as I was . . . harrowed up by the memory of my many sins, behold, I remembered also to have heard my father prophesy . . . concerning the coming of one Jesus Christ, a Son of God, to atone for the sins of the world.

"Now, as my mind caught hold upon this thought, I cried within my heart: O Jesus, thou Son of God, have mercy on me. . . .

"And now, behold, when I thought this, I could remember my pains no more. . . .

"And oh, what joy, and what marvelous light I did behold; yea, my soul was filled with joy as exceeding as was my pain!

" . . . There can be nothing so exquisite and sweet as was my joy" (Alma 36:12–14, 17–21).

Discussion

• Read Alma 36:10–28. Discuss the agony Alma suffered while remembering his sins; discuss also his repentance and how forgiveness brought him joy.

When Should We Repent?

The prophets have declared that "this life is the time for men to prepare to meet God" (Alma 34:32). We should repent now, every day. When we get up in the morning, we should examine ourselves to see whether the Spirit of God is with us. At night before we go to sleep, we should review our acts and words of the day and ask the Lord to show us the things for which we need to repent. By repenting every day and having the Lord forgive our sins, we will experience the daily process of becoming perfect. As with Alma, our happiness and joy can be sweet and exquisite.

Discussion

• Discuss how difficult it is to learn something new all at once. By contrast, discuss how easy it is to practice each day until we gain mastery. How is this like repentance?

Additional Scriptures

• Matthew 9:10–13; Luke 13:3; Ezekiel 18:30 (repent or perish)
• 2 Corinthians 7:9–10 (godly sorrow)
• Mosiah 4:10–12 (steps to repentance)
• Isaiah 1:18; Mosiah 26:28–32 (repentance brings forgiveness)
• D&C 58:42 (sins remembered no more)
• 2 Nephi 9:23 (repentance necessary to salvation)
• 2 Nephi 2:21 (repent while in the flesh)

Alma baptized in the waters of Mormon.

BAPTISM

Chapter 20

Today, as in the days of Jesus, there are certain principles and ordinances of the gospel that we must learn and obey. A principle is a belief or a teaching. An ordinance is a rite or a ceremony. The first two principles of the gospel are faith in the Lord Jesus Christ and repentance. Baptism is the first ordinance of the gospel. One of the instructions the Lord gave his Apostles was, "Go ye therefore, and teach all nations, baptizing them in the name of the Father, and of the Son, and of the Holy Ghost: teaching them to observe all things whatsoever I have commanded you" (Matthew 28:19–20).

Discussion
• How does a principle of the gospel differ from an ordinance of the gospel?

Why Must We Be Baptized?

We Must Be Baptized for the Remission of Our Sins

If we place our faith in Jesus Christ, repent, and are baptized, our sins are forgiven through the atonement of Jesus Christ.

From the scriptures we learn that John the Baptist "did baptize in the wilderness, and preach the baptism of repentance for the remission of sins" (Mark 1:4). The Apostle Peter taught, "Repent, and be baptized every one of you in the name of Jesus Christ for the remission of sins" (Acts 2:38). Following

We must be baptized by immersion for the remission of our sins.

Paul's conversion, Ananias said to him, "Arise, and be baptized, and wash away thy sins" (Acts 22:16).

We Must Be Baptized to Become Members of the Church of Jesus Christ

"All those who humble themselves before God, and desire to be baptized . . . that . . . have truly repented of all their sins . . . shall be received by baptism into his church" (D&C 20:37).

We Must Be Baptized before We Can Receive the Gift of the Holy Ghost

The Lord said, "If thou wilt turn unto me, and . . . repent of all thy transgressions [sins], and be baptized, even in water, in the name of mine Only Begotten Son, . . . ye shall receive the gift of the Holy Ghost" (Moses 6:52).

We Must Be Baptized to Show Obedience

Jesus Christ was without sin, yet he was baptized. He said his baptism was necessary "to fulfill all righteousness" (Matthew 3:15). The prophet Nephi explained that the Lord told him, "Follow me, and do the things which ye have seen me do . . . with full purpose of heart, acting no hypocrisy and no deception before God, but with real intent, repenting of your sins, witnessing unto the Father that ye are willing to take upon you the name of Christ, by baptism" (2 Nephi 31:12–13).

We Must Be Baptized to Enter the Celestial Kingdom

Jesus said, "Whoso believeth in me, and is baptized . . . shall inherit the kingdom of God. And whoso believeth not in me, and is not baptized, shall be damned" (3 Nephi 11:33–34). Baptism is the gateway through which we enter the celestial kingdom.

Discussion

• Discuss five reasons why we need to be baptized.

How Should We Be Baptized?

There is only one correct mode of baptism. Jesus revealed to the Prophet Joseph Smith that a person having the proper priesthood authority to baptize "shall go down into the water with the person who has presented himself or herself for baptism. . . . Then shall he immerse him or her in the water, and come forth again out of the water" (D&C 20:73–74). Immersion is necessary. The Apostle Paul taught that being immersed in water and coming out again is symbolic of death and resurrection. Our sins are washed away when we are baptized. After baptism we start a new life. Paul said:

"Know ye not, that so many of us as were baptized into Jesus Christ were baptized into his death?

"Therefore we are buried with him by baptism into death: that like as Christ was raised up from the dead by the glory of the Father, even so we also should walk in newness of life.

"For if we have been planted together in the likeness of his death, we shall be also in the likeness of his resurrection" (Romans 6:3–5).

Baptism by immersion by a person having the proper authority is the only acceptable way of being baptized.

Discussion
• Read D&C 20:73–74. Why is authority to perform a baptism important?

Who Should Be Baptized?
Every person who has reached eight years of age and is accountable (responsible) for his actions should be baptized. Some churches teach that little children should be baptized. This is not in keeping with the teachings of the Savior. When Jesus spoke of little children, he said, "Of such is the kingdom of heaven" (Matthew 19:14).

The prophet Mormon said that it is mockery before God to baptize little children because they are not capable of sinning. Baptism is not required of people who are mentally incapable of knowing right and wrong (see Moroni 8:9–22).

All other people are to be baptized. We must receive the ordinance of baptism and remain true to the covenant we make at that time.

Discussion

- Why does the Apostle Paul liken our baptism to the burial of the Savior?
- Read Moroni 8:11–20. Why do we not baptize little children?

We Make Covenants When We Are Baptized

Many scriptures teach about baptism. In one of these scriptures, the prophet Alma taught that faith and repentance are steps that prepare us for baptism. He taught that when we are baptized we make a covenant with the Lord. We promise to do certain things, and God promises to bless us in return.

Alma explained that we must want to be called the people of God. We must be willing to help and comfort each other. We must stand as witnesses of God at all times and in all things and in all places. As we do these things and are baptized, God will forgive our sins. Alma told the people who believed his teachings about the gospel:

"Behold, here are the waters of Mormon. . . . And now, as ye are desirous to come into the fold of God, and to be called his people, . . . what have you against being baptized in the name of the Lord, as a witness before him that ye have entered into a covenant with him, that ye will serve him and keep his commandments, that he may pour out his Spirit more abundantly upon you?" (Mosiah 18:8–10). The people clapped their hands for joy and said it was their desire to be baptized. Alma baptized them in the Waters of Mormon. (See Mosiah 18:7–17.)

Alma taught that when we are baptized we make covenants with the Lord to—

1. Come into the fold of God.
2. Bear one another's burdens.
3. Stand as witnesses of God at all times and in all places.
4. Serve God and keep his commandments.

When we are baptized and keep the covenants of baptism, the Lord promises to—

1. Forgive our sins.
2. Pour out his Spirit more abundantly upon us.
3. Give us daily guidance and the help of the Holy Ghost.
4. Let us come forth in the First Resurrection.
5. Give us eternal life.

Discussion

• Review the baptismal covenants. List and discuss the promises we make and those made by our Heavenly Father. How can we help each other keep these covenants?

Baptism Gives Us a New Beginning

With baptism we begin a new way of life. That is why we call it a rebirth. Jesus said that unless we are born again, we cannot enter the kingdom of God. He further explained that unless we are born of the water and of the spirit, we cannot enter the kingdom of God (see John 3:3–5). This principle was explained clearly to Adam:

Inasmuch as ye were born into the world by water, and blood, and the spirit, which I have made, and so became of dust a living soul, even so ye must be born again into the kingdom of heaven, of water, and of the Spirit, and be cleansed by blood, even the blood of mine Only Begotten (Moses 6:59).

The Apostle Paul said that following our baptism we should begin a new life: *We are buried with him by baptism; . . . even so we also should walk in newness of life* (Romans 6:4). One of the great blessings of baptism is that it provides us with a new start on our way toward our eternal goal.

Discussion

• In what ways is baptism a new beginning?

Additional Scriptures

• 2 Nephi 31:4–7 (purpose and necessity of baptism)
• 3 Nephi 11:21–27 (how to perform a baptism)
• Acts 2:38–39 (be baptized for the remission of sins)
• D&C 20:71–72 (baptism is not required of little children; baptism is required of all who repent)
• Alma 7:14, 15–16 (baptism is cleansing, entering into a covenant of eternal life)

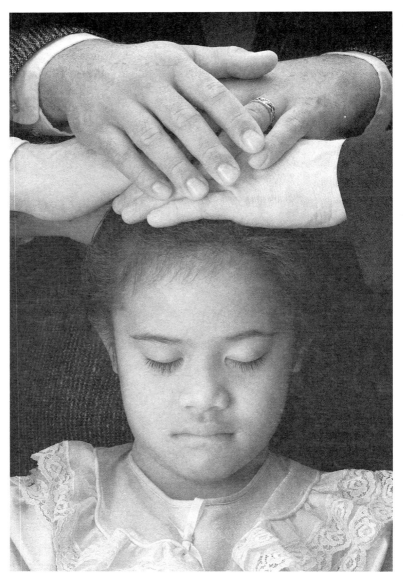

We must receive the gift of the Holy Ghost by the laying on of hands.

THE GIFT OF THE HOLY GHOST

Joseph Smith said we believe in the gift of the Holy Ghost being enjoyed now as much as it was enjoyed in the days of the first Apostles. We believe in this gift in all its fullness, power, greatness, and glory (see *Teachings of the Prophet Joseph Smith*, p. 243).

In chapter 7 we learned that the Holy Ghost is a member of the Godhead. He is a spirit in the form of a man. He does not have a body of flesh and bones. He can be in only one place at a time, but his influence can be everywhere at once. His mission is to bear witness of the Father and the Son and of all truth. Furthermore, the Holy Ghost purifies, or sanctifies, us to prepare us to dwell in the presence of God. The Holy Ghost purifies our hearts so we no longer have the desire to do evil.

There is a difference between the Holy Ghost and the *gift* of the Holy Ghost. In this chapter we will learn what the gift of the Holy Ghost is and how we can receive this great gift from God.

Discussion

• Have class members tell what they know about the Holy Ghost (see chapter 7, "The Holy Ghost").

What Is the Gift of the Holy Ghost?
The gift of the Holy Ghost is the privilege given to a person who has placed his faith in Jesus Christ, been baptized, and

been confirmed a member of the Church, to receive guidance and inspiration from the Holy Ghost.

A person may be temporarily guided by the Holy Ghost without receiving the gift of the Holy Ghost. However, this guidance will not be continuous unless he receives baptism and the laying on of hands for the gift of the Holy Ghost. We read in Acts 10 that the Roman soldier Cornelius received inspiration from the Holy Ghost so that he knew the gospel of Jesus Christ was true. But Cornelius did not receive the gift of the Holy Ghost until after he was baptized. The Prophet Joseph Smith taught that if Cornelius had not received baptism and the gift of the Holy Ghost, the Holy Ghost would have left him (see *Teachings of the Prophet Joseph Smith*, p. 199).

Today many nonmembers of the Church learn by the power of the Holy Ghost that the Book of Mormon is true (see Moroni 10:4–5). But that flash of testimony leaves them if they do not receive the gift of the Holy Ghost. They do not receive the continuing assurance that can come to those who have the gift of the Holy Ghost.

Discussion
• Discuss the difference between inspiration from the Holy Ghost and the gift of the Holy Ghost.

How Do We Receive the Gift of the Holy Ghost?
People who have been baptized and confirmed are given the gift of the Holy Ghost through the laying on of hands by the elders of the Church. The Lord said, ⁽ᵃ⁾Whoso having faith you shall confirm in my church, by the laying on of the hands, and I will bestow the gift of the Holy Ghost upon them⁽ᵃ⁾ (D&C 33:15).

Every worthy elder of the Church, when authorized, may give the gift of the Holy Ghost to another person. However, there is no guarantee that the person will receive inspiration and guidance from the Holy Ghost just because the elders have laid their hands on his head. Each person must *receive the Holy Ghost.* This means that the Holy Ghost will come to a person only when he is faithful and desires help from this heavenly messenger (see Bruce R. McConkie, *Mormon Doctrine,* p. 313).

To be worthy to have the help of the Holy Ghost, we must seek earnestly to obey the commandments of God. We must keep our thoughts and actions pure. President David O. McKay said: "One chief purpose of life is to overcome evil tendencies, to govern our appetites, to control our passions—anger, hatred, jealousy, immorality. We have to overcome them; we have to subject them, conquer them because God has said: '. . . the Spirit of the Lord doth not dwell in unholy temples—' (Helaman 4:24), nor will it '. . . always strive with man' (2 Nephi 26:11)" ("Emotional Maturity," *Instructor,* Sept. 1959, p. 281).

Discussion
• What must we do to receive the constant companionship of the Holy Ghost?

One of God's Greatest Gifts

The gift of the Holy Ghost is one of God's greatest gifts to us. Through the Holy Ghost we may know that God lives, that Jesus is the Christ, and that his Church has been restored to the earth. We may have the promptings of the Holy Ghost to tell us all the things we should do (see 2 Nephi 32:5). The Holy Ghost sanctifies us to prepare us for God's presence. We may enjoy the gifts of the Spirit (see chapter 22, "The Gifts of the Spirit"). This great gift from our Heavenly Father can also bring peace to our hearts and an understanding of the things of God (see 1 Corinthians 2:9–12).

Discussion
• In what ways has the Holy Ghost helped you?

Additional Scriptures
- 1 Corinthians 3:16–17; D&C 130:22–23 (the Holy Ghost dwells with the faithful)
- Moroni 8:25–26 (how to receive the Holy Ghost)
- Moroni 10:5 (the Holy Ghost is a witness to truth)
- Mosiah 5:2 (the Holy Ghost changes hearts)
- Alma 5:54 (the Holy Ghost sanctifies)

THE GIFTS OF THE SPIRIT

Chapter 22

Following baptism, each of us had hands laid on our heads to receive the gift of the Holy Ghost. If we are faithful, we can have his influence constantly with us. Through him, each of us can be blessed with certain spiritual powers called *gifts of the Spirit*. These gifts are given to those who are faithful to Christ. They help us know and teach the truths of the gospel. They will help us bless others. They will guide us back to our Heavenly Father. To use our gifts wisely, we need to know what they are, how we can develop them, and how to recognize Satan's imitations of them.

Discussion
• Discuss the reasons the Lord has given us spiritual gifts.

The Gifts of the Spirit
The scriptures mention many gifts of the Spirit. These gifts have been given to members of the true Church whenever it has been on the earth (see Mark 16:16–18). The gifts of the Spirit include the following.

The Gift of Tongues (D&C 46:24)
Sometimes it is necessary to communicate the gospel in a language we have not learned. When this happens, the Lord can bless us with the ability to speak that language. Many missionaries have received the gift of tongues when there was a great need for it. For example, Elder Alonzo A. Hinckley was

---

Joseph Smith translated the Book of Mormon by the power of the Spirit.

a missionary in Holland who understood and spoke very little Dutch even though he had prayed and studied hard. When he returned to a home he had visited before, a lady opened the door and spoke to him very angrily in Dutch. To his amazement he could understand every word. He felt a strong desire to bear his testimony to her in Dutch. He began to speak, and the words came out very clearly in Dutch. But when he returned to show his mission president that he could speak Dutch, the ability had left him. Many faithful members have been blessed with the gift of tongues (see Joseph Fielding Smith, *Answers to Gospel Questions,* 2:32–33).

The Gift of Interpretation of Tongues (D&C 46:25)

This gift is sometimes given to us when we do not understand a language and we need to receive an important message from God. For example, President David O. McKay had a great desire to speak to the Saints in New Zealand without an interpreter. He told them that he hoped that the Lord would bless them that they could understand him. He spoke in English. His message lasted about forty minutes. As he spoke, he could tell by the expression on many of their faces and the tears in their eyes that they were receiving his message (see *Answers to Gospel Questions,* 2:30–31).

The Gift of Translation (D&C 5:4)

If we have been called by the leaders of the Church to translate the word of the Lord, we can receive a gift to translate beyond our natural ability. As with all gifts, we must live righteously, study hard, and pray to receive it. When we do these things, the Lord causes us to feel a burning inside concerning the correctness of the translation (D&C 9:8–9). Joseph Smith had the gift of translation when he translated the Book of Mormon. This gift came to him only when he was in tune with the Spirit.

The Gift of Wisdom (D&C 46:17)

Some of us have been blessed with the ability to understand

people and the principles of the gospel as they apply in our lives. We are told:

"If any of you lack wisdom, let him ask of God, that giveth to all men liberally, and upbraideth not; and it shall be given him.

"But let him ask in faith, nothing wavering. For he that wavereth is like a wave of the sea driven with the wind and tossed.

"For let not that man think that he shall receive any thing of the Lord" (James 1:5–7).

The Lord said, "Seek not for riches but for wisdom, and behold, the mysteries of God shall be unfolded unto you" (D&C 6:7).

The Gift of Knowledge (D&C 46:18)

Everyone who becomes like Heavenly Father eventually knows all things. The knowledge of God and his laws is revealed by the Holy Ghost (see D&C 121:26). We cannot be saved if we are ignorant of these laws (see D&C 131:6).

The Lord revealed, "If a person gains more knowledge and intelligence in this life through his diligence and obedience than another, he will have so much the advantage in the world to come" (D&C 130:19). The Lord has commanded us to learn as much as we can about his work. He wants us to learn about the heavens, the earth, things that have happened or will happen, things at home and in foreign lands (see D&C 88:78–79). However, there are those who try to gain knowledge by their own study alone. They do not ask for the help of the Holy Ghost. They are those who are always learning but never arrive at the truth (see 2 Timothy 3:7). When we receive knowledge by revelation from the Holy Ghost, his Spirit speaks to our minds and our hearts and we feel the truth burn within us (see D&C 8:2).

Discussion

• What kinds of things should we learn about? (See also D&C 90:15.)
• Read 2 Nephi 9:28–29 and D&C 88:118. What is the right way to gain knowledge?

The Gift of Teaching Wisdom and Knowledge (Moroni 10:9–10)

Some people are given a special ability to explain and testify of the truths of the gospel. This gift can be used when we teach a class. It can be used by parents to teach their children. This gift also helps us instruct others so they can understand the gospel.

Discussion

• Why must we have the Spirit of the Lord to teach? (See D&C 42:14.)

The Gift of Knowing that Jesus Christ Is the Son of God (D&C 46:13)

This has been the gift of prophets and apostles who have been called as special witnesses of Jesus Christ. However, others are also given this gift. Every person can have a testimony. It usually comes through the whispering of the Holy Spirit but may come in a dream or vision. Elder Orson F. Whitney saw a vision of the Savior in Gethsemane. He saw the great suffering of the Savior, and it caused him to weep. Then the Savior took him into his arms and blessed him (see Bryant S. Hinckley, *The Faith of Our Pioneer Fathers,* pp. 211–13).

The Gift of Believing the Testimony of Others (D&C 46:14)

By the power of the Holy Ghost we may know the truth of all things. If we want to know whether someone else is speaking the truth, we must ask God in faith. If the thing we are praying about is true, the Lord will speak peace to our minds (see D&C 6:22–23). In this way we can know when someone else, even the prophet, has received revelation. Nephi asked the Lord to let him see, feel, and know that his father's dream was true (see 1 Nephi 10:17–19).

The brother of Jared had such great faith that he saw the finger of the Lord.

Discussion

• How can we receive a testimony that another person is speaking the truth?

The Gift of Prophecy (D&C 46:22)

Those who receive true revelations about the past, present, or future have the gift of prophecy. Prophets have this gift, but we too can have it to help us govern our own lives (see 1 Corinthians 14:39). We may receive revelations from God for ourselves and our own callings, but never for the Church or its leaders. It is contrary to the order of heaven for a person to receive revelation for one higher in authority than himself. If we truly have the gift of prophecy, we will not receive any revelation that does not agree with what the Lord has said in the scriptures (see Joseph Fielding Smith, *Doctrines of Salvation*, 3:203–4).

Read

The Gift of Healing (D&C 46:19–20)

Some have the faith to heal, and others have the faith to be healed. We can all exercise the faith to be healed when we are ill (see D&C 42:48). Many who hold the priesthood have the gift of healing the sick. Others may be given a knowledge of how to cure illness.

Discussion

• Read D&C 42:43–44. What should we do when we are ill?

The Gift of Working Miracles (D&C 46:21)

The Lord has blessed his people many times in miraculous ways. When the Utah pioneers planted their first crops, a plague of locusts nearly destroyed them. The pioneers prayed that the Lord would save them, and he sent sea gulls to devour the locusts. When we need help and ask in faith, if it is for our good the Lord will work miracles for us (see Matthew 17:20; D&C 24:13–14).

The Gift of Faith (Moroni 10:11)

The brother of Jared had great faith. Because of his faith, he received other gifts. His faith was so great that the Savior appeared to him (see Ether 3:9–15). Without faith, no other gift can be given. Moroni promises, "Whoso believeth in Christ, doubting nothing, whatsoever he shall ask the Father in the name of Christ it shall be granted him" (Mormon 9:21). We should seek to increase our faith, find out our gifts, and use them.

Some people lack faith and deny that these gifts of the Spirit actually exist. Moroni says to them:

"And again I speak unto you who deny the revelations of God, and say that they are done away, that there are no revelations, nor prophecies, nor gifts, nor healings, nor speaking with tongues, and the interpretation of tongues;

"Behold I say unto you, he that denieth these things knoweth not the gospel of Christ; yea, he has not read the scriptures; if so, he does not understand them" (Mormon 9:7–8).

We Can Develop Our Gifts

The Lord has said: "For all have not every gift given unto them; for there are many gifts, and to every man is given a gift by the Spirit of God. To some is given one, and to some is given another, that all may be profited thereby" (D&C 46:11–12).

To develop our gifts, we must find out which gifts we have. We do this by praying and fasting. We should seek after the best gifts (see D&C 46:8). Sometimes patriarchal blessings will tell us which gifts we have been given.

We must be obedient and faithful to be given our gifts. We then should use these gifts to do the work of the Lord. They are not given to satisfy our curiosity or to prove anything to us because we lack faith. Our gifts are to be used to build up the kingdom of God and to strengthen our testimonies.

Discussion
• How can we discover our spiritual gifts?
• How might Satan tempt us to misuse them?

Satan Imitates the Gifts of the Spirit

Satan can imitate the gifts of tongues, prophecy, visions, healings, and other miracles. Moses had to compete with Satan's imitations in Pharaoh's court (see Exodus 7:8–22). Satan wants us to believe in his false prophets, false healers, and false miracle workers. They may appear to be so real to us that the only way to know is to ask God for the gift of discernment. The devil himself can appear as an angel of light (see 2 Nephi 9:9).

Satan wants to blind us to the truth and keep us from seeking the true gifts of the Spirit. Mediums, astrologers, fortune tellers, and sorcerers are inspired by Satan even if they claim to follow God. Their works are abominable to the Lord (see Isaiah 47:12–14; Deuteronomy 18:9–10). We should avoid all associations with the powers of Satan.

Discussion

• How can we discern between the true gifts of the Spirit and Satan's imitations?

We Must Be Careful with Our Gifts of the Spirit

The Lord said, "A commandment I give unto them, that they shall not boast themselves of these things, neither speak them before the world; for these things are given unto you for your profit and for salvation" (D&C 84:73). We must remember that spiritual gifts are sacred.

The Lord asks only one thing in return for giving us these gifts. He says, "Ye must give thanks unto God in the Spirit for whatsoever blessing ye are blessed with" (D&C 46:32).

Discussion

• How do we keep our spiritual gifts sacred?

Additional Scriptures

• 3 Nephi 29:6–7 (fate of those who deny gifts)
• Moroni 10:7–19 (gifts depend on faith)
• 1 Corinthians 12 (spiritual gifts)
• Acts 10 (a gift given at baptism)
• D&C 46:9–26 (gifts of the Spirit)

Jesus administered the sacrament at the last supper with his Apostles.

By Carl Bloch. Original at the Chapel of Frederiksborg Castle, Denmark.
Used by permission of the Frederiksborgmuseum.

THE SACRAMENT

Chapter 23

Our Savior wants us to remember his great atoning sacrifice and keep his commandments. To help us do this, he has commanded us to meet often and partake of the sacrament.

The sacrament is a holy priesthood ordinance that helps remind us of the Savior's atonement. During the sacrament, we partake of bread and water. We do this in remembrance of his flesh and his blood, which he gave as a sacrifice for us. As we partake of the sacrament, we renew sacred covenants with our Heavenly Father.

Discussion
• What is the sacrament?
• What is the purpose of the sacrament?

Christ Introduced the Sacrament
Shortly before his crucifixion, Jesus gathered his Apostles around him in an upstairs room. He knew he would soon die on the cross. This was the last time he would meet with these beloved men before his death. He wanted them to always remember him so they could be strong and faithful.

To help them remember, he introduced the sacrament. He broke bread into pieces and blessed it. Then he said, "Take, eat; this is in remembrance of my body which I give a ransom for you" (JST, <u>Matthew 26:22</u>). Next he took a cup of wine, blessed it, and gave it to his Apostles to drink. He said: "Drink

We partake of the sacrament in remembrance of Jesus Christ.

ye all of it. For this is in remembrance of my blood, . . . which is shed for as many as shall believe on my name, for the remission of their sins" (JST, Matthew 26:23–24. See also Matthew 26:26–28; Mark 14:22–24; Luke 22:15–20).

After his resurrection, Jesus came to the Americas and taught the Nephites the same ordinance (see 3 Nephi 18:1–11). After the Church was restored in the latter days, Jesus once again commanded his people to partake of the sacrament in remembrance of him, saying, "It is expedient that the church meet together often to partake of bread and wine in the remembrance of the Lord Jesus" (D&C 20:75).

Discussion
• Read Matthew 26:26–28. Ask class members to think about the Lord's Supper the next time they partake of the sacrament.

How the Sacrament Is Administered
The scriptures explain exactly how the sacrament is to be administered. Members of the Church meet each Sabbath day to worship and partake of the sacrament (see D&C 20:75). The sacrament is administered by those who hold the necessary priesthood authority. A priest or elder breaks bread into pieces, kneels, and blesses it (see D&C 20:76). A deacon or other priesthood holder then passes the sacrament bread to the congregation. Then the priest or elder blesses the water and it too is passed to the members. Jesus gave his disciples wine when he introduced the sacrament. However, in a latter-day revelation he has said that it doesn't matter what we eat and drink during the sacrament as long as we remember him (D&C 27:2–3). Today, Latter-day Saints drink water instead of wine.

Jesus has revealed the exact words for both sacrament prayers. We should listen carefully to these beautiful prayers and try to understand what we are promising and what is being promised to us. Here is the prayer that is offered to bless the bread:

"O God, the Eternal Father, we ask thee in the name of thy Son, Jesus Christ, to bless and sanctify this bread to the souls of all those who partake of it, that they may eat in remembrance of the body of thy Son, and witness unto thee, O God, the Eternal Father, that they are willing to take upon them the name of thy Son, and always remember him and keep his commandments which he has given them; that they may always have his Spirit to be with them. Amen" (D&C 20:77).

Here is the prayer that is offered to bless the water:

"O God, the Eternal Father, we ask thee in the name of thy Son, Jesus Christ, to bless and sanctify this wine [water] to the souls of all those who drink of it, that they may do it in remembrance of the blood of thy Son, which was shed for them; that they may witness unto thee, O God, the Eternal Father, that they do always remember him, that they may have his Spirit to be with them. Amen" (D&C 20:79).

The ordinance of the sacrament is performed very simply and reverently.

Discussion

• Read the sacrament prayers one sentence at a time. Discuss the meaning of each sentence. Challenge each member to memorize the prayers.

The Covenants We Renew during the Sacrament

Each time we partake of the sacrament, we renew covenants with the Lord. A covenant is a sacred promise between the Lord and his children. The covenants we make are clearly stated in the sacramental prayers. It is important to know what those covenants are and what they mean.

We covenant to take upon ourselves the name of Jesus Christ. By this we show we are willing to be identified with him and his Church. We promise that we will not bring shame or reproach upon that name.

We covenant to remember Jesus Christ. All our thoughts, feelings, and actions will be influenced by him and his mission.

We promise to keep his commandments.

We take these obligations upon ourselves when we are baptized (see D&C 20:37; Mosiah 18:6–10). Thus, when we partake of the sacrament, we renew the covenants we made when we were baptized. Jesus gave us the pattern for partaking of the sacrament (see 3 Nephi 18:1–12) and said that when we follow this pattern, believing on his name, we will gain a remission of our sins (see JST, Matthew 26:24).

The Lord promises that if we keep our covenants, we will always have his Spirit to be with us. A person guided by the Spirit will have the knowledge, faith, power, and righteousness to gain eternal life.

Discussion
• Refer to D&C 20:77 again.
• What promises do we make during the sacrament?

Our Attitude When Taking the Sacrament

Before partaking of the sacrament, we are to prepare ourselves spiritually. The Lord emphasizes that no one should partake of the sacrament unworthily. That means we must repent of our sins before taking the sacrament. The scriptures say, "If any have trespassed, let him not partake until he makes reconciliation" (D&C 46:4). The scriptures also say, "Ye shall not suffer any one knowingly to partake of my flesh and blood unworthily, when ye shall minister it; For whoso eateth and drinketh my flesh and blood unworthily eateth and drinketh damnation to his soul" (3 Nephi 18:28–29).

During the sacrament service we should dismiss from our minds all worldly thoughts. We should feel prayerful and reverent. We should think of the atonement of our Savior and be grateful for it. We should examine our lives and look for ways to improve. We should also renew our determination to keep the commandments.

We do not need to be perfect before partaking of the sacrament, but we must have the spirit of repentance in our hearts. The attitude with which we partake of the sacrament influences our experience with it. If we partake of the sacrament with a pure heart, we receive the promised blessings of the Lord.

Discussion

- Ask someone to tell how we should prepare ourselves to partake of the sacrament.
- What can we think about during the sacrament to help us be more reverent?

Additional Scripture

- 1 Corinthians 11:27–29 (partake of the sacrament worthily)

PERFECTING OUR LIVES

Unit Seven

Sunday is a day for worship.

THE SABBATH DAY

---

*"*Remember the sabbath day, to keep it holy*"* (Exodus 20:8; see also D&C 68:29).

What Is the Sabbath Day?

The word *Sabbath* comes from the Hebrew word meaning *day of rest*. The Sabbath day commemorates God's day of rest after he finished the Creation. We read in the book of Genesis that God created the heavens and the earth in six periods of time, which he called days: *"*And on the seventh day God ended his work which he had made; and he rested on the seventh day from all his work which he had made. And God blessed the seventh day, and sanctified it*"* (Genesis 2:2–3).

The Sabbath day is every seventh day. It is a holy day ordained by God for us to rest from our daily labors and worship him.

Discussion

• What is the Sabbath day?

The Purpose of the Sabbath Day

Jesus taught that the Sabbath day was made to benefit man (see Mark 2:27). The purpose of the Sabbath is to give us a certain day of the week on which to direct our thoughts and actions toward God. It is not a day merely to rest from work. It is a sacred day to be spent in worship and reverence. As we rest from our usual daily activities, our minds are freed to

---

ponder spiritual matters. On this day we should renew our covenants with the Lord and feed our souls on the things of the Spirit.

Discussion
• What is the Lord's purpose for the Sabbath day?

History of the Sabbath
The seventh day was consecrated by God as a Sabbath in the beginning of the earth (see Genesis 2:2–3). Since earliest times, the tradition of a sacred seventh day has been preserved among various peoples of the earth. God renewed a commandment concerning this day to the Israelites, saying, "Remember the sabbath day, to keep it holy" (Exodus 20:8). Keeping the Sabbath day was also a sign that the Israelites were his covenant people (see Exodus 31:12–13, 16; Isaiah 56:1–8; Jeremiah 17:19–27).

However, some Jewish leaders made many unnecessary rules about the Sabbath. They decided how far a person could walk, what kind of knot he could tie, and so forth. When certain Jewish leaders criticized Jesus Christ for healing sick people on the Sabbath, Jesus reminded them that the Sabbath was made for the benefit of man.

The Nephites also observed the Sabbath day according to the commandments of God (see Jarom 1:5).

In modern times the Lord has repeated his commandment that we should remember the Sabbath day and keep it holy (see D&C 68:29).

Discussion
• Have someone tell about the history of the Sabbath using the following scriptures: Genesis 2:2–3; Exodus 20:8; Isaiah 56:1–8; Jarom 1:5; Mark 2:27; D&C 68:29.

The Lord's Day

Until the resurrection of Jesus Christ, he and his disciples honored the seventh day as the Sabbath. After his resurrection, Sunday was held sacred as the Lord's day in remembrance of his resurrection on that day (see Acts 20:7; 1 Corinthians 16:2). From that time on, his followers appointed the first day as their Sabbath. In both cases there were six days of labor and one for rest and devotion.

The Lord has given us a direct commandment in these days that we, too, should honor Sunday, the Lord's day, as our Sabbath (see D&C 59:12).

Discussion

- Why was the Sabbath changed from the seventh day to the first day?
- What special event does the first day commemorate?

How Do We Keep the Sabbath Day Holy?

The Lord asks us, first, to *sanctify* the Sabbath day. In a revelation given to Joseph Smith in 1831, the Lord commanded the Saints to go to the house of prayer and offer up their sacraments, rest from their labors, and pay their devotions to the Most High (see D&C 59:9–12).

Second, he asks us to rest from daily work. This means we should perform no labor that would keep us from giving our full attention to spiritual matters. The Lord told the Israelites, "Thou shalt not do any work, thou, nor thy son, nor thy daughter, thy manservant, nor thy maidservant, nor thy cattle" (Exodus 20:10). Our prophets have told us that we should not shop, hunt, fish, attend sports events, or participate in similar activities on that day.

Elder Spencer W. Kimball cautioned, however, that if we merely lounge about doing nothing on the Sabbath, we are not keeping the day holy. The Sabbath calls for constructive thoughts and acts (see *The Miracle of Forgiveness,* pp. 96–97).

What kinds of things *may* we do on the Sabbath? The Lord has told us to prepare only simple foods on that day, keeping the purpose of the Sabbath in mind (see D&C 59:13). The prophet Isaiah suggested that we should turn away from doing our own pleasure and should *"call the sabbath a delight, the holy of the Lord, honourable"* (Isaiah 58:13). We should do righteous things. We keep the Sabbath day holy by—

1. Attending Church meetings.
2. Reading the scriptures and the words of our Church leaders.
3. Visiting the sick, the aged, and our loved ones.
4. Listening to uplifting music and singing hymns.
5. Praying to our Heavenly Father with praise and thanksgiving.
6. Performing Church service that we have been assigned to do.
7. Preparing family history records and personal histories.
8. Telling faith-promoting stories and bearing our testimony to family members and sharing spiritual experiences with them.
9. Writing letters to loved ones.
10. Fasting with a purpose.
11. Sharing time with children and others in the home.

In deciding what other activities we should properly engage in on the Sabbath, we should ask ourselves: Will it uplift and inspire me?

There may be times when we are required to work on the Sabbath. We should avoid this whenever possible, but when it is absolutely necessary, we should still maintain the spirit of Sabbath worship in our hearts as much as possible.

Discussion
• Read D&C 59:9–13.
• What things can we do to draw nearer to our Heavenly Father?

Blessings for Observing the Sabbath

If we honor the Sabbath day, we may receive great spiritual and temporal blessings. The Lord has said that if we keep the Sabbath day with thanksgiving and cheerful hearts, we will be full of joy. He has promised:

"The fulness of the earth is yours, . . . whether for food or for raiment, or for houses, or for barns, or for orchards, or for gardens, or for vineyards;

"Yea, all things which come of the earth, in the season thereof, are made for the benefit and the use of man, both to please the eye and to gladden the heart;

"Yea, for food and for raiment, for taste and for smell, to strengthen the body and to enliven the soul" (D&C 59:16–19).

Discussion

• Read together D&C 59:15–19.
• Discuss some of the blessings that come from keeping the Sabbath day holy.

Additional Scriptures

• Exodus 31:14–17 (under Mosaic law the Sabbath was kept holy under pain of death)
• Mosiah 13:16–19; 18:23; Exodus 35:1–3 (observe the Sabbath as a holy day)
• Luke 6:1–11 (lawful to do good on the Sabbath)
• Luke 13:11–17; John 5:1–18 (Jesus' example of doing good on the Sabbath)

Fasting and prayer bring blessings.

FASTING

Chapter 25

Since the time of Adam, God's people have fasted to help them draw near to him and to worship him. Jesus showed the importance of fasting by his own example (see Luke 4:1–4). Through latter-day revelation we learn that the Lord still expects his people to fast and pray often (see D&C 88:76).

Discussion
• Read D&C 88:76. Discuss why fasting is given as a commandment.

How to Fast Properly
Fasting means to go without food and drink (see Joseph F. Smith, *Gospel Doctrine*, p. 243). Occasional fasting is good for our bodies and helps our minds become more active (see *Principles of the Gospel*, p. 175).

The Savior taught us that purposeful fasting is more than just going without food and drink. We must also concentrate on spiritual matters.

We Should Pray When We Fast
Prayer is a necessary part of fasting. Throughout the scriptures, prayer and fasting are mentioned together. Our fasting should be accompanied by sincere prayer, and we should begin and end our fasting with prayer.

We Should Fast with a Purpose

Fasting can have many purposes. We can overcome weaknesses or problems by fasting and praying. Sometimes we may wish to fast and pray for help or guidance for others, such as a family member who is ill and needs a blessing (see Mosiah 27:22–23). Through fasting we can come to know the truth of things just as did the prophet Alma in the Book of Mormon. He said: *"I have fasted and prayed many days that I might know these things of myself. And now I do know of myself that they are true; for the Lord God hath made them manifest unto me by his Holy Spirit"* (Alma 5:46).

We can fast for our nonmember friends to become converted to the truth. Fasting can help comfort us in times of sorrow and mourning (see Alma 28:4–6). Fasting can help us become humble and feel closer to our Heavenly Father (see Helaman 3:35).

Our purpose in fasting should not be to impress others. The Lord counseled:

*"Moreover when ye fast, be not, as the hypocrites, of a sad countenance: for they disfigure their faces, that they may appear unto men to fast.

"Verily I say unto you, They have their reward.

"But thou, when thou fastest, anoint thine head, and wash thy face; that thou appear not unto men to fast"* (Matthew 6:16–18).

We should be cheerful when we fast and not advertise our fasting to others.

Discussion

• What things should we do to make our fasting more spiritual? What things do we need to fast for?

The Fast Day

One Sunday each month Latter-day Saints observe a fast day. On this day we neither eat nor drink for two consecutive meals, thus making a fast of twenty-four hours. If we were to eat our evening meal on Saturday, then we would not eat or drink until the evening meal on Sunday.

Everyone who can do so should fast. However, "many are subject to weakness, others are delicate in health, and others have nursing babies; of such it should not be required to fast. Neither should parents compel their little children to fast" (_Gospel Doctrine_, p. 244).

We should encourage our children to fast after they have been baptized, but we should never force them. The fast day is a special day for us to humble ourselves before the Lord in fasting and prayer. It is a day to pray for forgiveness from our sins and for the power to overcome our faults and to forgive others.

On fast Sunday, members of the Church meet together and partake of the sacrament. They strengthen themselves and one another by bearing testimony in fast and testimony meeting.

Fast Offerings
When we fast each month, the Lord asks us to help those in need. One way we do this is by giving through the proper priesthood authority either the food or the money we would have spent on food for the two meals. We should give as generously as we are able. Through our fast offerings we become partners with the Lord in administering to the needs of our less fortunate brothers and sisters.

Discussion
• What should we do on fast day to make fasting more meaningful?
• What are some of the reasons we pay fast offerings?

We Are Blessed When We Fast
Isaiah, an Old Testament prophet wrote of the Lord's rich promises to those who fast and help the needy. We are promised peace, inproved health, and spiritual guidance. Isaiah

tells us that when we fast: "Then shall thy light break forth as the morning, and thine health shall spring forth speedily: and thy righteousness shall go before thee; the glory of the Lord shall be thy reward. Then shalt thou call, and the Lord shall answer; thou shalt cry, and he shall say, Here I am" (Isaiah 58:8–9).

Fasting improves our lives and gives us added strength. It helps us live other principles of the gospel because it draws us nearer to the Lord.

Fasting Teaches Self-Control

Fasting helps us gain strength of character. This reason alone makes fasting important (see David O. McKay, *True to the Faith,* p. 81). When we fast properly, we will learn to control our appetites, our passions, and our tempers. Solomon said, "He that is slow to anger is better than the mighty; and he that ruleth his spirit than he that taketh a city" (Proverbs 16:32). Even fasting for only two meals can give us a feeling of success. We are a little stronger by having proved to ourselves that we have self-control. If we teach our children to fast, they will develop the willpower to overcome greater temptations later in their lives.

Fasting Gives Us Spiritual Power

When we fast wisely and prayerfully, we develop our faith. With that faith we will have greater spiritual power. For example, Alma (the Book of Mormon prophet) tells the story of meeting again with the sons of Mosiah many years after their miraculous conversion. He felt great joy when he learned that they had strengthened their faith and had developed great spiritual power. They had gained this power because "they had given themselves to much prayer, and fasting; therefore they had the spirit of prophecy, and the spirit of revelation" (Alma 17:3).

The sons of Mosiah had been preaching for fourteen years to the Lamanites. Because the sons of Mosiah had fasted and prayed, the Spirit of the Lord increased the power of their words. This gave them great success in their missionary work. (See Alma 17:4.)

The Savior has said to those who fast properly, *"Thy Father, which seeth in secret, shall reward thee openly"* (Matthew 6:18).

Discussion
• Why is it important to have self-control?
• How does fasting give or increase our spiritual power?
• Have class members tell how they have been blessed by observing a proper fast.

Additional Scriptures
• Luke 2:37; Alma 45:1; (worshiping God through fasting)
• Mosiah 27:19, 23 (fasting for the sick)
• 3 Nephi 27:1–3; Exodus 34:27–28 (fasting for revelation and testimony)
• Alma 6:6; 17:9 (fasting for nonmembers)
• Acts 13:2–3 (fasting for selection of Church officers)

The rich young ruler lacked the faith to sacrifice his possessions and follow Jesus.

SACRIFICE

Chapter 26

Sacrifice is the crowning test of the gospel. It means giving to the Lord whatever he requires of our time, our earthly possessions, and our energies to further his work. The Lord commanded, "Seek ye first the kingdom of God, and his righteousness" (Matthew 6:33). People have always been tried and tested to see if they will put the things of God first in their lives.

Discussion
• Have members think of favorite things they possess.
• How would you feel if you were asked to give it up?
• Consider the sacrifices of many people as you read Matthew 19:29 and Romans 12:1–2.

Animal Sacrifice Was an Ordinance of the Gospel
From the time of Adam and Eve to the time of Jesus Christ, the Lord's people practiced the law of animal sacrifice (see Moses 5:5). It was an ordinance of the gospel. They were commanded to offer as sacrifices the firstlings of their flocks. These animals had to be perfect, without blemish. The ordinance was given to remind the people that Jesus Christ, the firstborn of the Father, would come into the world. He would be perfect in every way, and he would offer himself as a sacrifice for our sins (see Moses 5:5–8).

Jesus did come and offer himself as a sacrifice, just as the people had been taught he would. Because of his sacrifice,

Abraham had such great faith that he was prepared to sacrifice his son Isaac at the Lord's command.

everyone will be saved from physical death by the Resurrection and all can be saved from their sins through faith in Jesus Christ (see chapter 12, "The Atonement").

Christ's atoning sacrifice marked the end of blood sacrifices. Blood sacrifice was replaced by the ordinance of the sacrament. The ordinance of the sacrament was also given to remind us of the Savior's great sacrifice. We should partake of the sacrament often. The emblems of bread and water remind us of the Savior's bruised body and of his blood, which he shed for us (see chapter 23, "The Sacrament").

Discussion
• Read Moses 5:5–7.
• What did the sacrifice of a lamb represent in ancient times?
• What event brought blood sacrifice to an end?
• What ordinance was given to replace the ancient law of sacrifice?

We Still Must Sacrifice
Even though blood sacrifice was ended, the Lord still asks us to sacrifice. But now he requires a different kind of offering. He said: "Ye shall offer up unto me no more the shedding of blood, . . . and your burnt offerings shall be done away. . . . And ye shall offer for a sacrifice unto me a broken heart and a contrite spirit" (3 Nephi 9:19–20). A "broken heart and a contrite spirit" means that we offer deep sorrow for our sins as we humble ourselves and repent of them.

Discussion
• How do we observe the law of sacrifice today?

We Must Be Willing to Sacrifice Everything We Have to the Lord
The Apostle Paul wrote that we should become living sacrifices, holy and acceptable unto God (see Romans 12:1).

If we are to be a living sacrifice, we must, if asked, be willing to give everything we have for The Church of Jesus Christ of Latter-day Saints.

A rich young ruler asked the Savior, "What shall I do to inherit eternal life?" Jesus answered, "Thou knowest the commandments, Do not commit adultery, Do not kill, Do not steal, Do not bear false witness, Honour thy father and thy mother." And the rich man said, "All these have I kept from my youth." When Jesus heard this, he said, "Yet lackest thou one thing: sell all that thou hast, and distribute unto the poor, and thou shalt have treasure in heaven: and come, follow me." When the young man heard this, he was sorrowful. He was very rich and had his heart set on his riches (see Luke 18:18–23).

The young ruler was a good man. But when he was put to the test, he was not willing to sacrifice his worldly possessions. On the other hand, the Lord's disciples Peter and Andrew were willing to sacrifice everything for the sake of the kingdom of God. When Jesus said unto them, "Follow me, . . . they straightway left their nets, and followed him" (Matthew 4:19–20).

Like the disciples, we can offer our daily activities as a sacrifice to the Lord. We can say, "Thy will be done." Abraham did this. He lived on the earth before Christ, in the days when blood sacrifices and burnt offerings were required. As a test of Abraham's faith, the Lord commanded him to offer up his son Isaac as a sacrifice. Isaac was the only son of Abraham and Sarah. To offer him as a sacrifice was extremely painful for Abraham.

Nevertheless, he and Isaac made the long journey to Mount Moriah, where the sacrifice was to be made. They traveled for three days. Imagine Abraham's thoughts and his heartache. His son was to be sacrificed to the Lord. When they reached Mount Moriah, Isaac carried the wood and Abraham carried the fire and the knife to the place where they were to build the altar. Isaac said, "My father . . . behold the fire and the wood: but where is the lamb for a burnt offering?" Abraham answered, "My son, God will provide himself a lamb." Then Abraham built an altar and arranged the wood on it. He bound Isaac and laid him upon the wood. He then took the knife to kill Isaac. At that moment an angel of the Lord stopped him, saying, *"Abraham . . . lay not thine hand upon the lad, neither do thou anything unto him: for now I know that thou fearest God, seeing thou hast not withheld thy son, thine only son from me"* (see Genesis 22:1–14).

Abraham must have been overcome with joy when he was no longer required to sacrifice his son. But he loved the Lord so much that he was willing to do anything the Lord asked.

Discussion
- Have someone tell the story of Abraham's being commanded to sacrifice Isaac (see Genesis 22:1–14). Have someone tell the story of the rich young ruler (see Luke 18:18–23).
- Ask class members to think what they might have done in these situations.

Sacrifice Helps Us Prepare to Live in the Presence of God

Only through sacrifice can we become worthy to live in the presence of God. Only through sacrifice can we enjoy eternal life. Many who have lived before us have sacrificed all they had. We must be willing to do the same if we would earn the rich reward they enjoy (see Joseph Smith, *Lectures on Faith*, p. 58).

We may not be asked to sacrifice all things. But like Abraham, we should be willing to sacrifice everything to become worthy to live in the presence of the Lord.

The Lord's people have always sacrificed greatly and in many different ways. Some have suffered hardship and ridicule for the gospel. Some new converts to the Church have been cut off from their families. Lifetime friends have turned away. Some members have lost their jobs; some have lost their lives. But the Lord notices our sacrifices; he promises,

"Every one that hath forsaken houses, or brethren, or sisters, or father, or mother, or wife, or children, or lands, for my

name's sake, shall receive an hundredfold, and shall inherit everlasting life" (Matthew 19:29).

As our testimonies of the gospel grow, we become able to make greater sacrifices to the Lord. Note the sacrifices made in these true examples:

A member of the Church in Germany saved his tithing for years until someone with priesthood authority could come and accept it.

A Relief Society visiting teacher served for thirty years without missing an assignment.

A group of Saints in South Africa rode for three days, standing up, to be able to hear and see the prophet of the Lord.

At an area conference in Mexico, members of the Church slept on the ground and fasted during the days of the conference. They had used all their money just to get to the conference and had nothing left for food and shelter.

One family sold their car to get the money they wanted to contribute to a temple building fund.

Another family sold their home to get money to go to the temple.

Many faithful Latter-day Saints have very little to live on, yet they pay their tithes and offerings.

One brother sacrificed his job because he refused to work on Sunday.

In one branch, the youth gave freely and willingly of their time to care for the young children while their parents helped build the meetinghouse.

Young men and women give up good job opportunities to serve as missionaries.

Many more examples could be given of those who sacrifice for the Lord. Yet a place in our Heavenly Father's kingdom is worth any sacrifice we have to make of our time, talents, energy, money, and lives. Through sacrifice we can obtain a knowledge from the Lord that we are acceptable to him (see D&C 97:8).

Discussion

• Have class members tell of sacrifices they or their family members have made for the gospel and some of the blessings they have received as a result of the sacrifice.

Additional Scriptures

• Luke 12:16–34 (where the treasure is, there is the heart)
• Luke 9:57–62 (sacrifice to be fit for the kingdom)
• D&C 64:23; D&C 97:12 (today is a day of sacrifice)
• D&C 98:13–15 (those who lose life for the Lord will find it)
• Alma 24 (the people of Ammon sacrifice their lives rather than break their oath to the Lord)
• Alma 27:5–10 (the people of Ammon offer to become slaves in payment of their sins)

Families become stronger by working together.

WORK AND PERSONAL RESPONSIBILITY

Chapter 27

Work Is an Eternal Principle

Our Heavenly Father and Jesus Christ have shown us by their examples and teachings that work is important in heaven and on earth. God worked to create the heavens and the earth. He caused the seas to gather in one place and the dry land to appear. He caused grass, herbs, and trees to grow on the land. He created the sun, the moon, and the stars. He created every living thing in the sea or on the land. Then he placed man on the earth to take care of it and to govern the other creatures (see Genesis 1:1–28).

Jesus said, "My Father worketh hitherto, and I work" (John 5:17). He also said, "I must work the works of him that sent me" (John 9:4).

Discussion
• Read John 9:4. Why is work an eternal principle?
• Who set the example for work?

We Are Commanded to Work

Work has been the way of life on earth since Adam and Eve left the Garden of Eden. The Lord said to Adam, "In the sweat of thy face shalt thou eat bread" (Genesis 3:19). Adam and Eve worked in the fields so they could provide for their own needs and the needs of their children (see Moses 5:1).

The Lord said to the people of Israel, "Six days shalt thou labour" (Exodus 20:9).

In the early days of the restored Church, the Lord told the Latter-day Saints, "Now, I, the Lord, am not well pleased with the inhabitants of Zion, for there are idlers among them" (D&C 68:31).

In this century, a prophet of God has said, "Work is to be reenthroned as the ruling principle of the lives of our Church membership" (Heber J. Grant, in Conference Report, Oct. 1936, p. 3).

Discussion
• What would happen if people did not work?

Family Responsibility
Parents work together to provide for the physical, spiritual, and emotional well-being of their family. They should never expect anyone to take care of this responsibility for them. The Apostle Paul wrote, "If any provide not for his own, and specially for those of his own house, he hath denied the faith" (1 Timothy 5:8).

Couples should seek inspiration from the Lord and follow the counsel of the prophets when establishing individual responsibilities. Creating a home where principles of the gospel are taught daily and where love and order abound is as important as providing the basic necessities of food and clothing.

Children should do their part in the work of the family. It is necessary for children to have work assignments to fit their abilities. They need to be praised for their successes. Good work attitudes, habits, and skills are learned through successful experiences in the home.

Sometimes people encounter hardships when trying to provide for their families. Chronic illness, the loss of a spouse, or the addition of an elderly parent can add to the responsibilities in a home. Our Heavenly Father remembers the families in these situations and gives them the strength to carry out their duties. He will always bless them if they ask him in faith.

Discussion
• List the responsibilities of maintaining a home. Let members decide what they can do to share in the work.

We Can Enjoy Our Work

To some people work is a drudgery. To others it is an exciting part of life. One way to enjoy life's fullest benefits is to learn to love work.

Not all of us can choose the kind of work we do. Some of us labor for long hours for the bare necessities. It is difficult to enjoy such work. Yet the happiest people have learned to enjoy their work, whatever it is.

We can help one another in our work. The heaviest load becomes lighter when someone shares it.

Our attitude toward work is very important. The following story shows how one man saw beyond his daily labor. A traveler passed a stone quarry and saw three men working. He asked each man what he was doing. Each man's answer revealed a different attitude toward the same job. "I am cutting stone," the first man answered. The second replied, "I am earning three gold pieces per day." The third man smiled and said, "I am helping to build a house of God."

In any honest work we can serve God. King Benjamin, a Nephite prophet, said, "When ye are in the service of your fellow beings ye are only in the service of your God" (Mosiah 2:17). If our work provides only enough for necessities for ourselves or our families, we are still helping some of God's children.

Discussion
• How does our attitude affect our work?
• How can we improve our attitude?

God Condemns Idleness and Gain Obtained from Evil or Idle Practices

The Lord is not pleased with those who are lazy or idle. He said, "The idler shall not have place in the church, except he repent and mend his ways" (D&C 75:29). He also commanded, "Thou shalt not be idle; for he that is idle shall not eat the bread nor wear the garments of the laborer" (D&C 42:42).

From the earliest days of the Church, the prophets have taught Latter-day Saints to be independent and self-sustaining and to avoid idleness. No true Latter-day Saint will, while physically able, voluntarily shift from himself the burden of his own support. So long as he can, he will supply himself and his family with the necessities of life.

As far as they are able, all Church members should accept the responsibility to care for their relatives who are unable to provide for themselves.

God condemns receiving gain from evil and idle pursuits. Elder Spencer W. Kimball said, "I feel strongly that men who accept wages or salary and do not give . . . [fair] time, energy, devotion, and service are receiving money that is not clean." He also said that money obtained by evil or idle practices, such as theft, gambling (including lotteries), graft, illegal drugs, oppression of the poor, and the like is unclean money.

Elder Kimball defined the difference between honorable work and evil work: "Clean money is that [pay] received for a full day's honest work. It is that reasonable pay for faithful service. It is that fair profit from the sale of goods, commodities, or service. It is that income received from transactions where all parties profit. Filthy lucre is . . . money . . . obtained through theft and robbery, . . . gambling, . . . sinful operations, . . . bribery, and from exploitation" (in Conference Report, Oct. 1953, p. 52).

Discussion
- Discuss the effects of idleness in your community. Discuss the effects of idleness on an individual or family.
- How can idleness lead people into sinful practices?

Work, Rest, and Relaxation
We should each find the proper balance between work, rest, and relaxation. There is an old saying: "Doing nothing is the hardest work of all, because one can never stop to rest." Without work, rest and relaxation have no meaning.

Not only is it pleasant and necessary to rest, but we are commanded to rest on the Sabbath day (see Exodus 20:10; D&C 59:9–12). This day of rest after each six days of labor brings refreshment for the days that follow. The Lord also promises the "fulness of the earth" to those who observe the Sabbath day (see D&C 59:16–20; see also chapter 24, "The Sabbath Day").

On other days of the week we should schedule some time when we can visit with family, friends, and relatives. We may spend time to improve our talents and enjoy our hobbies, recreation, or other activities that will refresh us.

Discussion
- Why is it important to rest and relax from work?
- Why is it important to keep a balance in life between work, play, rest, and education?

The Blessings of Work
God revealed to Adam, "In the sweat of thy face shalt thou eat bread" (Genesis 3:19). In addition to being a temporal law, this was a law for the salvation of Adam's soul. There is no real division between spiritual, mental, and physical work. Work is essential to each of us for growth, character development, and many satisfactions that the idle never know.

"The happiest man is he who has toiled hard and successfully in his life work. The work may be done in a thousand different ways; with the brain or the hands, in the study, the field, or the workshop; if it is honest work, honestly done and well worth doing, that is all we have a right to ask" (Theodore Roosevelt, *A Nation of Pioneers,* quoted by Richard L. Evans, *Improvement Era,* Nov. 1963, p. 984). President David O. McKay said, "Let us realize that the privilege to work is a gift, that the power to work is a blessing, that the love of work is success" (quoted by Franklin D. Richards, "The Gospel of Work," *Improvement Era,* Dec. 1969, p. 103).

"Men are, that they might have joy" (2 Nephi 2:25). Work is a key to full joy in the plan of God. If we are righteous, we will return to live with our Heavenly Father, and we will have work to do. As we become like him, our work will become like his work. His work is "to bring to pass the immortality and eternal life of man" (Moses 1:39).

Discussion
• List the blessings that come from work.
• Discuss the blessings that we enjoy because of honest labor.

Additional Scriptures
• Moses 4:23–25 (Adam told that he would work all his life for his food)
• D&C 56:16–17 (God warns the rich and poor against greed, envy, and laziness)
• D&C 58:26–29 (men should be anxiously engaged in a good cause)
• Matthew 25:14–30 (parable of the talents)
• Ephesians 4:28 (steal no more but rather labor)
• 1 Thessalonians 4:11–12 (work with your own hands)
• 2 Nephi 5:17 (Nephi taught his people to work and be industrious)

SERVICE

Chapter 28

Jesus said, "I am among you as he that serveth" (Luke 22:27). As true followers of Jesus, we also must serve others.

Service is helping others who need assistance. Christlike service grows out of genuine love for the Savior and of love and concern for those whom he gives us opportunities and direction to help. Love is more than a feeling; when we love others, we want to help them.

All of us must be willing to serve, no matter what our income, age, condition of health, or social position. Some people believe that only the poor and lowly should serve. Other people think service should only be given by the rich. But Jesus taught otherwise. When the mother of two of his disciples asked him to honor her sons in his kingdom, Jesus replied, "Whosoever will be great among you, let him be your minister; And whosoever will be chief among you, let him be your servant" (Matthew 20:26–27).

How We Can Serve

There are many ways to serve. We can help others economically, socially, physically, and spiritually. For example, we can give money, food, or other articles to those who need them. We can be a friend to a newcomer. We can plant a garden for an elderly person or care for someone who is sick. We can teach the gospel to someone who needs the truth or comfort someone who grieves.

When we help one another, we serve God.

We can do small and large acts of service. We should never fail to help someone because we are unable to do great things. A widow tells of two children who came to her door shortly after she had moved to a new town. The children brought her a lunch basket and a note that read, "If you want anyone to do errands, call us." The widow was gladdened by the small kindness and never forgot it.

Sometimes, however, we must sacrifice greatly to serve someone. The Savior gave up his life in serving us.

Discussion
- Have class members tell how they have benefited at some time from kind acts of service.
- Ask members to list as many ways to serve as they can.

Why the Savior Wants Us to Serve Others
Through the service of men and women and boys and girls God's work is done. President Spencer W. Kimball explained: "God does notice us, and he watches over us. But it is usually through another person that he meets our needs" ("Small Acts of Service," *Ensign,* Dec. 1974, p. 5).

Throughout our lives all of us depend on others for help. When we were infants, our parents fed, clothed, and cared for us. Without this care we would have died. When we grew up, other people taught us skills and attitudes. Many of us have needed nursing care during illness or money in a financial crisis. Some of us ask God to bless suffering people and then do nothing for them. We must remember that God works through us.

When we help one another, we serve God. King Benjamin, a great king in Book of Mormon times, taught his people this principle by the way he lived. He served them all his life, earning his own living instead of being supported by the people. In an inspired sermon he explained why he loved service, saying:

To show humility, Jesus washed the feet of his Apostles.

*⁽ᵃ⁾*When ye are in the service of your fellow beings ye are only in the service of your God. . . .

"And if I, whom ye call your king, do labor to serve you, then ought not ye to labor to serve one another?*⁽ᵇ⁾* (Mosiah 2:17–18).

Discussion
• Read Matthew 25:40. Why does the Lord want and need us to serve others?
• Who benefits when we perform acts of service?

We Receive Blessings through Service

When we serve others we gain important blessings. Through service we increase our ability to love. We become less selfish. As we think of the problems of others, our own problems seem less serious. We must serve others to gain eternal life. God has said that those who live with him must love and serve his children.

When we consider the lives of people who serve unselfishly, we can see that they gain more than they give. One such person was a Latter-day Saint named Paul who lost the use of both legs in an accident. Some men might have become bitter and useless, but Paul chose to think of others instead. He learned a trade and earned enough money to buy a house. There he and his wife made room for many homeless, unwanted children. Some were badly handicapped. Until his death twenty years later, he served these children and others. In return he was greatly loved, and his thoughts turned away from his crippled legs. He grew close to the Lord.

Discussion
• What blessings do we receive through service to others?
• How does serving others increase our ability to love them?

Opportunities to Serve

Some of us serve only those we enjoy being around and avoid all others. However, Jesus commanded us to love and serve everyone. There are many opportunities to serve (see Mosiah 4:15–19).

We can serve members of our families. Husbands and wives should be aware of each other's needs. Parents should serve their children not only by feeding and clothing them but also by teaching and by playing and working with them. Children can serve by helping with household chores and by helping brothers and sisters.

A husband can care for a sick baby when his wife needs rest. A wife can prepare a favorite dish for her husband. A mother and father may sacrifice to send a child on a mission. An older boy may comfort a little sister who is afraid of the dark or help her learn to read. Our prophets have told us that a family is the most important unit in society. We must serve our families well (see Mosiah 4:14–15).

We have many opportunities to serve our neighbors, our friends, and even strangers. If a neighbor is having difficulty harvesting crops before a storm, we can help. If a mother is ill, we can watch her children or help with the housework. If a young man is falling away from the Church, we can lead him back. If a child is ridiculed, we can befriend him and persuade others to be kind. We do not need to know the people we serve, nor do we need to be fond of them. We should look for ways to serve as many of our Heavenly Father's children as we can.

If we have special talents, we should use them to serve others. God blesses us with talents and abilities to help improve the lives of others.

We have opportunities to serve in the Church. One purpose of the Church organization is to give us opportunities to help each other. Members of the Church serve by doing missionary work, accepting leadership assignments, visiting other Church members, teaching classes, and doing other Church work. In The Church of Jesus Christ of Latter-day Saints there is no professional clergy, so the lay members must carry on all of the activities of the Church.

Discussion

• Have each person write on a sheet of paper one way he can serve someone in his family and someone outside his family during the week. Have him place the paper where he can see it often as a reminder.

Christ Is the Perfect Example of Service

The Savior provided the perfect example of service. He explained that he didn't come to earth to be served but to serve and to give his life for us (see Matthew 20:28).

Jesus loves all of us more than we can understand. When he was on earth he served the poor, the ignorant, the sinner, the despised. He taught the gospel to all who would listen, fed crowds of hungry people who came to hear him, healed the sick, and raised the dead.

He is our God and Savior and Lord of the universe, yet he did many humble acts of service. Just before his crucifixion he met with his disciples. After teaching them, he took a basin of water and a towel and washed their feet (see John 13:4–10). In those days washing a visitor's feet was a sign of honor and was usually done by a servant. Jesus did it as an example of love and service. When we willingly serve others in the spirit of love, we become more like Christ.

Discussion

• Give three people a scripture reference and have each tell of the Savior's example of service: John 13:4–10 (washing of feet); Matthew 15:30–31 (healing); Matthew 15:32–38 (feeding the 4,000).

Additional Scriptures

• Mosiah 2 (King Benjamin's discourse on service)
• D&C 81:5 (succor, lift, strengthen)
• Colossians 3:23–24 (serve others as you would serve the Lord)
• Galatians 5:13 (serve one another by love)

THE LORD'S LAW OF HEALTH

Chapter 29

One of the great blessings we received when we came to earth was a physical body. We need a physical body to become like our Heavenly Father. Our bodies are so important that the Lord calls them temples of God (see 1 Corinthians 3:16–17). Our bodies are holy.

Because our bodies are important, our Father in Heaven wants us to take good care of them. He knows that we can be happier, better people if we are healthy. The Spirit of our Heavenly Father can be with us if our bodies are clean. Our Father knows that we face temptations to treat our bodies unwisely or to take harmful things into them. For this reason he has told us which things are good for our health and which things are bad. Much of the information God has given us concerning good health is found in Doctrine and Covenants 89. This revelation is called the Word of Wisdom.

We must obey the Word of Wisdom to be worthy to enter the temple. If we do not obey the Word of Wisdom, the Lord's Spirit may not dwell with us. If we defile the "temple of God" which is our body, we hurt ourselves physically and spiritually.

Discussion
• Read Doctrine and Covenants 89.

We Are Commanded Not to Take Certain Things into Our Bodies

The Lord commands us not to use wine and strong drinks, meaning drinks containing alcohol. President Heber J. Grant taught that strong drink often brings cruelty, poverty, disease, and plague onto the home. It often is a cause of dishonesty, loss of chastity, and loss of good judgment. It is a curse to all who drink it (see "Message of the First Presidency," *Improvement Era*, Nov. 1942, p. 686). Expectant mothers who drink can cause physical and mental damage to their children. Many automobile accidents are caused each year by people who drink alcohol.

The Lord has also told us that "tobacco is not for the body" (D&C 89:8). It is harmful to our bodies and our spirits. We should not smoke cigarettes or cigars or use chewing tobacco. Scientists have shown that tobacco causes many diseases and can harm unborn children.

The Lord also counsels us against the use of "hot drinks." Church leaders have said that this means coffee and tea, which contain harmful drugs. We should avoid all drinks that contain harmful drugs.

We should not use drugs except when they are necessary as medicine. Some drugs are even more harmful than alcohol and tobacco (which are also drugs). Those who misuse drugs need to repent of this habit.

We should avoid anything that we know is harmful to our bodies. We should not use any substance that is habit forming. The Word of Wisdom does not tell us everything to avoid, but it does give us guidelines. It is a valuable temporal law. It is also a great spiritual law. By living the Word of Wisdom, we become stronger spiritually. We purify our bodies so the Spirit of the Lord can dwell with us.

Discussion

• List the things we should not take into our bodies.

• Discuss why these things should not be used.

We Are Taught That Certain Things Are Good for Our Bodies

Fruits, vegetables, and wholesome herbs are good for us. We should use them with wisdom and thanksgiving.

The flesh of birds and animals is also provided for our food. However, we should eat meat sparingly (see D&C 49:18; 89:12). Fish is also good for man.

Grains are good for us. Wheat is especially good for us. Grains may be used also to make mild drinks.

Discussion
• According to the Word of Wisdom, what are some of the things the Lord says are good for us?

Work, Cleanliness, Rest, and Exercise Are Important

In addition to Doctrine and Covenants 89, other scriptures tell us how to be healthy. They tell us that we should "cease to be idle; cease to be unclean; . . . cease to sleep longer than is needful; retire to thy bed early, that ye may not be weary; arise early, that your bodies and your minds may be invigorated" (D&C 88:124). We are also told, "Six days shalt thou labour and do all thy work" (Exodus 20:9). The Lord counsels us not to labor more than we have strength for (see D&C 10:4).

A latter-day prophet has told us that people should learn to keep their bodies healthy by right living, . . . by inhaling pure air, taking plenty of exercise, and bathing . . . often in fresh water" (Joseph F. Smith, *Gospel Doctrine*, p. 241).

Discussion
• What do work, cleanliness, rest, and exercise have to do with the Lord's law of health?

Blessings for Living the Lord's Law of Health

Our Heavenly Father has given us health laws to teach us how to care for our bodies. The scriptures tell us about God's laws: "No temporal commandment gave I, . . . for my commandments are spiritual" (D&C 29:35). This means that his commandments concerning our physical state are for our spiritual good.

When we keep the Lord's law of health and obey his other commandments, the Lord promises to bless us physically and spiritually.

Physically we have been promised good health. As a result of this good health we "shall run and not be weary, and shall walk and not faint" (D&C 89:20). This is a great blessing, but the spiritual blessings he has promised us are even greater than the physical ones.

The Lord promises us that we "shall find wisdom and great treasures of knowledge, even hidden treasures" (D&C 89:19). We will be taught important truths by the Holy Ghost through revelation. The Lord also promises that the destroying angel shall pass us by. Elder Spencer W. Kimball said that in our time this means we will be saved from spiritual death: "For observing the Word of Wisdom the reward is life, not only prolonged mortal life but life eternal" (*The Miracle of Forgiveness*, p. 211).

Discussion

- What eternal blessings come to us from living the Word of Wisdom?
- Ask the members to share ideas about how they can obey the Word of Wisdom and overcome any problems they might have.

Additional Scriptures

- Judges 13:13–14; Proverbs 20:1; Isaiah 5:11–12; Daniel 1 (avoid strong drink)
- D&C 59:16–20 (things of the earth for the benefit of man)
- Proverbs 23:20–21 (warning against drunkenness, gluttony, laziness)

The good Samaritan showed us by his example how to love our neighbor.

CHARITY

Chapter 30

The life of the Savior reflects his pure love for all mankind. He even gave his life for us. Charity is that pure love which our Savior Jesus Christ has. He has commanded us to love one another as he loves us. The scriptures tell us that charity is felt within the heart. We have pure love when, from the heart, we show genuine concern and compassion for all our brothers and sisters. (See 1 John 3:16–24.)

Discussion
• What is charity?

Charity Is the Greatest of All Virtues
The prophet Moroni tells us, "Wherefore, cleave unto charity, which is the greatest of all, for all things must fail—but charity is the pure love of Christ, and it endureth forever" (Moroni 7:46–47).

The Savior gave us the example of his life to follow. He was a perfect man. He had perfect love, and he showed us how we must love. By his example, he showed us that the spiritual and physical needs of our fellowmen are as important as our own. Before he gave his life for us, he said:

"This is my commandment, That ye love one another, as I have loved you.

"Greater love hath no man than this, that a man lay down his life for his friends" (John 15:12–13).

Speaking to the Lord, Moroni said:

"I remember that thou hast said that thou hast loved the world, even unto the laying down of thy life for the world. . . .

"And now I know that this love which thou hast had for the children of men is charity; wherefore, except men shall have charity they cannot inherit that place which thou hast prepared in the mansions of thy Father" (Ether 12:33–34).

It may not be necessary for us to give our lives as the Savior did. But we can have charity if we make him the center of our lives and follow his example and teachings. Like the Savior, we too can bless the lives of our brothers and sisters here on earth.

Discussion
• Why is charity the greatest of all virtues?
• Why is it so important that we develop this virtue?

Charity Includes Giving to the Sick, Afflicted, and Poor
The Savior gave us many teachings in the form of stories or parables. The parable of the Good Samaritan teaches us that we should give to those in need, regardless of whether they are our friends or not (see Luke 10:30–37; see also James E. Talmage, *Jesus the Christ,* pp. 430–32). In the parable, the Savior said that a man was traveling to another city. On the road he was attacked by bandits. They stole his clothes and money and beat him, leaving him half dead. A priest came along, saw him, and passed him by. Then a temple attendant walked over, looked at him, and went on. However, a Samaritan, who was despised by the Jews, came along, and when he saw the man he felt compassion. Kneeling beside him, the good Samaritan bandaged his wounds and took him on a donkey to an inn. He paid the innkeeper to take care of the man until he recovered.

Jesus taught that we should give food to the hungry, shelter to those who have none, and clothes to the poor. When we visit the sick and those who are in prison, it is as if we were doing these things to him instead. He promises that as we do these things, we will inherit his kingdom. (See Matthew 25:34–46.)

We should not try to decide whether someone really deserves our help or not (see Mosiah 4:16–24). If we have taken care of our own family's needs first, then we should help all who need help. In this way we will be like our Father in Heaven, who causes rain to fall on the just and on the unjust alike (see Matthew 5:44–45).

President Harold B. Lee reminded us that there are those who need more than material goods: "It is well to remember that there are broken hearts and wounded souls among us that need the tender care of a brother who has an understanding heart and is kind" (*Stand Ye in Holy Places*, p. 228).

Discussion
- Have a person tell the parable of the good Samaritan (see Luke 10:30–37).
- Discuss the attitude of those who passed the injured man and of the Samaritan who cared for him.

Charity Comes from the Heart

Even when we give to those in need, unless we feel compassion for them we do not have charity (see 1 John 3:16–17). The Apostle Paul taught that when we have charity we are filled with good feelings for all people. We are patient and kind. We are not boastful or proud, selfish or rude. When we have charity we do not remember or rejoice in the evil others have done. Neither do we do good things just because it is to our advantage. Instead, we share the joy of those who live by truth. When we have charity we are loyal, we believe the best of others, and we defend them. When we really have charity these good feelings stay with us forever (see 1 Corinthians 13:4–8).

The Savior was our example of how to feel toward and treat others. He despised wickedness, but he loved sinners in spite of their sins. He had compassion for children, the elderly, the poor, and the needy. He had such great love that he could beg our Heavenly Father to forgive the soldiers who drove the nails into his hands and feet (see Luke 23:34). He taught us that if we do not forgive others, our Father in Heaven will not forgive us (see Matthew 18:33–35). He said: "I say unto you, Love your enemies, bless them that curse you, do good to them that hate you, and pray for them which despitefully use you and persecute you. . . . For if ye love them which love you, what reward have ye?" (Matthew 5:44, 46). We must learn to feel toward others as Jesus did.

Discussion
• Read Moroni 7:45.
• What attitudes show that we have charity?
• How can we love people in spite of their sins and faults?

How Can We Become Charitable?
One way we can become charitable is by studying the life of Jesus Christ and keeping his commandments. We can study what he did in certain situations and do the same things when we are in the same kinds of situations.

Second, when we have uncharitable feelings, we can pray to have them taken away. Moroni urges us, "Pray unto the Father with all the energy of heart, that ye may be filled with this love [charity], which he hath bestowed upon all who are true followers of his Son, Jesus Christ" (Moroni 7:48).

Third, we can learn to love ourselves. The Savior taught that we must love others *as we love ourselves* (see Matthew 22:39). To love ourselves, we must respect and trust ourselves. This means that we must be obedient to the principles of the gospel. We must repent of any wrongdoings. We must forgive ourselves when we have repented. We will come to love ourselves only when we can feel the deep, comforting assurance that the Savior truly loves us.

Fourth, as we love ourselves, our love for others will increase. We will not think we are better than other people. We will have patience with their faults. Joseph Smith said, "The nearer we get to our heavenly Father, the more we are disposed to look with compassion on perishing souls; we feel that we want to take them upon our shoulders, and cast their sins behind our backs" (*Teachings of the Prophet Joseph Smith,* p. 241).

In the Book of Mormon we read of Enos, a young man who wanted to know that his sins had been forgiven. He tells us:

"My soul hungered; and I kneeled down before my Maker, and I cried unto him in mighty prayer and supplication for mine own soul; and all the day long did I cry unto him; yea, and when the night came I did still raise my voice high that it reached the heavens.

"And there came a voice unto me, saying: Enos, thy sins are forgiven thee, and thou shalt be blessed" (Enos 1:4–5).

The Lord explained to Enos that because of his faith in Christ his sins had been forgiven. When Enos heard these words he no longer was concerned about himself. He knew the Lord loved him and would bless him. He began instead to feel concern for the welfare of his friends and relatives, the Nephites. He poured out his whole soul unto God for them. The Lord answered and said they would be blessed according to their faithfulness in keeping the commandments they had already been given. Enos's love increased even further after these words, and he prayed with many long strugglings for the Lamanites, who were the enemies of the Nephites. The Lord granted his desires, and he spent the rest of his life trying to save the souls of the Nephites and the Lamanites.

Enos was so grateful for the Lord's love and forgiveness that he willingly spent the rest of his life helping others receive this same gift. (See Enos 1:7–23.) Enos had become truly charitable. We too can do so. In fact, we must do so to inherit the place that has been prepared for us in our Father's kingdom.

Discussion
- Read Moroni 8:25–26 and 2 Peter 1:5–7.
- What can we do to become charitable?

Additional Scriptures
- Colossians 3:12–14 (charity is the bond of perfectness)
- Alma 34:28 (prayers are not answered unless we act charitably)
- 1 Corinthians 12:29–13:3 (charity is greater than any spiritual gift)
- D&C 121:45–46 (charity is necessary to have the companionship of the Holy Ghost)

HONESTY

Chapter 31

The thirteenth article of faith says, "We believe in being honest." The Book of Mormon tells us about a group of people who were "distinguished for their zeal towards God, and also towards men; for they were perfectly honest and upright in all things; and they were firm in the faith of Christ, even unto the end" (Alma 27:27). Because of their honesty, these people were noted by their fellowmen and by God. It is important to learn what honesty is, how we are tempted to be dishonest, and how we can overcome this temptation.

Discussion
• Read Alma 27:27.
• What would a society be like where everyone was perfectly honest?

Honesty Is a Principle of Salvation

Complete honesty is necessary for our salvation. An Apostle of the Lord has said: "Honesty is a principle of salvation in the kingdom of God. . . . Just as no man or woman can be saved without baptism, so no one can be saved without honesty" (Mark E. Petersen, in Conference Report, Oct. 1971, p. 63; or *Ensign*, Dec. 1971, p. 72).

God is honest and just in all things (see Alma 7:20). We too must be honest in all things to become like him. The brother of Jared testified, "Yea, Lord, I know that thou . . . art a God of truth, and canst not lie" (Ether 3:12). In contrast, the devil is a liar. In fact, he is the father of lies (see 2 Nephi 9:9). "Those who choose to cheat and lie and deceive and misrepresent become his slaves" (Mark E. Petersen, in Conference Report, Oct. 1971, p. 65; or *Ensign,* Dec. 1971, p. 73).

Discussion
• Why is honesty a principle of salvation?

What Is an Honest Person?
An honest person loves truth and justice. He is honest in his words and actions. He does not lie, steal, or cheat.

To Lie Is Dishonest
Lying is intentionally deceiving others. Bearing false witness is one form of lying. The Lord gave this commandment to the children of Israel: "Thou shalt not bear false witness against thy neighbour" (Exodus 20:16). Jesus also taught this when he was on earth (see Matthew 19:18). There are many other forms of lying. When we speak untruths, we are guilty of lying. We can also intentionally deceive others by a gesture or a look, by silence, or by telling only part of the truth. Whenever we lead people in any way to believe something that is not true, we are not being honest.

The Lord is not pleased with such dishonesty, and we will have to account for our lies. Satan would have us believe it is all right to lie. He says, "Yea, lie a little; . . . there is no harm in this" (2 Nephi 28:8). Satan encourages us to justify our lies to ourselves. An honest person will recognize Satan's temptations and will speak the whole truth, even if it seems to be to his disadvantage.

To Steal Is Dishonest
Jesus taught, "Thou shalt not steal" (Matthew 19:18). Stealing is taking something that does not belong to us. When we take what belongs to someone else or to a store or to the community without permission, we are stealing. Taking merchandise or supplies from an employer is stealing. Accepting more

change or goods than one should is dishonest. Taking more than our share of anything is stealing.

To Cheat Is Dishonest

We cheat when we give less than we owe, or when we get something we do not deserve. Some employees cheat their employers by not working their full time; yet they accept full pay. Some employers are not fair to their employees; they pay them less than they deserve. Satan says, "Take the advantage of one because of his words, dig a pit for thy neighbor" (2 Nephi 28:8). Taking unfair advantage is a form of dishonesty. Providing inferior service or merchandise is cheating.

Discussion
• Have three people tell how we can be honest. Discuss lying, stealing, and cheating.

We Must Not Excuse Our Dishonesty

People use many excuses for being dishonest. People lie to protect themselves and to have others think well of them. Some excuse themselves for stealing, thinking they deserve what they took, intend to return it, or need it more than the owner. Some cheat to get better grades in school or because "everyone else does it" or to get even.

These excuses and many more are given as reasons for dishonesty. To the Lord, there are no acceptable reasons. President Kimball taught that when we excuse ourselves, we cheat ourselves and the Spirit of God ceases to be with us. We become more and more unrighteous. (See *Faith Precedes the Miracle*, p. 234.)

Discussion
• What happens to us spiritually when we excuse our dishonesty?

We Can Be Completely Honest

To become completely honest, we must look carefully at our lives. If there are ways in which we are being even the least bit dishonest, we should repent of them immediately.

When we are completely honest, we cannot be corrupted. We are true to every trust, duty, agreement, or covenant, even if it costs us money, friends, or our lives. Then we can face the Lord, ourselves, and others without shame. President Joseph F. Smith counseled, "Let every man's life be so that his character will bear the closest inspection, and that it may be seen as an open book, so that we will have nothing to shrink from or be ashamed of" (*Gospel Doctrine*, p. 252).

Discussion

• What does it mean to be completely honest? What must we do to be completely honest?

Additional Scriptures

• D&C 50:17 (speak only by the spirit of truth)
• D&C 76:103–6 (destination of liars)
• D&C 42:27 (commandment not to speak evil of neighbors)
• Exodus 20:15–16 (commandment not to steal or bear false witness)
• D&C 42:20, 84–85; 59:6 (forbidden to steal)
• D&C 3:2 (God is honest)
• D&C 10:25–28 (Satan deceives)

TITHES AND OFFERINGS

Chapter 32

Our Heavenly Father knows all of the things we need. He has given us this commandment and promise: *"Seek ye first the kingdom of God, and his righteousness; and all these things shall be added unto you"* (Matthew 6:33).

We have been given commandments to help us prepare in every way to live in the presence of our Heavenly Father. He has given us a way to thank him for our blessings. Willingly paying tithes and offerings is one way we thank him. As we pay these offerings, we show the Savior that we love him and will obey his counsel: *"And verily it is a day of sacrifice, and a day for the tithing of my people"* (D&C 64:23).

Discussion
• How do we show our gratitude to our Heavenly Father for all his blessings to us?

Obeying the Law of Tithing
Anciently Abraham and Jacob obeyed the commandment to pay a tithe of one-tenth of their increase (see Hebrews 7:1–10; Genesis 28:20–22).

In modern times the Prophet Joseph Smith prayed, *"O Lord, show unto thy servants how much thou requirest of the properties of thy people for a tithing"* (D&C 119, section introduction). The Lord answered: *"This shall be the beginning of the tithing of my people. And after that, those who have thus been tithed shall pay one-tenth of all their interest annually; and this shall be a standing law unto them forever" (D&C 119:3–4).

A tithe is one-tenth of our increase. This means that we give one-tenth of all we earn before we pay for our own needs such as food, clothing, and shelter. If our increase is in the form of flocks, herds, or crops rather than money, we give one-tenth of those things (see Leviticus 27:30–32).

When we pay tithing we show our faithfulness to the Lord. We also teach our children the value of this law. They will want to follow our example and pay tithing on any money they earn.

Discussion
• What is an honest tithe?
• What can we do to teach our children to pay tithing?

We Should Give Willingly
It is important to give willingly. "When one pays his tithing without enjoyment he is robbed of a part of the blessing. He must learn to give cheerfully, willingly and joyfully, and his gift will be blessed" (Stephen L. Richards, *The Law of Tithing* [pamphlet, 1983], p. 8).

The Apostle Paul taught that how we give is as important as what we give. He said, "Let him give; not grudgingly, or of necessity: for God loveth a cheerful giver" (2 Corinthians 9:7).

Discussion
• Read 2 Corinthians 9:6–7. What does it mean to give grudgingly?
• Discuss the importance of our attitude in giving.

Tithing and Other Offerings
As members of the Church, we give tithing and other offerings to the Lord in money, goods, and time.

Tithing

Tithing is used by the Church for many purposes. Some of these are to—

1. Build, maintain, and operate temples, meetinghouses, and other buildings.
2. Provide operating funds for stakes, wards, and other units of the Church. (These units use the funds to carry out the ecclesiastical programs of the Church, which include teaching the gospel and recreation and social activities.)
3. Help the missionary program.
4. Educate young people in Church schools, seminaries, and institutes.
5. Print and distribute lesson materials.
6. Help in family history and temple work.

Other Offerings

Fast Offerings. Church members fast each month by going without food and drink for two consecutive meals. They contribute at least the amount of money they would have spent for the meals. They may give as generously as they are able. This offering is called the *fast offering.* Bishops use these fast offerings to provide food, shelter, clothing, and medical care for the needy.

As part of the fast, members attend a meeting called the *fast and testimony meeting,* where they share with each other their testimonies of Christ and his gospel.

Missionary Funds. Members contribute missionary funds to the Church to help spread the gospel around the world. These funds are used to support missions and missionaries in almost every country.

Service. Members also offer their time, skills, and goods to help others. This service allows the Church to help needy members and nonmembers around the world at community, national, and international levels, especially when disasters occur.

Discussion
• How do the offerings in addition to tithing show that we are grateful to our Heavenly Father?

We Are Blessed When We Give Tithes and Offerings

The Lord promises to bless us as we faithfully pay our tithes and offerings. He said, "Bring ye all the tithes into the storehouse, that there may be meat in mine house, and prove me now herewith . . . if I will not open you the windows of heaven, and pour you out a blessing, that there shall not be room enough to receive it" (Malachi 3:10).

Latter-day revelation tells of another blessing for those who tithe: "Verily it is a day of sacrifice, and a day for the tithing of my people; for he that is tithed shall not be burned at his coming" (D&C 64:23).

The blessings we have been promised are both material and spiritual. If we give willingly, Heavenly Father will provide our daily needs for food, clothes, and shelter. He will also help us grow "in a knowledge of God, in a testimony, in the power to live the gospel and to inspire our families to do the same" (Heber J. Grant, *Gospel Standards*, p. 58).

Those who pay their tithes and offerings are greatly blessed. They have a good feeling that they are helping to build the kingdom of God on earth.

Discussion
• Name three blessings we receive from being obedient to the law of tithing.

Additional Scriptures
• D&C 119:1–4 (the law of tithing)
• Genesis 14:19–20; Alma 13:13–16 (Abraham paid tithes)
• 2 Chronicles 31:5–6, 12; Nehemiah 10:37–38 (children of Israel paid tithing)
• 3 Nephi 24:8–10 (will a man rob God?)

MISSIONARY WORK

Chapter 33

The Lord revealed the gospel plan to Adam: *"*And thus the Gospel began to be preached, from the beginning*"* (Moses 5:58). Later, when people became wicked, Adam's righteous sons were sent to preach the gospel to the others on the earth: *"*They . . . called upon all men, everywhere, to repent; and faith was taught unto the children of men*"* (Moses 6:23).

All the prophets have been missionaries. Each in his day was commanded to preach the gospel message. Whenever the priesthood has been on the earth, the Lord has needed missionaries to preach the eternal principles of the gospel to his children.

Discussion
• When was the gospel message first preached on the earth?

The Lord's Church Is a Missionary Church
The Lord's church has always been a missionary church. When the Savior lived on the earth, he ordained Apostles and Seventies and gave them the authority and responsibility to preach the gospel. Most of their preaching was to their own people, the Jews (see Matthew 10:5–6). After Jesus was resurrected, he sent Apostles to preach the gospel to the Gentiles. He commanded the Apostles, *"*Go ye into all the world, and preach the gospel to every creature*"* (Mark 16:15).

Jesus commanded his Apostles to teach the gospel in all the world.

The Apostle Paul was a great missionary sent to the Gentiles. After he was converted to the Church, he spent the remainder of his life preaching the gospel to them. At different times during his mission he was whipped, stoned, and imprisoned. Yet each time he escaped from his persecutors, he preached the gospel as diligently as before (see Acts 23:10–12; Acts 26).

Missionary work began again when the Lord's Church was restored through the Prophet Joseph Smith. Today the Apostles and Seventies have been given the chief responsibility for preaching the gospel and seeing that it is preached in all the world. The Lord told Joseph Smith:"Proclaim my gospel from land to land, and from city to city. . . . Bear testimony in every place, unto every people" (D&C 66:5, 7). In June 1830, Samuel Harrison Smith, the Prophet's brother, began the first missionary journey for the Church.

Since that time thousands of missionaries have been called and sent forth to preach the gospel. The message they take to the world is that Jesus Christ is the Son of God and the Savior of mankind. They testify that the gospel has been restored to the earth through a prophet of God (see David O. McKay, *Gospel Ideals,* p. 132). The missionaries are given the responsibility to preach the gospel to all people, to baptize them, and to teach them to do all things that the Lord has commanded (see Matthew 28:19–20). Latter-day Saint missionaries go at their own expense to all parts of the world to preach the gospel message.

Discussion
• What two important messages do missionaries teach and testify of?

The Gospel Will Be Preached to All the World
We have been told in latter-day revelation that we must take the restored gospel to every nation and people (see D&C 133:37). The Lord never gives us a commandment without preparing a way for us to accomplish it (see 1 Nephi 3:7). The Lord has prepared ways for us to teach the gospel in nations

that were once closed to us. As we continue to pray and exercise faith, the Lord will open other nations to missionary work.

The Lord is also *"*inspiring the minds of great people to create inventions that further the work of the Lord in ways this world has never known*"* (Russell M. Nelson, "Computerized Scriptures Now Available," *Ensign*, Apr. 1988, p. 73). Newspapers, magazines, television, radio, satellites, computers, and related discoveries help give the gospel message to millions of people (see Spencer W. Kimball, "When the World Will Be Converted," *Ensign*, Oct. 1974, pp. 10–14). We who have the fulness of the gospel need to use these inventions to fulfill the Lord's commandment: *"*For, verily, the sound must go forth from this place into all the world, and unto the uttermost parts of the earth—the gospel must be preached unto every [person]*"* (D&C 58:64).

Discussion

• Who needs to hear the gospel? Have each member think of one person with whom he could share the gospel.

Missionary Work Is Important

*"*This is our first interest as a Church—to save and exalt the souls of the children of men*"* (Ezra Taft Benson, in Conference Report, Apr. 1974, p. 151; or *Ensign*, May 1974, p. 104). Missionary work is necessary in order to give the people of the world an opportunity to hear and accept the gospel. They need to learn the truth, turn to God, and receive forgiveness from their sins.

Many of our brothers and sisters on earth are blinded by false teachings and *"*are only kept from the truth because they know not where to find it*"* (D&C 123:12). Through missionary work we can bring them the truth.

The Lord has commanded, *"*Labor ye in my vineyard for the last time—for the last time call upon the inhabitants of the earth*"* (D&C 43:28). As we teach the gospel to our brothers and sisters, we are preparing the way for the second coming of the Savior (see D&C 34:6).

Discussion

• Why is it important for each person to hear and understand the gospel?

We Should All Be Missionaries

Every member of the Church is to be a missionary. We should be missionaries even if we are not formally called and set apart. We are responsible to teach the gospel by word and deed to all of our Heavenly Father's children. The Lord has told us, "It becometh every man who hath been warned to warn his neighbor" (D&C 88:81). We have been told by a prophet that we should show our neighbors that we love them before we warn them. They need to experience our friendship and fellowship.

The sons of Mosiah willingly accepted their responsibility to teach the gospel. When they were converted to the Church, their hearts were filled with compassion for others. They wanted to preach the gospel to their enemies the Lamanites, "for they could not bear that any human soul should perish; yea, even the very thoughts that any soul should endure endless torment did cause them to quake and tremble" (Mosiah 28:3). As the gospel fills our lives with joy, we will feel this kind of love and compassion for our brothers and sisters. We will want to share the message of the gospel with everyone who desires to listen.

Discussion

• Why do we feel a desire to share the gospel with others when we are truly converted?

How Can We All Be Missionaries?

There are many ways we can share the gospel. Following are some suggestions:

1. We can show friends and others the joy we experience from living the truths of the gospel. In this way we will be a light to the world (see Matthew 5:16).

2. We can overcome our natural shyness by being friendly to others and doing kind things for them. We can help them see that we are sincerely interested in them and are not seeking personal gain.

3. We can explain the gospel to nonmember friends and others.

4. We can invite friends who are interested in learning more about the gospel into our homes to be taught by the missionaries. If our nonmember friends live too far away, we can request that missionaries in their areas visit them.

5. We can teach our children the importance of sharing the gospel, and we can prepare them spiritually and financially to go on missions.

6. We can pay our tithing and contribute to the missionary fund. These donations are used for furthering missionary work.

7. We can help support financially a missionary whose family is unable to support him.

8. We can do family history research and temple work to help our ancestors receive the full blessings of the gospel.

9. We can invite nonmembers to activities such as family home evenings and Church socials, conferences, and meetings.

Our Heavenly Father will help us be effective missionaries when we have the desire to share the gospel and pray for guidance. He will help us find ways to share the gospel with those around us.

Discussion
• Ask each person to decide on a way to share the gospel with the individual he chose earlier in the lesson.

The Lord Promises Us Blessings for Doing Missionary Work
The Lord told the Prophet Joseph Smith that missionaries would receive great blessings. Speaking to elders who were returning from their missions, the Lord said, "Ye are blessed,

for the testimony which ye have borne is recorded in heaven for the angels to look upon; and they rejoice over you" (D&C 62:3).

The Lord has told us:

"If it so be that you should labor all your days in crying repentance unto this people, and bring, save it be one soul unto me, how great shall be your joy with him in the kingdom of my Father!

"And now, if your joy will be great with one soul that you have brought unto me into the kingdom of my Father, how great will be your joy if you should bring many souls unto me!" (D&C 18:15–16).

Discussion
• Why is it important to bear testimony to the truth of the gospel?
• What blessings come from sharing the gospel?

Additional Scriptures
• D&C 1:17–23 (Joseph Smith commanded to preach)
• D&C 34:4–6; Acts 5:42 (gospel to be preached)
• D&C 60:1–2 (Lord warns those who are afraid to preach the gospel)
• Matthew 24:14 (gospel to be preached before the end shall come)
• Abraham 2:9 (priesthood to be given to all nations)

DEVELOPING OUR TALENTS

Chapter 34

We all have special talents and abilities given to us by our Heavenly Father. When we were born, we brought these talents and abilities with us (see chapter 2, "Our Heavenly Family"). Each of us has been given at least one special talent.

We All Have Different Talents and Abilities
The prophet Moses was a great leader, but he needed Aaron, his brother, to help as a spokesman (see Exodus 4:14–16). Some of us are leaders like Moses or good speakers like Aaron. Some of us can sing well or play an instrument. Others of us may be good in sports or able to work well with our hands. Other talents we might have are understanding others, patience, cheerfulness, or the ability to teach others.

Discussion
• Ask each member to identify a talent of the person sitting beside him.

We Should Use and Improve Our Talents
Our Heavenly Father has said it is up to us to receive the gifts he has given us (see D&C 88:33). This means we must develop and use our talents. Sometimes we think we do not have many talents or that other people have been blessed with more abilities than we possess. Sometimes we do not use our talents because we are afraid that we might fail or be criticized by others. We should not hide our talents. We should use

them. Then others can see our good works and glorify our Heavenly Father (see Matthew 5:16).

Discussion
• Why should we improve our talents?

How Can We Develop Our Talents?
There are certain things we must do to develop our talents. First, we must discover our talents. We should evaluate ourselves to find our strengths and abilities. Our family and friends can help us do this. We should also ask our Heavenly Father to help us learn about our talents.

Second, we must be willing to spend the time and effort to develop the talent we are seeking.

Third, we must have faith that our Heavenly Father will help us, and we must have faith in ourselves.

Fourth, we must learn the skills necessary for us to develop our talents. We might do this by taking a class, asking a friend to teach us, or reading a book.

Fifth, we must practice using our talent. Every talent takes effort and work to develop. The mastery of a talent must be earned.

Sixth, we must share our talent with others. It is by our using our talents that they grow (see Matthew 25:29).

All of these steps are easier if we pray and seek the Lord's help. He wants us to develop our talents, and he will help us.

Discussion
• Name a talent or a skill you possess. How can a person develop this talent or skill? Have class members explain how they have developed talents or skills.

We Can Develop Our Talents in Spite of Our Weaknesses
Sometimes the Lord gives us weaknesses so we will work hard and overcome them. With his help, our weaknesses can become our strengths (see Ether 12:27). Beethoven composed

his greatest music after he was deaf. Demosthenes overcame weak lungs and a lisp to become one of the greatest orators of all time.

Some great athletes have had to overcome handicaps before they have succeeded in developing their talents. Shelly Mann was such an example. "At the age of five she had polio. . . . Her parents took her daily to a swimming pool where they hoped the water would help hold her arms up as she tried to use them again. When she could lift her arm out of the water with her own power, she cried for joy. Then her goal was to swim the width of the pool, then the length, then several lengths. She kept on trying, swimming, enduring, day after day after day, until she won the gold medal for the butterfly stroke—one of the most difficult of all swimming strokes" (Marvin J. Ashton, in Conference Report, Apr. 1975, p. 127; or *Ensign,* May 1975, p. 86).

Heber J. Grant overcame many of his weaknesses and turned them into talents. He had as his motto these words: "That which we persist in doing becomes easier for us to do; not that the nature of the thing is changed, but that our power to do is increased" (*Gospel Standards*, p. 355).

Discussion
• Read Ether 12:27. How can weak things be made strong?

The Lord Will Bless Us If We Use Our Talents Wisely
President Joseph F. Smith said, "Every son and every daughter of God has received some talent, and each will be held to strict account for the use or misuse to which it is put" ("The Returned Missionary," *Juvenile Instructor,* Nov. 1903, p. 689). A talent is one kind of stewardship (responsibility in the kingdom of God). The parable of the talents tells us that when we serve well in our stewardship we will be given greater responsibilities. If we do not serve well, our stewardship will eventually be taken from us. (See Matthew 25:14–30.)

We are also told in the scriptures that we will be judged according to our works (see Matthew 16:27). By developing and using our talents for other people, we perform good works.

The Lord is pleased when we use our talents wisely. He will bless us if we use our talents to benefit other people and to build up his kingdom here on earth. Some of the blessings we gain are joy and love from serving our brothers and sisters here on earth. We also learn self-control. All these things are necessary if we are going to be worthy to live with our Heavenly Father again.

Discussion
- Read and discuss the parable of the talents found in Matthew 25:14–30.

Additional Scriptures
- James 1:17 (gifts come from God)
- D&C 46:8–9; 1 Timothy 4:14 (develop gifts)
- 2 Corinthians 12:9 (weak things made strong)
- Revelation 20:13; 1 Nephi 15:33; D&C 19:3 (judged by our works)
- Hebrews 13:21 (show good works)

Jesus showed obedience to his Father by being baptized.

OBEDIENCE

Chapter 35

When Jesus was on the earth, a lawyer asked him a question: "Master, which is the great commandment in the law?

"Jesus said unto him, Thou shalt love the Lord thy God with all thy heart, and with all thy soul, and with all thy mind.

"This is the first and great commandment.

"And the second is like unto it, Thou shalt love thy neighbor as thyself.

"On these two commandments hang all the law and the prophets" (Matthew 22:36–40).

From these scriptures we learn how important it is for us to love the Lord and our neighbors. But how do we show our love for the Lord?

Jesus answered this question when he said, "He that hath my commandments, and keepeth them, he it is that loveth me: and he that loveth me shall be loved of my Father" (John 14:21).

We Should Obey God Willingly
Each of us should ask ourselves why we obey God's commandments. Is it because we fear punishment? Is it because we desire the rewards for living a good life? Is it because we love God and Jesus Christ and want to serve them?

It is better to obey the commandments because we fear pun-ishment than not to obey them at all. But we will be much happier if we obey God because we love him and want to obey him. When we obey him freely, he can bless us freely. He said, "I, the Lord, . . . delight to honor those who serve me in righteousness and in truth unto the end" (D&C 76:5). Obedi-ence also helps us progress and become more like our Heav-enly Father. But those who do nothing until they are commanded and then keep the commandments unwillingly lose their reward (see D&C 58:26–29).

Discussion
• Read D&C 58:26–29. Why is it important to obey willingly rather than unwillingly? How can we increase our desire to obey?

We Can Obey without Understanding Why
By keeping God's commandments, we prepare for eternal life and exaltation. Sometimes we do not know the reason for a particular commandment. However, we show our faith and trust in God when we obey him without knowing why.

Adam and Eve were commanded to offer sacrifices to God. One day an angel appeared to Adam and asked why he of-fered sacrifices. Adam replied that he did not know the rea-son. He did it because the Lord commanded him to. (See Moses 5:5–6.)

The angel then taught Adam the gospel and told him of the Savior who was to come. The Holy Ghost fell upon Adam, and Adam prophesied concerning the inhabitants of the earth down to the last generation (see Moses 5:9–10; D&C 107:56). This knowledge and great blessings came to Adam because he was obedient.

Discussion
• Discuss why we need not understand the Lord's purposes in order to be obedient.

God Will Prepare a Way

The Book of Mormon tells us that Nephi and his older brothers received a very difficult assignment from the Lord (see 1 Nephi 3:1–6). Nephi's brothers complained, saying, "It is a hard thing you require of us." But Nephi said, "I will go and do the things which the Lord hath commanded, for I know that the Lord giveth no commandments unto the children of men, save he shall prepare a way for them that they may accomplish the thing which he commandeth them" (1 Nephi 3:7). When we find it difficult to obey a commandment of the Lord, we should remember Nephi's words.

Discussion

• Have members memorize 1 Nephi 3:7.

• Ask members to tell about times when the Lord prepared a way for them to obey him.

No Commandment Is Too Small or Too Great to Obey

Sometimes we may think a commandment is not very important. The scriptures tell of a man named Naaman who thought that way. Naaman had a dreadful disease and traveled from Syria to Israel to ask the prophet Elisha to heal him. Naaman was an important man in his own country, so he was offended when Elisha did not greet him in person but sent his servant instead. Naaman was even more offended when he received Elisha's message: wash seven times in the river Jordan. "Are not [the] rivers of Damascus better than all the waters of Israel? may I not wash in them, and be clean?" he demanded. He went away in a rage. But his servants asked him: "If the prophet had bid thee do some great thing, wouldest thou not have done it? how much rather then, when he saith to thee, Wash, and be clean?" Naaman was wise enough to understand that it was important to obey the prophet of God, even if it seemed a small matter. So he washed in the Jordan and was healed. (See 2 Kings 5:1–14.)

Sometimes we may think a commandment is too difficult for us to obey. Like Nephi's brothers, we may say, "It is a hard thing you require of us." Yet, like Nephi, we can be sure that God will give us no commandment unless he prepares a way for us to obey him.

It was a "hard thing" when the Lord commanded Abraham to offer his beloved son Isaac as a sacrifice (see Genesis 22:1–13; see also chapter 26, "Sacrifice"). Abraham had waited many years for the birth of Isaac, the son God had promised him. How could he lose his son in such a way? The deed must have been most repugnant to Abraham. Yet he chose to obey God.

We too should be willing to do anything God requires. The Prophet Joseph Smith said, "I made this my rule: when the Lord commands, do it" (*History of the Church*, 2:170). This can be our rule also.

Discussion
• How does obeying the commandments strengthen us?

Jesus Christ Obeyed His Father
Jesus Christ was the sublime example of obedience to our Heavenly Father. He said, "I came down from heaven, not to do mine own will, but the will of him that sent me" (John 6:38). His whole life was devoted to obeying his Father; yet it was not always easy for him. He was tempted in all ways as other mortals (see Hebrews 4:15). In the Garden of Gethsemane he prayed to his Father, asking if he might avoid the agony he was enduring and the suffering to come on the cross. Then he ended his prayer by saying, "Not as I will, but as thou wilt" (Matthew 26:39).

The Apostle Paul said of him, "Though he were a Son, yet learned he obedience by the things which he suffered; and being made perfect, he became the author of eternal salvation unto all them that obey him" (Hebrews 5:8–9).

Because Jesus obeyed the Father's will in all things, he made salvation possible for all of us.

Discussion

• How can remembering the example of the Savior help us be obedient?

Results of Obedience and Disobedience

The kingdom of heaven is governed by law, and when we receive any blessing, it is by obedience to the law upon which that blessing is based (see D&C 130:21; 132:5). The Lord has told us that through our obedience and diligence we may gain knowledge and intelligence (see D&C 130:18–19). We may also grow spiritually (see Jeremiah 7:23–24). On the other hand, disobedience brings disappointment and results in a loss of blessings. "Who am I, saith the Lord, that have promised and have not fulfilled? I command and men obey not; I revoke and they receive not the blessing. Then they say in their hearts: This is not the work of the Lord, for his promises are not fulfilled" (D&C 58:31–33).

When we keep the commandments of God, he fulfills his promises, as King Benjamin told his people: "He doth require that ye should do as he hath commanded you; for which if ye do, he doth immediately bless you" (Mosiah 2:24).

Discussion

• Read together Jeremiah 7:23–24.
• What happens to those who do not repent of their disobedience?

The Obedient Gain Eternal Life

The Lord counsels us, "If you keep my commandments and endure to the end you shall have eternal life, which gift is the greatest of all the gifts of God" (D&C 14:7).

The Lord has described other blessings that will come to those who obey him in righteousness and truth until the end:

"Great shall be their reward and eternal shall be their glory.

"And to them will I reveal all mysteries, yea, all the hidden mysteries of my kingdom from days of old, and for ages to come, will I make known unto them the good pleasure of my will concerning all things pertaining to my kingdom.

"Yea, even the wonders of eternity shall they know, and things to come will I show them, even the things of many generations.

"And their wisdom shall be great, and their understanding reach to heaven. . . .

"For by my Spirit will I enlighten them, and by my power will I make known unto them the secrets of my will—yea, even those things which eye has not seen, nor ear heard, nor yet entered into the heart of man" (D&C 76:6–10).

Discussion
• Read 2 Nephi 31:16.
• Why is it important to endure to the end?

Additional Scriptures
• Abraham 3:25 (we came to earth to test our obedience)
• 1 Samuel 15:22 (obedience is better than sacrifice)
• Ecclesiastes 12:13; John 14:15; Romans 6:16; D&C 78:7; 132:36; Deuteronomy 4:1–40 (we should obey God)
• 2 Nephi 31:7 (Jesus Christ was obedient)
• Proverbs 3:1–4; 6:20–22; 7:1–3; Ephesians 6:1–3; Colossians 3:20 (children should obey their parents)
• D&C 21:4–6 (obey the prophet)
• John 8:31–32; Mosiah 2:22, 41; D&C 82:10; 1 Nephi 2:20 (blessings for obedience)
• D&C 58:21–22; 98:4–6; 134 (obey the laws of the land)
• Isaiah 60:12; D&C 1:14; 93:39; 132:6, 39 (consequences of disobedience)
• 2 Nephi 31:16; D&C 53:7; Matthew 24:13; Luke 9:62 (endure to the end)

FAMILY SALVATION

Unit Eight

Families can be together forever.

THE FAMILY
CAN BE ETERNAL

Chapter 36

The first family on earth was established by our Heavenly Father when he gave Eve to Adam in marriage (see Moses 3:21–24). Since then, each of us has been commanded to marry and have children so that through our own experience we can learn to be heavenly parents. President Brigham Young explained that our families are not yet ours. The Lord has committed them to us to see how we will treat them. Only if we are faithful will they be given to us forever. What we do on earth determines whether or not we will be worthy to become heavenly parents (see chapter 2, "Our Heavenly Family").

The Importance of Families

After Heavenly Father gave Eve to Adam, he commanded them to have children (see Genesis 1:28). He revealed that one of the purposes of marriage is to provide mortal bodies for his spirit children. Parents are partners with our Heavenly Father. He wants each of his spirit children to receive a physical body and to experience earth life. When a man and a woman bring children into this world, they help our Heavenly Father carry out his plan.

Every new child should be welcomed into the family with gladness. Each is a child of God. We should take time to enjoy our children, to play with them, and to teach them.

President David O. McKay said, "With all my heart I believe that the best place to prepare for . . . eternal life is in the home" ("Blueprint for Family Living," *Improvement Era,* Apr. 1963, p. 252). At home, with our families, we can learn self-control, sacrifice, loyalty, and the value of work. We can learn to love, to share, and to serve one another.

Fathers and mothers are responsible to teach their children about Heavenly Father. They should show by example that they love him because they keep his commandments. Parents should also teach their children to pray and to obey the commandments (see Proverbs 22:6).

Discussion
• Why did the Lord give us families?
• Why is the home the best place to prepare for eternal life?

The Eternal Family
Families can be together forever. To enjoy this blessing we must be married in the temple. When people are married outside the temple, the marriage ends when one of the partners dies. When we are married in the temple by the authority of the Melchizedek Priesthood, we are married for time and eternity. Death cannot separate us. If we obey the commandments of the Lord, our families will be together forever as husband, wife, and children.

Discussion
• What must we do to make our families eternal?

Loving Family Relationships
Husbands and wives should be thoughtful and kind to each other. They should never do or say anything to hurt each other's feelings. They should also try to do everything possible to make each other happy.

Parents are to teach children to love one another. In the Book of Mormon, King Benjamin explained:

"Ye will not suffer your children . . . [to] fight and quarrel one with another. . . .

"But ye will teach them to walk in the ways of truth and soberness; ye will teach them to love one another, and to serve one another" (Mosiah 4:14–15).

As family members we can help each other feel confident by giving encouragement and sincere praise. Each child should feel important. Parents need to show they are interested in what their children do and express love and concern for their children. Children should likewise show their love for their parents. They should be obedient and try to live the kind of life that will bring honor to their parents and to their family name.

Discussion
• Read Ephesians 4:29–32.
• How can we develop greater harmony in our homes?

How to Have a Successful Family
President Harold B. Lee taught, "The most important of the Lord's work that you will ever do will be the work you do within the walls of your own home" (*Strengthening the Home* [pamphlet, 1973], p. 7).

The following story illustrates this point:

After performing a temple marriage ceremony, President Spencer W. Kimball greeted the parents of the young couple. One of the fathers said, "My wife and I are common people, and have never been successful, but we are very proud of our family." The father explained that all eight of his children had now been married in the temple. All are faithful and serve in the Church, teaching the gospel in their families.

President Kimball looked at the calloused hands and wrinkled face of the father and said: "That is the greatest success story I have heard. . . . You are fulfilling the purpose for which you were sent to this world by keeping your own lives righteous, bearing and rearing this great family, and training them in faith. Why, my dear folks, you are very successful. God bless you" (Spencer W. Kimball, in Conference Report, Oct. 1971, pp. 152–53; or *Ensign,* Dec. 1971, pp. 37–38).

Satan knows how important families are to our Heavenly Father's plan. He seeks to destroy them by keeping us from drawing near to the Lord. He will tempt us to do things that will draw our families apart.

All of us want to have happy, successful families. The following things will help us achieve this:

1. Have family prayer every night and morning (see 3 Nephi 18:21).
2. Teach children the gospel by meeting together as a family at least once a week to study gospel principles. "There shouldn't be—there mustn't be—one family in this Church that doesn't take the time to read from the scriptures every day" (H. Burke Peterson, in Conference Report, Apr. 1975, p. 79; or *Ensign,* May 1975, pp. 53–54).
3. Do things together as a family, such as work projects, outings, and decision making.
4. Kneel together as husband and wife each night in prayer.
5. Learn to be kind, patient, long-suffering, and charitable (see Moroni 7:45–48).
6. Attend church meetings regularly (see D&C 59:9–10).
7. Follow the counsel of the Lord in D&C 88:119: "Organize yourselves; prepare every needful thing; and establish a house, even a house of prayer, a house of fasting, a house of faith, a house of learning, a house of glory, a house of order, a house of God."
8. Keep a family history and gather family genealogy.

The family is the most important unit in The Church of Jesus Christ of Latter-day Saints. The Church exists to help families gain eternal blessings and exaltation. The organizations and programs within the Church are designed to strengthen us individually and help us live as families forever.

Discussion
- What can we do to have a successful family?
- As a family, decide which principles to work on during the weeks ahead.

Additional Scriptures
- Moses 2:27–28 (man and woman created and blessed)
- Genesis 2:24 (man to cleave unto his wife)
- D&C 49:15–16 (God ordained marriage)
- Ephesians 6:4 (train children in righteousness)
- D&C 132:15–21 (eternal marriage)
- D&C 88:119–126 (instructions for a successful family)

FAMILY RESPONSIBILITIES

Chapter 37

Each person has an important place in his family. Through prophets the Lord has explained how fathers, mothers, and children should behave and feel toward one another. As husbands, wives, and children we need to learn what the Lord expects us to do to fulfill our purpose as a family. If we all do our part, we will be able to live together as a family forever.

Discussion
• What is the purpose of a family?

Responsibilities of the Parents
In marriage neither the man nor the woman is more important than the other. They are equal partners and should work together to provide for the spiritual, emotional, intellectual, and physical needs of the family.

Some responsibilities must be shared by the husband and the wife. Parents should teach their children the gospel. The Lord warned that if parents do not teach their children about faith, repentance, baptism, and the gift of the Holy Ghost, the sin will be upon the heads of the parents. Parents should also teach their children to pray and to obey the Lord's commandments. (See D&C 68:25, 28.)

One of the best ways parents can teach their children is by example. Husbands and wives should show love and respect for each other and for their children by both actions and words. It is important to remember that each member of the family is a child of God. Parents should treat their children with love and respect, being firm but kind to them.

Parents should understand that sometimes children will make wrong choices even after they have been taught the truth. When this happens, parents should not give up or become discouraged. They should continue to teach their children, to express love for them, to be good examples to them, and to fast and pray for them.

The Book of Mormon tells us how the prayers of a father helped a rebellious son return to the ways of the Lord. Alma the Younger had fallen away from the teachings of his righteous father, Alma, and had gone about seeking to destroy the Church. The father prayed with faith for his son. Alma the Younger was visited by an angel and repented of his evil way of living. He became a great leader of the Church. (See Mosiah 27:8–32.)

Parents can provide an atmosphere of reverence and respect in the home if they teach and guide their children with love. Parents should also provide happy experiences for their children.

Discussion
• Discuss the responsibilities of the parents.

Responsibilities of the Father
The father is the patriarch of the family and has important responsibilities that are his alone. He is the priesthood holder and has the duties of priesthood leadership. He should guide his family with humility and kindness rather than with force or cruelty. The scriptures teach that those who hold the priesthood should lead others by persuasion, gentleness, love, and kindness (see D&C 121:41–44; Ephesians 6:4).

The father shares the blessings of the priesthood with the members of his family. When a man holds the Melchizedek Priesthood, he can share these blessings by naming and blessing babies, administering to the sick, baptizing children, and giving special priesthood blessings and ordinations. He should set a good example for his family by keeping the commandments. He should also make sure the family prays together twice daily and holds family home evening.

The father should spend time with each child individually. He should teach his children correct principles, talk with them about their problems and concerns, and counsel them lovingly. Some good examples are found in the Book of Mormon (see 2 Nephi 1:14–3:25; Alma 36–42).

It is also the father's duty to provide the physical needs of his family, making sure they have the necessary food, housing, clothing, and education. Even if he is unable to provide all the support himself, he does not give up the responsibility of the care of his family.

Responsibilities of the Mother

President David O. McKay said that motherhood is woman's noblest calling (see *Treasures of Life*, p. 54). It is a sacred calling, a partnership with God in bringing his spirit children into the world. A mother's most important responsibility is to bring children into the world and to care for and teach them. Bearing children is one of the greatest of all blessings.

Elder Boyd K. Packer praised women who were unable to have children of their own yet sought to care for others. He said: "When I speak of mothers, I speak not only of those women who have borne children, but also of those who have fostered children born to others, and of the many women who, without children of their own, have mothered the children of others" (*Mothers*, p. 8).

A mother needs to spend time with her children and teach them the gospel. She should play and work with them so they can discover the world around them. She also needs to help her family know how to make the home a pleasant place to be. If she is warm and loving, she helps her children feel good about themselves.

The Book of Mormon describes a group of two thousand young men who rose to greatness because of the teachings of their mothers (see Alma 53:16–23). Led by the prophet Helaman, they went into battle against their enemies. They had learned to be honest, brave, and trustworthy from their mothers. Their mothers also taught them that if they did not doubt, God would deliver them (see Alma 56:47). They all survived the battle. Later they expressed faith in the teachings of their mothers, saying, *"*We do not doubt our mothers knew it*"* (Alma 56:48). Every mother who has a testimony can have a profound effect on her children.

Discussion
• Why is motherhood called a partnership with God?
• Assign someone to tell the story of Helaman's young warriors.

Responsibilities of the Children

Children share with their parents the responsibilities of building a happy home. They should obey the commandments and cooperate with other family members. The Lord is not pleased when children quarrel (see Mosiah 4:14).

The Lord has commanded children to honor their parents. He said, *"*Honor thy father and thy mother: that thy days may be long upon the land*"* (Exodus 20:12). To honor parents means to love and respect them. It also means to obey them. The scriptures tell children to *"*obey your parents in the Lord: for this is right*"* (Ephesians 6:1).

President Spencer W. Kimball said that children should learn to work and to share responsibilities in the home and yard. They should be given assignments to keep the house neat and clean. Children may also be given assignments to take care of the garden (see Conference Report, Apr. 1976, p. 5; or *Ensign*, May 1976, p. 5).

Discussion
• What should children do to honor and respect their parents?

Accepting Responsibilities Brings Blessings

A loving and happy family does not happen by accident. Each person in the family must do his part. The Lord has given responsibilities to both parents and children. The scriptures teach that we must be thoughtful, cheerful, and considerate of others. When we speak, pray, sing, or work together, we can enjoy the blessings of harmony in our families. (See Colossians 3.)

Discussion
• Have each family member tell how he can help make home a happier place.

Additional Scriptures
• Proverbs 22:6 (train up a child)
• Ephesians 6:1–3 (children are to obey parents)

ETERNAL MARRIAGE

Chapter 38

Marriage is ordained of God. The Lord has said, "Whoso forbiddeth to marry is not ordained of God, for marriage is ordained of God unto man" (D&C 49:15). Since the beginning, marriage has been a law of the gospel. Marriages are intended to last forever, not just for our mortal lives.

Adam and Eve were married by God before there was any death in the world. They had an eternal marriage. They taught the law of eternal marriage to their children and their children's children. As the years passed, wickedness entered the hearts of the people and the authority to perform this sacred ordinance was taken from the earth. Through the restoration of the gospel, eternal marriage has been restored to earth.

Discussion
• When was eternal marriage first performed on the earth?

Eternal Marriage Is Essential for Exaltation
Many people in the world consider marriage to be only a social custom, a legal agreement between a man and a woman to live together. But to Latter-day Saints, marriage is much more. Our exaltation depends on marriage. We believe that marriage is the most sacred relationship that can exist between a man and a woman. This sacred relationship affects our happiness now and in the eternities.

Heavenly Father has given us the law of eternal marriage so we can become like him. We must live this law to be able to have spirit children. The Lord has said:

"In the celestial glory there are three heavens or degrees;

"And in order to obtain the highest, a man must enter into this order of the priesthood [meaning the new and everlasting covenant of marriage];

"And if he does not, he cannot obtain it" (D&C 131:1–3).

Discussion
• Why do we believe marriage is the most sacred relationship
  between a man and woman?

Eternal Marriage Must Be Performed by Proper Authority in the Temple
An eternal marriage must be performed by one who holds the sealing power. The Lord promised, "If a man marry a wife by . . . the new and everlasting covenant . . . by him who is anointed, . . . it . . . shall be of full force when they are out of the world" (D&C 132:19).

Not only must an eternal marriage be performed by the proper priesthood authority, but it must also be done in one of the holy temples of our Lord. The temple is the only place this holy ordinance can be performed.

In the temple, latter-day Saint couples kneel at one of the sacred altars in the presence of their family and friends and two special witnesses. They make their marriage covenants before God. They are pronounced husband and wife for time and all eternity. This is done by one who holds the holy priesthood of God and has been given the authority to perform this sacred ordinances. He acts under the direction of the Lord and promises the couple the blessings of exaltation. He instructs them in the things they must do to receive these blessings. He reminds them that all blessings depend on obedience to the laws of God.

If we are married by authority other than the priesthood in a temple, the marriage is for this life only. After death, the marriage partners have no claim on each other or on their children. An eternal marriage gives us the opportunity to continue as families after this life.

Discussion
• Who has the authority to perform an eternal marriage? Why must it be performed in the temple?

Benefits of an Eternal Marriage
As Latter-day Saints, we are living for eternity and not just for the moment. However, the blessings of an eternal marriage can be ours now as well as for eternity.

The blessings we can enjoy in this life are as follows:

1. We know that our marriage can last forever. Death can part us from one another only temporarily. Nothing can part us forever except our own disobedience. This knowledge helps us work harder to have a happy, successful marriage.
2. We know that we can have our children with us throughout eternity. This knowledge helps us be careful in teaching and training our children. It also helps us show them greater patience and love. As a result, we should have a happier home.

Some of the blessings we can enjoy for eternity are as follows:

1. We can live in the highest degree of the celestial kingdom of God.
2. We can be exalted as God is and receive a fulness of joy.
3. We can, at some future time, increase our family by having spirit children.

Discussion
• Have class members discuss the blessings of an eternal marriage in this life and in eternity.

We Must Prepare for an Eternal Marriage
President Spencer W. Kimball taught that "marriage is per-

haps the most vital of all the decisions and has the most far-reaching effects. . . . It affects not only the two people involved, but their children and . . . their children's children. . . . Of all the decisions, this one must not be wrong." He recommended "that all boys and girls from their infancy up plan to be married only in the temple . . . to keep their lives spotless so that this can be accomplished" (" . . . The Matter of Marriage," devotional address, Salt Lake Institute of Religion, 22 Oct. 1976).

President Kimball also said:

"We say to all youth regardless of what country is your home, and regardless of the customs in your country, your Heavenly Father expects you to marry for eternity and rear a good, strong family.

"It would be our hope that parents would train you . . . to earn some money, and to put it away for your missions and your marriages. . . .

"There will be a new spirit in Zion when the young women will say to their boyfriends: 'I am sorry, but as much as I love you, I will not marry out of the holy temple' " ("Marriage — The Proper Way," *New Era*, Feb. 1976, p. 4).

An eternal marriage should be the goal of every Latter-day Saint. This is true even for those already married by civil law. To prepare for an eternal marriage takes much thought and prayer. Only members of the Church who live righteously are permitted to enter the temple (see D&C 97:15–17). We do not suddenly decide one day that we want to be married in the temple, then enter the temple that day and get married. We must first meet certain requirements.

Before we can go to the temple, we must be active, worthy members of the Church for at least one year. Men must hold the Melchizedek Priesthood. We must be interviewed by the branch president or bishop. If he finds us worthy, he will give us a temple recommend. If we are not worthy, he will counsel with us and help us set goals to become worthy to go to the temple.

After we receive a recommend from our bishop or branch president, we must have it signed by a member of the stake presidency or the mission president.

We are asked questions like the following in interviews for a temple recommend:

1. Do you believe in God, the Eternal Father, in his Son, Jesus Christ, and in the Holy Ghost? Do you have a firm testimony of the restored gospel?

2. Do you sustain the President of The Church of Jesus Christ of Latter-day Saints as the prophet, seer, and revelator? Do you recognize him as the only person on earth authorized to exercise all priesthood keys?

3. Do you live the law of chastity?

4. Are you a full-tithe payer?

5. Do you keep the Word of Wisdom?

6. Are you totally honest in your dealings with others?

7. Do you earnestly strive to do your duty in the Church; to attend your sacrament, priesthood, and other meetings; and to obey the rules, laws, and commandments of the gospel?

8. Do you live in accordance with the teachings of the gospel?

When you ask for a temple recommend, you should remember that entering the temple is a sacred privilege. It is a serious act, not something to be taken lightly.

We must seek earnestly to obey every covenant that we make in the temple. The Lord has said that if we are true and faithful, we will pass by the angels to our exaltation. We will become gods. (See D&C 132:19–20.) Temple marriage is worth any sacrifice. It is a way of obtaining eternal blessings beyond measure.

Discussion

• Ask each person to think about the temple interview questions as you reread them.

• How can we prepare for an eternal marriage?

Additional Scriptures

• Genesis 1:26–28 (we should multiply and replenish the earth)

• Genesis 2:21–24 (the first marriage was performed by God)

• Matthew 19:3–8 (what God has joined)

• D&C 132 (the eternal nature of the marriage law)

• D&C 42:24–26 (marriage vows should be kept)

• Jacob 3:5–11 (blessings for keeping the law of marriage)

• Matthew 22:23–30 (no marriage in the Resurrection)

THE LAW
OF CHASTITY

Chapter 39

A Note to Parents

This chapter includes some parts that are beyond the maturity of young children. It is best to wait until children are old enough to understand sexual relations and procreation before teaching them these parts of the chapter. Our Church leaders have told us that parents are responsible to teach their children about procreation (the process of conceiving and bearing children). Parents must also teach them the law of chastity.

Parents can begin teaching children to have proper attitudes toward their bodies when children are very young. Talking to children frankly but reverently and using the correct names for the parts and functions of their bodies will help them grow up without unnecessary embarrassment about their bodies.

Children are naturally curious. They want to know how their bodies work. They want to know where babies come from. If parents answer all such questions immediately and clearly so children can understand, children will continue to take their questions to their parents. However, if parents answer questions so that children feel embarrassed, rejected, or dissatisfied, they will probably go to someone else with their questions and perhaps get incorrect ideas and improper attitudes.

It is not wise or necessary, however, to tell children everything at once. Parents need only give them the information

---

they have asked for and can understand. While answering these questions, parents can teach children the importance of respecting their bodies and the bodies of others. Parents should teach children to dress modestly. They should correct the false ideas and vulgar language that children learn from others.

By the time children reach maturity, parents should have frankly discussed procreation with them. Children should understand that these powers are good and were given to us by the Lord. He expects us to use them within the bounds he has given us.

Little children come to earth pure and innocent from Heavenly Father. As parents pray for guidance, the Lord will inspire them to teach children at the right time and in the right way.

The Power of Procreation

After the Creation, God commanded each living thing to reproduce after its own kind (see Genesis 1:22). Reproduction was part of his plan so that all forms of life could continue to exist upon the earth.

Then he placed Adam and Eve on the earth. They were different from his other creations because they were his spirit children. God married Adam and Eve in the Garden of Eden and commanded them to multiply and replenish the earth (see Genesis 1:28). However, their lives were to be governed by moral laws rather than by instinct.

God wanted his spirit children to be born into families so they could be properly cared for and taught. We, like Adam and Eve, are to provide physical bodies for these spirit children through sexual reproduction.

The powers of procreation are sacred. God has commanded us that only in marriage are we to have sexual relations. This commandment is called the law of chastity.

Discussion

• What are some important purposes of the marriage relationship?

What Is the Law of Chastity?

We are to have sexual relations only with our spouse to whom we are legally married. No one, male or female, is to have sexual relations before marriage. After marriage, sexual relations are permitted only with our spouse.

To the Israelites the Lord said, *"Thou shalt not commit adultery"* (Exodus 20:14). Those Israelites who broke this commandment were put to death (see Leviticus 20:10). The Lord repeated this commandment to the Prophet Joseph Smith (see D&C 42:24).

We have been taught that the law of chastity encompasses more than sexual intercourse. Elder Spencer W. Kimball warned young people of other sexual sins:

"Among the most common sexual sins our young people commit are necking and petting. Not only do these improper relations often lead to fornication, pregnancy, and abortions—all ugly sins—but in and of themselves they are pernicious evils, and it is often difficult for youth to distinguish where one ends and another begins. They awaken lust and stir evil thoughts and sex desires. They are but parts of the whole family of related sins and indiscretions" (*The Miracle of Forgiveness*, p. 65).

Discussion

• What is the law of chastity?
• How can we be chaste?

Satan Wants Us to Break the Law of Chastity

Satan's plan is to deceive as many of us as he can to prevent us from returning to live with our Heavenly Father. One of the most damaging things he can do is entice us to break the law of chastity. He is cunning and powerful. He would like us to believe it is no sin to break this law. Many people have been deceived. We must guard ourselves against evil influences.

Satan attacks the standards of modesty. He wants us to believe that because the human body is beautiful, it should be seen and appreciated. Our Heavenly Father wants us to keep our bodies covered so that we do not put improper thoughts into the minds of others.

Satan not only encourages us to dress immodestly, but he also encourages us to think immoral or improper thoughts. He does this with pictures, movies, stories, jokes, music, and dances that suggest immoral acts. The law of chastity requires that our thoughts as well as our actions be pure. The prophet Alma taught that when we are judged by God, "our thoughts will also condemn us; and in this awful state we shall not dare to look up to our God" (Alma 12:14). Jesus taught,

"Ye have heard that it was said by them of old time, Thou shalt not commit adultery:

"But I say unto you, That whosoever looketh on a woman to lust after her hath committed adultery with her already in his heart" (Matthew 5:27–28).

Satan sometimes tempts us through our emotions. He knows when we are lonely, confused, or depressed. He chooses this time of weakness to tempt us to break the law of chastity. Our Heavenly Father can give us the strength to pass through these trials unharmed.

The scriptures tell about a righteous young man named Joseph who was greatly trusted by his master, Potiphar. Potiphar had given Joseph command over everything he had. Potiphar's wife lusted after Joseph and tempted him to commit adultery with her. But Joseph resisted her and fled from her. (See Genesis 39:1–18.)

Our Heavenly Father has promised, "There hath no temptation taken you but such as is common to man: but God is faithful, who will not suffer you to be tempted above that ye are able; but will with the temptation also make a way to escape, that ye may be able to bear it*" (1 Corinthians 10:13).

Discussion

• What are some ways Satan tempts us to break the law of chastity?
• What promise has the Lord given us to help us overcome Satan's temptations?

Breaking the Law of Chastity Is Extremely Serious

The prophet Alma grieved because one of his sons had broken the law of chastity. Alma said to his son Corianton, *"Know ye not, my son, that these things are an abomination in the sight of the Lord; yea, most abominable above all sins save it be the shedding of innocent blood or denying the Holy Ghost?*" (Alma 39:5). Unchastity is next to murder in seriousness.

If a child is conceived by those who break the law of chastity, they may be tempted to commit another abominable sin: abortion. There is seldom any excuse for abortion. The only exceptions are when—

1. Pregnancy has resulted from incest or rape.
2. The life or health of the woman is in jeopardy in the opinion of competent medical authority; or
3. The fetus is known, by competent medical authority, to have severe defects that will not allow the baby to survive beyond birth.

Even in these cases the couple should consider an abortion only after consulting with each other and their bishop or branch president and receiving divine confirmation through prayer. (See *General Handbook of Instructions* [30943], p. 11-4.)

It is extremely important to our Heavenly Father that his children obey the law of chastity. Members of the Church who break this law may be disfellowshipped or excommunicated (see D&C 42:22–26, 80–81). All those who do not repent after committing adultery will not be able to live with our Heavenly Father and Jesus Christ but will live in the telestial kingdom (see D&C 76:81–86, 103–5; see also chapter 46, "The Last Judgment").

Discussion

• Read D&C 76:103–5.

• Why is breaking the law of chastity such a serious transgression?

• What blessings do people lose if they break the law of chastity?

Those Who Break the Law of Chastity Can Be Forgiven

Peace can come to those who have broken the law of chastity. The Lord tells us, "If the wicked will turn from all his sins that he hath committed, and keep all my statutes, . . . all his transgressions that he hath committed, they shall not be mentioned unto him" (Ezekiel 18:21–22). Peace comes only through forgiveness. But forgiveness has a high price.

Elder Kimball said: "To every forgiveness there is a condition. . . . The fasting, the prayers, the humility must be equal to or greater than the sin. There must be a broken heart and a contrite spirit. . . . There must be tears and genuine change of heart. There must be conviction of the sin, abandonment of the evil, confession of the error to properly constituted authorities of the Lord" (*The Miracle of Forgiveness*, p. 353).

For many people, confession is the most difficult part of repentance. We must confess not only to the Lord but also to the person we have offended, such as a husband or wife, and to the proper priesthood authority. The priesthood leader (bishop or stake president) will judge our standing in the Church. The Lord told Alma, "Whosoever transgresseth against me . . . if he confess his sins before thee and me, and repenteth in the sincerity of his heart, him ye shall forgive, and I will forgive him also" (Mosiah 26:29).

But Elder Kimball warns: "Even though forgiveness is so abundantly promised, there is no promise nor indication of forgiveness to any soul who does not totally repent. . . . We can hardly be too forceful in reminding people that they cannot sin and be forgiven and then sin again and again and expect forgiveness" (*The Miracle of Forgiveness,* pp. 353, 360). Those who receive forgiveness and then repeat the sin are held accountable for their former sins (see D&C 82:7; Ether 2:15).

Those Who Keep the Law of Chastity Are Greatly Blessed
When we obey the law of chastity, we can live without guilt or shame. Our lives and our children's lives are blessed when we keep ourselves pure and spotless before the Lord. Children can look to our example and follow in our footsteps.

Discussion
• Read D&C 76:58–60. How will those who keep all of God's commandments, including the law of chastity, be blessed?

Additional Scriptures
• Matthew 19:5–9; Genesis 2:24 (marriage relationship is sacred)
• Titus 2:4–12 (instructions for chastity)
• Proverbs 6:25–32; Leviticus 19:29; 20:13, 15–16 (perversion condemned)
• 1 Corinthians 7:2–5; Ephesians 5:28 (loyalty to spouse)
• Revelation 14:4–5 (blessings for obedience to the law of chastity)
• Proverbs 31:10 (virtue praised)

The Portland Temple.

TEMPLE WORK AND FAMILY HISTORY

Chapter 40

The atonement of Jesus Christ assures each of us that we will be resurrected and live forever. But if we are to live forever with our families in Heavenly Father's presence, we must do all that the Savior commands us to do. This includes being baptized and receiving the ordinances of the temple.

As members of The Church of Jesus Christ of Latter-day Saints, we have each been baptized by one having the proper priesthood authority. Each of us may also go to the temple to receive the saving priesthood ordinances performed there. But many of God's children have not had these same opportunities. They lived at a time when the gospel was not available to them.

Heavenly Father wants all of his children to return and live with him. For those who died without baptism or the temple ordinances, he has provided a way for this to happen. He has asked us to perform ordinances for our ancestors in the temples.

Discussion

• What blessings does the Savior's atonement provide for us?
• What must we do to return and live with our Heavenly Father?

Temples of the Lord

Temples of The Church of Jesus Christ of Latter-day Saints are special buildings dedicated to the Lord. Worthy Church members may go there to receive sacred ordinances and make covenants with God. Like baptism, these ordinances and covenants are necessary for our salvation. They must be performed in the temples of the Lord.

We also go to the temple to learn more about Heavenly Father and his Son, Jesus Christ. We gain a better understanding of our purpose in life and our relationship with Heavenly Father and Jesus. We are taught about our premortal existence, the meaning of earth life, and life after death.

Discussion
• Show a picture of a temple. Why are temples important in our lives?

Temple Ordinances Seal Families Together Forever
All temple ordinances are performed by the power of the priesthood. Through this power, ordinances performed on earth are sealed, or bound, in heaven. The Savior taught his Apostles, "Whatsoever thou shalt bind on earth shall be bound in heaven" (Matthew 16:19; see also D&C 132:7).

Only in the temple can we be sealed together forever as families. Marriage in the temple joins a man and woman as husband and wife eternally if they honor their covenants. Baptism and all other ordinances prepare us for this sacred event.

When a man and woman are married in the temple, their children also become part of their eternal family. Couples who have been married civilly can receive these blessings by preparing themselves and their children to go to the temple and be sealed to each other.

Discussion
• What does it mean to be sealed?

Our Ancestors Need Our Help
Mario Cannamela married Maria Vitta in 1882. They lived in Tripani, Italy, where they raised a family and shared many wonderful years together. Mario and Maria did not hear the

message of the restored gospel of Jesus Christ during their lifetimes. They were not baptized. They did not have the opportunity to go to the temple and be sealed together as an eternal family. At death, their marriage ended.

Over a century later a great reunion took place. Descendants of Mario and Maria went to the Los Angeles Temple, where a great-grandson and his wife knelt at an altar and served as proxies for the sealing of Mario and Maria. Tears filled their eyes as they shared in Mario and Maria's joy.

Many of our ancestors are among those who died without hearing about the gospel while on the earth. They now live in the spirit world (see chapter 45, "The Postmortal Spirit World"). There they are taught the gospel of Jesus Christ. Those who have accepted the gospel are waiting for the temple ordinances to be performed for them. As we perform these ordinances in the temple for our ancestors, we can share their joy.

Discussion
• How are baptism and other ordinances made available to our ancestors?

Family History—How We Begin Helping Our Ancestors
Latter-day Saints are encouraged to participate in family history activities. Through these activities we learn about our ancestors so that we can perform ordinances for them. Family history involves three basic steps:

1. Identify our ancestors.
2. Find out which ancestors need temple ordinances performed.
3. Make certain that the ordinances are performed for them.

Most wards have family history consultants who can answer questions and direct us to the resources we need. If a ward does not have a family history consultant, the bishop or branch president can provide direction.

Identify Our Ancestors

To perform temple ordinances for our ancestors, we need to know their names. Many wonderful resources are available today to help us identify our ancestors' names.

A good way to begin gathering information about our ancestors is to see what we have in our own homes. We may have birth, marriage, or death certificates. We may also find family Bibles, obituaries, family histories, or diaries and journals. In addition, we can ask relatives for information they have.

How much we learn will depend on what information is available to us. We may have only a little family information and may be able to do no more than identify our parents and grandparents. If we already have a large collection of family records, we may be able to identify ancestors from generations further back in time.

We can keep track of the information we gather on family group records and pedigree charts. Samples of these forms are shown at the end of this chapter.

Find Out Which Ancestors Need Temple Ordinances Performed

Temple ordinances have been performed for the dead since the early days of the Church. Consequently, some ordinances for our ancestors may have already been done. To find out which ancestors need temple ordinances, we can look in two places. Our own family records might have information about what has been done. If not, the Church has a record of all ordinances that have been performed in the temple.

Make Certain the Ordinances Are Performed

Many of our ancestors in the spirit world may be anxious to receive their temple ordinances. As soon as we identify these ancestors, we should arrange for this work to be done for them.

One of the blessings of family history work comes from going to the temple and performing ordinances in behalf of our ancestors. We should prepare ourselves to receive a temple recommend so that, when possible, we can do this work. If our children are twelve years or older, they can share in these blessings by being baptized and confirmed for their ancestors.

If it is not possible for us to go to the temple to participate in the ordinances, the temple will arrange to have the ordinances performed by other Church members.

Discussion
• How do we go about performing ordinances for our ancestors?
• What help is available if we need it?

Additional Family History Opportunities
In addition to providing temple ordinances for the ancestors we know about, we can help those in the spirit world in many other ways. We should seek the guidance of the Spirit as we prayerfully consider what we might do. Depending on our circumstances, we can do the following things:

1. Attend the temple as often as possible. After we have gone to the temple for ourselves, we can perform the saving ordinances for others waiting in the spirit world.
2. Do research to identify ancestors who are more difficult to find. Family history consultants can guide us to helpful resources.
3. Serve in the Church's name extraction program where it is available. Through this program, members prepare genealogical information for use in the Church's family history computer programs. These programs make it easier for us to identify our ancestors.
4. Contribute family history information to Ancestral File™, one of the Church's computer programs. It contains genealogies contributed by people all over the world. Ancestral File allows people to share their family information. Family history consultants can provide more information about Ancestral File.

5. Participate in family organizations. We can accomplish much more for our ancestors as we work together with other family members.

Discussion

• What are some of the things we can do to help those in the spirit world?

Additional Scriptures

• 1 Peter 4:6 (gospel was preached to the dead)
• Malachi 4:5–6; D&C 2:2; 3 Nephi 25:5–6 (mission of Elijah)
• D&C 1:8–9 (sealing power)
• 1 Corinthians 15:29; D&C 128:15–18 (work for the dead)
• D&C 138 (redemption of the dead)

Family Group Record

If typing, set spacing at 1 1/2.   Page   of

Husband Given name(s)				Last name		☐ See "Other Marriages"
	Born (day month year)	Place				Temple
				LDS ordinance dates		
	Christened	Place		Baptized		
	Died	Place		Endowed		
	Buried	Place		Sealed to parents		
	Married	Place		Sealed to spouse		
	Husband's father Given name(s)		Last name			☐ Deceased
	Husband's mother Given name(s)		Maiden name			☐ Deceased

Wife Given name(s)				Last name		☐ See "Other Marriages"
	Born (day month year)	Place				Temple
				LDS ordinance dates		
	Christened	Place		Baptized		
	Died	Place		Endowed		
	Buried	Place		Sealed to parents		
	Wife's father Given name(s)		Last name			☐ Deceased
	Wife's mother Given name(s)		Maiden name			☐ Deceased

Children List each child (whether living or dead) in order of birth

					LDS ordinance dates	Temple
1 Sex	Given name(s)		Last name			☐ See "Other Marriages"
	Born (day month year)	Place		Baptized		
	Christened	Place		Endowed		
	Died	Place		Sealed to parents		
	Spouse Given name(s)		Last name			
	Married	Place		Sealed to spouse		
2 Sex	Given name(s)		Last name			☐ See "Other Marriages"
	Born (day month year)	Place		Baptized		
	Christened	Place		Endowed		
	Died	Place		Sealed to parents		
	Spouse Given name(s)		Last name			
	Married	Place		Sealed to spouse		
3 Sex	Given name(s)		Last name			☐ See "Other Marriages"
	Born (day month year)	Place		Baptized		
	Christened	Place		Endowed		
	Died	Place		Sealed to parents		
	Spouse Given name(s)		Last name			
	Married	Place		Sealed to spouse		

Select **only one** of the following options. The option you select applies to all names on this form.

☐ **Option 1—Family File** Send all names to my family file at the _____ Temple.

I will provide proxies for ☐ Baptism ☐ Endowment ☐ Sealing
The temple will assign proxies for ordinances not checked.

☐ **Option 2—Temple**
File. Send all names to any temple and assign proxies for all approved ordinances.

☐ **Option 3—Ancestral File** Send all names to the computerized Ancestral File for research purposes only, not for ordinances. I am including the required pedigree chart.

Your name _____

Address _____

Phone (____) _____   Date prepared _____

Your relationship to the husband and wife on this form

Husband _____   Wife _____

Published by the Church of Jesus Christ of Latter-day Saints 31827 9/89 Printed in USA

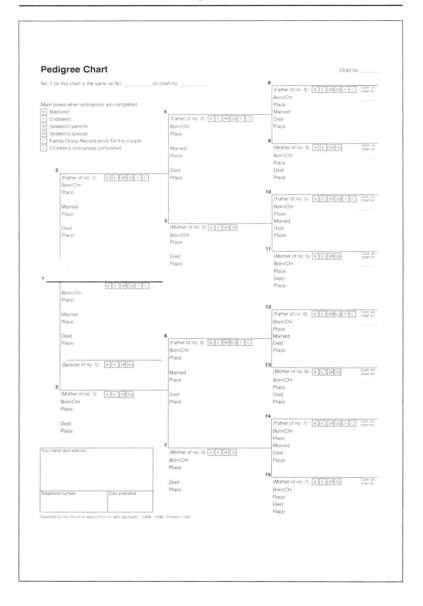

Pedigree Chart

Chart no. _____

No. 1 on this chart is the same as No. _____ on chart no. _____

Mark boxes when ordinances are completed:
- B Baptized
- E Endowed
- SP Sealed to parents
- SS Sealed to spouse
- F Family Group Record exists for this couple
- C Children's ordinances completed

2
(Father of no. 1) B E SP SS F C
Born/Chr
Place

Married
Place

Died
Place

1
B E SP SS F C
Born/Chr
Place

Married
Place

Died
Place

(Spouse of no. 1) B E SP SS

3
(Mother of no. 1) B E SP SS
Born/Chr
Place

Died
Place

Your name and address

Telephone number   Date prepared

Published by The Church of Jesus Christ of Latter-day Saints. 31826 10/89 Printed in USA

4
(Father of no. 2) B E SP SS F C
Born/Chr
Place

Married
Place

Died
Place

5
(Mother of no. 2) B E SP SS
Born/Chr
Place

Died
Place

6
(Father of no. 3) B E SP SS F C
Born/Chr
Place

Married
Place

Died
Place

7
(Mother of no. 3) B E SP SS
Born/Chr
Place

Died
Place

8
(Father of no. 4) B E SP SS F C   Cont on chart no
Born/Chr
Place
Married
Died
Place

9
(Mother of no. 4) B E SP SS   Cont on chart no
Born/Chr
Place
Died
Place

10
(Father of no. 5) B E SP SS F C   Cont on chart no
Born/Chr
Place
Married
Died
Place

11
(Mother of no. 5) B E SP SS   Cont on chart no
Born/Chr
Place
Died
Place

12
(Father of no. 6) B E SP SS F C   Cont on chart no
Born/Chr
Place
Married
Died
Place

13
(Mother of no. 6) B E SP SS   Cont on chart no
Born/Chr
Place
Died
Place

14
(Father of no. 7) B E SP SS F C   Cont on chart no
Born/Chr
Place
Married
Died
Place

15
(Mother of no. 7) B E SP SS   Cont on chart no
Born/Chr
Place
Died
Place

THE SECOND
COMING OF
JESUS CHRIST

Unit Nine

There are many signs that the second coming of the Lord is near.

SIGNS OF THE SECOND COMING

Chapter 41

Jesus Christ Will Return to the Earth

The Savior told Joseph Smith, "I will reveal myself from heaven with power and great glory . . . and dwell in righteousness with men on earth a thousand years, and the wicked shall not stand" (D&C 29:11; see also chapters 43 and 44, "The Second Coming of Jesus Christ" and "The Millennium"). Jesus has told us that certain signs and events will warn us when the time of his second coming is near. This second coming is also called "the great and dreadful day of the Lord" (D&C 110:16).

Discussion

• Read Acts 1:9–11.

• What great truth did the two angels tell the Apostles?

Signs Will Tell Us of Jesus' Coming

For thousands of years, followers of Jesus have looked forward to the Second Coming as a time of peace and joy. But before the Savior comes, the people of the earth will experience great trials and calamities. Our Heavenly Father wants us to be prepared for these troubles. He also expects us to be spiritually ready when the Savior comes in his glory. Therefore, he has given us signs, which are events that will tell us when the Savior's second coming is near. Throughout the ages God has revealed these signs to his prophets. He has said that all faithful followers of Christ will know what the signs

265

are and will be watching for them (see D&C 45:39). If we are obedient and faithful, we will study the scriptures and know of the signs.

Discussion
• Why is it important to know the signs of the Second Coming?
• How may we know the signs?

What Are the Signs Foretelling Jesus Christ's Coming?
Some of the signs foretelling the second coming of Jesus Christ have already been or are now being fulfilled. Others will be fulfilled in the future.

Wickedness, War, and Turmoil
Many of the signs are terrifying and dreadful. The prophets have warned that the earth will experience great turmoil, wickedness, war, and suffering. The prophet Daniel said that the time before the Second Coming would be a time of trouble such as the earth has never known (see Daniel 12:1). The Lord said, *"The love of men shall wax cold, and iniquity shall abound"* (D&C 45:27). *"And all things shall be in commotion; and . . . fear shall come upon all people"* (D&C 88:91). We can expect earthquakes, disease, famines, great storms, lightnings, and thunder (see Matthew 24:7; D&C 88:90). Hailstorms will destroy the crops of the earth (see D&C 29:16).

Jesus told his disciples that war would fill the earth: *"Ye shall hear of wars and rumours of wars. . . . For nation shall rise against nation, and kingdom against kingdom"* (Matthew 24:6–7). These wars will continue until a great and final war, the most destructive the world has known. In the midst of this war the Savior will appear. (See Bruce R. McConkie, *Mormon Doctrine*, p. 732.)

Many of these signs are being fulfilled. Wickedness is everywhere. Nations are constantly at war. Earthquakes and other calamities are occurring. Many people now suffer from devastating storms, drought, hunger, and diseases. We can be certain that these calamities will become more severe before the Lord comes.

However, not all the events preceding the Second Coming are dreadful. Many of them bring joy to the world.

The Restoration of the Gospel
The Lord said, "Light shall break forth among them that sit in darkness, and it shall be the fulness of my gospel" (D&C 45:28). Prophets of old foretold the restoration of the gospel. The Apostle John saw that the gospel would be restored by an angel (see Revelation 14:6–7). In fulfillment of this prophecy, the angel Moroni and other heavenly visitors brought the gospel of Jesus Christ to Joseph Smith.

The Coming Forth of the Book of Mormon
The Lord told the Nephites of another sign: the Book of Mormon would come to their descendants (see 3 Nephi 21). In Old Testament times the prophets Isaiah and Ezekiel foresaw the coming of the Book of Mormon (see Isaiah 29:4–18; Ezekiel 37:16–20). These prophecies are now being fulfilled. The Book of Mormon has been brought forth and is being taken to all the world.

The Gospel Preached to All the World
Another sign of Jesus' coming is that the "gospel of the kingdom shall be preached in all the world for a witness unto all nations" (Matthew 24:14). All people will hear the fulness of the gospel in their own language (see D&C 90:11). Ever since the restoration of the Church, missionaries have preached the gospel. The missionary effort has increased until now tens of thousands of missionaries preach in many countries of the world in many languages. Before the Second Coming, the Lord will provide a way to bring the truth to *all* nations.

The Coming of Elijah
The prophet Malachi predicted that before Christ came the second time, the prophet Elijah would visit the earth. Elijah would restore the sealing powers so families could be sealed

together. He would also inspire people to be concerned about their ancestors and descendants (see Malachi 4:5–6; D&C 2). The prophet Elijah came to Joseph Smith in April 1836. Since that time, interest in genealogy and family history has grown rapidly. We are also able to perform sealing ordinances in the temples for the living and the dead.

The Lamanites Will Become a Great People

The Lord said that when his coming was near, the Lamanites would become a righteous and respected people. He said, "Before the great day of the Lord shall come, . . . the Lamanites shall blossom as the rose" (D&C 49:24). Great numbers of Lamanites in North and South America and the South Pacific are now receiving the blessings of the gospel.

Building of the New Jerusalem

Near the time of the coming of Jesus, the faithful Saints will build a righteous city, a city of God, called the New Jerusalem. Jesus Christ himself will rule there. (See 3 Nephi 21:23–25.) The Lord said the city will be built in the state of Missouri in the United States (see D&C 84:3–4).

These are only a few of the signs that the Lord has given us. The scriptures describe many more.

Discussion

• List some of the signs of the Second Coming. Discuss each one.

Knowing the Signs of the Times Can Help Us

No one except our Heavenly Father knows exactly when the Lord will come. The Savior taught this with the parable of the fig tree. He said that when we see a fig tree putting forth leaves, we can tell that summer will soon come. Likewise, when we see the signs described in the scriptures, we can know that his coming is near. (See Matthew 24:32–33.)

The Lord gave these signs to help us. We can put our lives in order and prepare ourselves and our families for those things yet to come.

We do not need to worry about the calamities but can look forward to the coming of the Savior and be glad. The Lord said, "Be not troubled, for, when all these things [the signs] shall come to pass, ye may know that the promises which have been made unto you shall be fulfilled" (D&C 45:35). He said those who are righteous when he comes will not be destroyed "but shall abide the day. And the earth shall be given them for an inheritance; . . . and their children shall grow up without sin. . . . For the Lord shall be in their midst, and his glory shall be upon them, and he will be their king and their lawgiver" (D&C 45:57–59).

Discussion
• How can knowing the signs of the Second Coming help us?

Additional Scriptures
• 1 Corinthians 15:22–28 (the end cometh; death is done away)
• 1 Thessalonians 5:1–6 (signs of a woman in childbirth)
• Matthew 16:1–4 (discern signs of the times)
• Matthew 24 (signs of the Second Coming)
• D&C 38:30 (prepare so we might not fear)
• D&C 68:11 (we can know the signs)

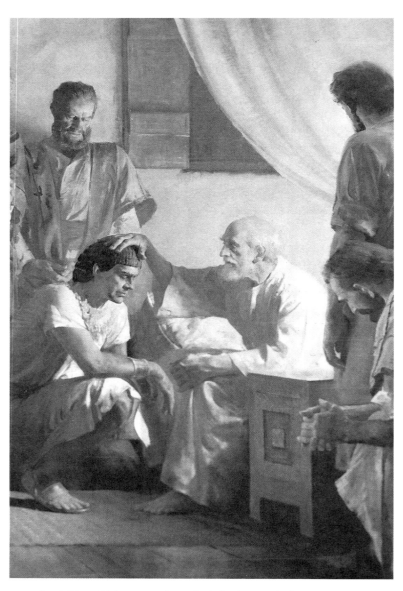

Jacob blessed his sons and prophesied what would happen to their descendants in the last days.

THE GATHERING
OF THE
HOUSE OF ISRAEL

Chapter 42

The House of Israel Are God's Covenant People

Jacob was a great prophet who lived hundreds of years before the time of Christ. Because Jacob was faithful, the Lord gave him the special name of Israel, which means "a prince of God" (see Genesis 32:28). Jacob had twelve sons. These sons and their families became known as the twelve tribes of Israel, or Israelites (see Genesis 49:28).

Jacob was a grandson of Abraham. The Lord made an everlasting covenant with Abraham that was renewed with Jacob and his children (see Deuteronomy 32:7–9; see also chapter 15, "The Lord's Covenant People"). God promised that the Israelites would be his covenant people as long as they would obey his commandments (see Deuteronomy 28:9–10). They would be a blessing to all the nations of the world by taking the gospel and the priesthood to them. Thus, they would keep their covenant with the Lord and he would keep his covenant with them.

Discussion

• Discuss the promise of the Lord to make the Israelites his chosen people.

The House of Israel Was Scattered

Again and again prophets of the Lord warned the house of Israel what would happen if they were wicked. Moses prophesied, *And the Lord shall scatter thee among all people, from the one end of the earth even unto the other* (Deuteronomy 28:64).

Gradually the Israelites began to break the commandments of God. They fought among themselves and split into two kingdoms: the Northern Kingdom, called the kingdom of Israel, and the Southern Kingdom, called the kingdom of Judah. Ten of the twelve tribes of Israel lived in the Northern Kingdom. During a war they were conquered by their enemies and carried away into captivity. Some of them later escaped into the lands of the north and became lost to the rest of the world.

About one hundred years after the capture of the Northern Kingdom, the Southern Kingdom was conquered. The capital city of Jerusalem was destroyed in 586 B.C., and the remaining two tribes of Israel were taken captive. Later, some of the members of these tribes returned and rebuilt Jerusalem. Just before Jerusalem was destroyed, Lehi and his family left the city and settled in the Americas. The Lamanites are descendants of Lehi's people.

After the time of Christ, Jerusalem was again destroyed, this time by Roman soldiers. The Jews were scattered over much of the world. Today Israelites are found in all countries of the world. Many of these people do not know that they are descended from the ancient house of Israel.

Discussion
• Have class members list the important events that are part of the scattering of the house of Israel.

The House of Israel Must Be Gathered
The Lord promised that the Israelites, his covenant people, would someday be gathered: *I will gather the remnant of my flock out of all countries whither I have driven them* (Jeremiah 23:3).

The Lord has some important reasons for gathering the Israelites. The people of Israel need to learn the teachings of the gospel and prepare themselves to meet the Savior when he comes again. The Israelites have the responsibility of building temples and performing sacred ordinances for ancestors who died without having this opportunity. The covenant people of God must take the gospel to all nations. They must fulfill the covenant to be a blessing to all the world.

The power and authority to direct the work of gathering the house of Israel was given to Joseph Smith by the prophet Moses, who appeared in 1836 in the Kirtland Temple (see D&C 110:11). Since that time, each prophet has held the keys for the gathering of the house of Israel, and this gathering has been an important part of the Church's work. The house of Israel is now being gathered as they accept the restored gospel and serve the God of Abraham, Isaac, and Jacob (see Deuteronomy 30:1–5).

Discussion
• List some of the reasons why the house of Israel must be gathered.

How Will the House of Israel Be Gathered?
The Israelites are to be gathered spiritually first and then physically. They are gathered spiritually when they join The Church of Jesus Christ of Latter-day Saints. This spiritual gathering began during the time of the Prophet Joseph Smith and continues today all over the world. Converts to the Church are Israelites either by blood or adoption. They belong to the family of Abraham and Jacob (see Abraham 2:9–11; Galatians 3:26–29).

President Joseph Fielding Smith said: "There are many nations represented in the . . . Church. . . . They have come because the Spirit of the Lord rested upon them; . . . receiving the *spirit of gathering,* they have left everything for the sake of the gospel" (*Doctrines of Salvation,* 3:256).

The physical gathering of Israel means that the Israelites will be gathered home to the lands of their inheritance, and shall be established in all their lands of promise^D (see 2 Nephi 9:2). The tribes of Ephraim and Manasseh will be gathered to the land of America. The tribe of Judah will return to the city of Jerusalem and the area surrounding it. The ten lost tribes will receive from the tribe of Ephraim their promised blessings (see D&C 133:26–35).

When the Church was first established, the Saints were instructed to gather in Ohio, then Missouri, and then the Salt Lake Valley. Today, however, modern prophets have taught that Church members are to build up the kingdom of God in their own lands. Elder Bruce R. McConkie said:

"Every stake on earth is the gathering place for the lost sheep of Israel who live in its area.

"The gathering place for Peruvians is in the stakes of Zion in Peru, or in the places which soon will become stakes. The gathering place for Chileans is in Chile; for Bolivians it is in Bolivia; for Koreans it is in Korea; and so it goes through all the length and breadth of the earth. Scattered Israel in every nation is called to gather to the fold of Christ, to the stakes of Zion, as such are established in their nations" ("Come: Let Israel Build Zion," *Ensign*, May 1977, p. 118).

The physical gathering of Israel will not be complete until the second coming of the Savior (see Joseph Smith—Matthew 1:37). Then the Lord's promise will be fulfilled:

^DBehold, the days come, saith the Lord, that it shall no more be said, The Lord liveth, that brought up the children of Israel out of the land of Egypt;

"But, the Lord liveth, that brought up the children of Israel from the land of the north, and from all the lands whither he had driven them: and I will bring them again into their land that I gave unto their fathers^D (Jeremiah 16:14–15).

Discussion
• In what two ways will the house of Israel be gathered? Discuss each of these.

Additional Scriptures
- Genesis 17:1–8 (God's covenant with Abraham)
- 2 Kings 17 (Northern Kingdom taken captive)
- 2 Chronicles 36:11–20 (Southern Kingdom taken captive)
- James 1:1 (twelve tribes scattered abroad)
- 1 Nephi 10:12–13 (Nephite migration was part of the scattering)
- Jeremiah 3:14–18 (one from a city, two from a family)
- Jeremiah 31:7–14 (lost tribes to come from the north countries)
- Ezekiel 20:33–36 (Israel will be gathered from all countries)
- 3 Nephi 20:29–46 (Jews will be gathered to Jerusalem)
- 3 Nephi 21:26–29 (gathering starts with restoration of the gospel)
- D&C 133:26–34 (ten tribes to return from the north)
- Isaiah 11:11–13 (the Lord will recover his people)
- Revelation 18:4–8 (a voice will proclaim the gathering)
- D&C 133:6–15 (Gentiles to Zion, Jews to Jerusalem)

Jesus Christ will return to the earth in glory.

THE SECOND COMING OF JESUS CHRIST

Chapter 43

Forty days after his resurrection, Jesus and his Apostles were gathered together on the Mount of Olives. The time had come for Jesus to leave the earth. He had completed all the work that he had to do at that time. He was to return to our Heavenly Father until the time of his second coming.

After he had instructed his Apostles, Jesus ascended into heaven. While the Apostles looked up into the heavens, two angels stood beside them and said, "Ye men of Galilee, why stand ye gazing up into heaven? this same Jesus, which is taken up from you into heaven, shall so come in like manner as ye have seen him go" (Acts 1:11).

From that time until the present day, the followers of Jesus Christ have looked forward to the Second Coming.

Discussion
• Why is it important for us to know about the Second Coming?

What Will Jesus Do When He Comes Again?
When Jesus Christ comes again to the earth, he will do the following things:

1. He will cleanse the earth. When Jesus comes again, he will come in power and great glory. At that time the wicked will be destroyed. All things that are corrupt will be burned, and the earth will be cleansed by fire (see D&C 101:24–25).

2. He will judge his people (see chapter 46, "The Last Judgment"). When Jesus comes again, he will judge the nations and will divide the righteous from the wicked (see Matthew 25:31–46). John the Revelator wrote about this judgment: "I saw thrones, and they sat upon them, and judgment was given unto them: and I saw the souls of them that were beheaded for the witness of Jesus, and for the word of God . . . and they lived and reigned with Christ a thousand years." The wicked he saw "lived not again until the thousand years were finished" (Revelation 20:4–5; see also D&C 88:95–98).

3. He will usher in the Millennium. The Millennium is the thousand-year period when Jesus will reign on the earth. At the beginning of this period of time, the righteous will be caught up to meet Jesus at his coming. His coming will begin the millennial reign. (See chapter 44, "The Millennium.")

Brigham Young said:

"In the Millennium, when the Kingdom of God is established on the earth in power, glory and perfection, and the reign of wickedness that has so long prevailed is subdued, the Saints of God will have the privilege of building their temples, and of entering into them, becoming, as it were, pillars in the temples of God, and they will officiate for their dead. . . . And we will have revelations to know our forefathers clear back to Father Adam and Mother Eve, and we will enter into the temples of God and officiate for them. Then man will be sealed to man until the chain is made perfect back to Adam, so that there will be a perfect chain of Priesthood from Adam to the winding-up scene" (*Discourses of Brigham Young*, p. 116).

4. He will complete the Resurrection. Those who have obtained the privilege of coming forth in the Resurrection of the Just will rise from their graves. They will be caught up to meet the Savior as he comes down from heaven.

After Jesus Christ rose from the dead, other righteous people who had died were also resurrected. They appeared in Jerusalem and also on the American continent (see Matthew 27:52–53; 3 Nephi 23:9). This was the beginning of the First Resurrection. Some people have been resurrected since then. Those who already have been resurrected and those who will be resurrected at the time of his coming will all inherit the glory of the celestial kingdom (see D&C 76:50–70).

After the beginning of the Millennium, those who will receive a terrestrial glory will be resurrected (see D&C 88:99; D&C 76:71–80). When all these people have been resurrected, the First Resurrection will be completed.

The wicked who are living at the time of the second coming of the Lord will be destroyed in the flesh. They, along with the wicked who are already dead, will have to wait until the end of the Millennium before they can come forth from their graves. At the end of the Millennium, the Second Resurrection will take place. All of the remaining dead will rise to meet God. They will either inherit the telestial kingdom or be cast into outer darkness with Satan (see D&C 76:32–33, 81–112).

5. He will take his rightful place as king of heaven and earth. When Jesus comes, he will establish his government on the earth. The Church will become part of that kingdom. He will rule all the people of the earth in peace for a thousand years.

When Jesus Christ first came to the earth, he did not come in glory. He was born in a lowly stable and laid in a manger of hay. He did not come with great armies as the Jews had expected of their Savior. Instead, he came saying, "Love your enemies, . . . do good to them that hate you, and pray for them which despitefully use you" (Matthew 5:44). He was rejected and crucified. But he will not be rejected at his second coming, "for every ear shall hear it, and every knee shall bow, and every tongue shall confess" that Jesus is the Christ (D&C 88:104). He will be greeted as "Lord of Lords and King of Kings." He will be called "Wonderful, Counsellor, The mighty God, The everlasting Father, The Prince of Peace" (Isaiah 9:6).

For information about how we will know when Jesus' second coming is near, see chapter 41, "Signs of the Second Coming."

Discussion

• Have members discuss some of the things the Lord will do when he comes the second time.

How Will We Know When Jesus' Coming Is Near?

When Jesus was born, very few people knew that the Savior of the world had come. When he comes again, there will be no doubt who he is. No one knows the exact time that the Savior will come again. "Of that day and hour knoweth no man, no, not the angels of heaven, but my Father only" (Matthew 24:36).

The Lord used a parable to give us an idea of the time of his coming:

"Now learn a parable of the fig tree; When her branch is yet tender, and putteth forth leaves, ye know that summer is near:

"So ye in like manner, when ye shall see these things come to pass, know that it is nigh, even at the doors" (Mark 13:28–29).

The Lord has also given us some signs to let us know when his coming is near. After revealing the signs, he cautioned:

"Watch therefore: for ye know not what hour your Lord doth come. . . .

"Be ye also ready: for in such an hour as ye think not the Son of man cometh" (Matthew 24:42–44).

Discussion

• Read Mark 13:1–29. How can we know when the Savior's coming is near?

We Can Be Ready When the Savior Comes

The best way we can prepare for the Savior's coming is to accept the teachings of the gospel and make them part of our lives. We should live each day the best we can, just as Jesus taught when he was on the earth. We can look to the prophet for guidance and follow his counsel. We can live worthy to have the Holy Ghost guide us. Then we will look forward to the Savior's coming with happiness and not with fear. The Lord said:*"Fear not, little flock, the kingdom is yours until I come. Behold, I come quickly. Even so. Amen"* (D&C 35:27).

Discussion

• Read Matthew 25:1–13. What are some things we can do to be ready when the Savior (the bridegroom) comes again?

Additional Scriptures

• John 14:2–3; Matthew 26:64 (Jesus to prepare a place and come again)
• Malachi 3:2–3; 4:1; D&C 64:23–25 (earth to be burned)
• D&C 133:41–51 (wicked to be destroyed)
• Matthew 13:40–43 (the Judgment predicted)
• Romans 2:6–9; Revelation 20:12–13 (the Judgment)
• 1 Corinthians 15:40–42; D&C 78; 88:17–35 (degrees of glory)
• 2 Corinthians 12:2 (a man was caught up to the third heaven)
• D&C 43:29–30; 29:11 (the Savior's coming will usher in the Millennium)
• Articles of Faith 1:10 (Jesus to reign)
• Alma 11:43–44; Alma 40 (the Resurrection explained)
• Helaman 14:25 (the dead to rise)
• Zechariah 14:9; Revelation 11:15; 1 Nephi 22:24–26 (Jesus to reign as King)

THE MILLENNIUM

A thousand years of peace, love, and joy will begin on the earth at the second coming of Jesus Christ. This thousand-year period is called the Millennium. It will be the final thousand years of the earth's temporal existence. The scriptures and the prophets help us understand what it will be like to live on the earth during the Millennium.

Discussion
• What is the Millennium?

Who Will Be on Earth during the Millennium?

Only righteous people will live on the earth during the Millennium. They will be those who have lived virtuous and honest lives. These people will inherit either the terrestrial or celestial kingdom.

During the Millennium, mortals will still live on earth, and they will continue to have children as we do now (see D&C 45:58). Joseph Smith said that immortal beings will frequently visit the earth. These resurrected beings will help with the government and other work (see *Teachings of the Prophet Joseph Smith*, p. 268).

Brigham Young taught that there will be nonmembers of The Church of Jesus Christ of Latter-day Saints living on earth as well as members. People will still have their agency, and for a time many will continue to believe their false religions and ideas. Eventually everyone will accept Jesus Christ as the Savior (see Daniel H. Ludlow, ed., _Latter-day Prophets Speak,_ pp. 261–62).

During the Millennium, Jesus will "reign personally upon the earth" (Articles of Faith 1:10). Joseph Smith explained that Jesus and the resurrected Saints will probably not live on the earth all the time but will visit whenever they please or when necessary to help in the governing of the earth (see _Teachings of the Prophet Joseph Smith,_ p. 268).

Discussion
• Who will be on the earth during the Millennium?

What Will Be Done during the Millennium?

There will be two great works for members of the Church during the Millennium: temple work and missionary work. Some ordinances are necessary for exaltation. These include baptism, the laying on of hands for the gift of the Holy Ghost, and the temple ordinances—the endowment, temple marriage, and the sealing together of family units.

Many people have died without receiving these ordinances. People on the earth must perform these ordinances for them. This work is now being done in the temples of the Lord. There is too much work to finish before the Millennium begins, so it will be completed during that time. Resurrected beings will help us correct the mistakes we have made in doing research concerning our dead ancestors. They will also help us find the information we need to complete our records.

The other great work during the Millennium will be missionary work. The gospel will be taught with great power to all people. Eventually there will be no need to teach others the first principles of the gospel because "they shall all know me, from the least of them unto the greatest of them, saith the Lord" (Jeremiah 31:34).

Discussion
• Discuss the great works to be done during the Millennium.

Conditions during the Millennium

The earth will again be as it was when Adam and Eve lived in the Garden of Eden (see Articles of Faith 1:10). The whole earth will be a delightful garden. There will not be different continents as we have now, but the land will be gathered in one place as it was in the beginning (see D&C 133:23–24).

Satan Bound

During the Millennium, Satan will be bound. This means he will not have power to tempt those who are living at that time (see D&C 101:28). The *"children shall grow up without sin unto salvation"* (D&C 45:58). *"Because of the righteousness of his people, Satan has no power; wherefore, he cannot be loosed for the space of many years; for he hath no power over the hearts of the people, for they dwell in righteousness, and the Holy One of Israel reigneth"* (1 Nephi 22:26).

Peace on the Earth

During the Millennium, there will be no war. People will live in peace and harmony together. Everything that has been used for war will be turned to useful purposes. *"They shall beat their swords into plowshares, and their spears into pruninghooks: nation shall not lift up sword against nation, neither shall they learn war any more"* (Isaiah 2:4).

Righteous Government

Jesus Christ will not only lead the Church during the Millennium, but he will also be in charge of the political government. This government will be based on principles of righteousness and will preserve the basic rights and freedoms of all people. Mortals, both members of the Church and non-members, will hold government positions (see Brigham Young, *in Journal of Discourses,* 2:310). They will receive help from resurrected beings. At this time there will be two capitals in the world, one in Jerusalem, the other in America (see Joseph Fielding Smith, *Doctrines of Salvation,* 3:66–72). *"For out of Zion shall go forth the law, and the word of the Lord from Jerusalem"* (Isaiah 2:3).

No Disease or Death

Even though mortals will live on the earth during the Millennium, they will not have diseases as we do now. There will be no death as we know it. When people have lived to an old age, they will not die and be buried. Instead, they will be changed from their mortal condition to an immortal condition in an instant (see D&C 63:51; 101:29–31).

All Things Revealed

Some truths have not been revealed to us. These will be revealed during the Millennium. The Lord said he will "reveal all things—things which have passed, and hidden things which no man knew, things of the earth, by which it was made, and the purpose and the end thereof—things most precious, things that are above, and things that are beneath, things that are in the earth, and upon the earth, and in heaven" (D&C 101:32–34).

Changes in the Animal Kingdom

The animal kingdom will also be at peace. All animals, even those that are now enemies, will live together in harmony. Animals that now eat flesh will eat grass and grain (see Isaiah 11:6–7).

Other Millennial Activities

In many ways, life will be much as it is now, except that everything will be done in righteousness. People will eat and drink and will wear clothing (see *Discourses of Brigham Young*, p. 115). People will continue to plant and harvest crops and build houses (see Isaiah 65:21).

Discussion

• Discuss the conditions that will exist during the Millennium. Use the scriptural reference listed for each condition.

One Final Struggle after the Millennium

At the end of the thousand years, Satan will be set free for a short time. Some people will turn away from Heavenly Father. Satan will gather his armies, and Michael (Adam) will gather the hosts of heaven. In this great struggle, Satan and his followers will be cast out forever. Then will come the final judgment, and all people will be assigned to the kingdoms they will have prepared for by the way they have lived. The earth will be changed into a celestial kingdom (see D&C 29:22–29; 88:17–20, 110–15).

Additional Scriptures
- Zechariah 14:4–9; 1 Nephi 22:24–26 (Jesus to reign on earth)
- Daniel 7:27 (Saints to be given the kingdom)
- D&C 88:87–110 (conditions during the Millennium)
- Revelation 20:1–3; 2 Nephi 30:10–18 (Satan to be bound)
- D&C 101:22–31 (enmity to cease; no death; Satan to have no power to tempt)
- Isaiah 11:1–9 (wolf and lamb to dwell together)
- D&C 43:31; Revelation 20:7–10 (Satan loosed to gather forces)

LIFE AFTER DEATH

Unit Ten

We will join our families and loved ones in the spirit world after death.

THE POSTMORTAL SPIRIT WORLD

Chapter 45

Heavenly Father prepared a plan for our salvation. As part of this plan, he sent us from his presence to live on earth and receive mortal bodies of flesh and blood. Eventually our mortal bodies will die, and our spirits will go to the spirit world. The spirit world is a place of waiting, working, learning, and resting from care and sorrow. Our spirits will live there until we are ready for our resurrection. Then our mortal bodies will once more unite with our spirits, and we will receive the degree of glory we have prepared for (see chapter 46, "The Last Judgment").

Many of us have wondered what the spirit world is like. The scriptures and latter-day prophets have given us information about the spirit world.

Discussion
• What is the purpose of the spirit world?

Where Is the Spirit World?
In a funeral sermon, Joseph Smith declared that the spirits of righteous people who have died "are not far from us, and know and understand our thoughts, feelings, and motions, and are often pained therewith" (*Teachings of the Prophet Joseph Smith*, p. 326). Other latter-day prophets have made similar statements. President Ezra Taft Benson said: "Sometimes the veil between this life and the life beyond becomes very thin.

Our loved ones who have passed on are not far from us" (in Conference Report, Apr. 1971, p. 18; or *Ensign,* June 1971, p. 33). President Brigham Young said: "Where is the spirit world? It is right here" (*Discourses of Brigham Young,* p. 376).

Discussion
• Where is the spirit world?

What Are Spirits Like?
Spirit beings have the same bodily form as mortals except that the spirit body is in perfect form (see Ether 3:16). Spirits carry with them from earth their attitudes of devotion or antagonism toward things of righteousness (see Alma 34:34). They have the same appetites and desires that they had when they lived on earth.

All spirits are in adult form. They were adults before their mortal existence, and they are in adult form after death, even if they die as infants or children (see Joseph F. Smith, *Gospel Doctrine,* p. 455).

Discussion
• Read Ether 3:16. What do spirit bodies look like?

Divisions in the Spirit World
The prophet Alma in the Book of Mormon taught about two divisions or states in the spirit world:

"The spirits of those who are righteous are received into a state of happiness, which is called paradise, a state of rest, a state of peace, where they shall rest from all their troubles and from all care, and sorrow.

"And then shall it come to pass, that the spirits of the wicked, yea, who are evil—for behold, they have no part nor portion of the Spirit of the Lord; for behold, they chose evil works rather than good; therefore the spirit of the devil did enter into them, and take possession of their house—and these shall be cast out into outer darkness; there shall be weeping, and wailing, and gnashing of teeth, and this because of their own iniquity, being led captive by the will of the devil.

"Now this is the state of the souls of the wicked, yea, in darkness, and a state of awful, fearful looking for the fiery indignation of the wrath of God upon them; thus they remain in this state, as well as the righteous in paradise, until the time of their resurrection" (Alma 40:12–14).

The spirits are classified according to the purity of their lives and their obedience to the will of the Lord while on earth. The righteous and the wicked are separated (see 1 Nephi 15:28–30), but the spirits may progress from one level to another as they learn gospel principles and live in accordance with them (see Bruce R. McConkie, *Mormon Doctrine*, p. 762).

Discussion
• What divisions are there in the spirit world?

Paradise
According to the prophet Alma, the righteous spirits rest from earthly care and sorrow. Nevertheless, they are occupied in doing the work of the Lord. President Joseph F. Smith saw in a vision that immediately after Jesus Christ was crucified, he visited the righteous in the spirit world. He appointed messengers, gave them power and authority, and commissioned them to "carry the light of the gospel to them that were in darkness, even to all the spirits of men" (D&C 138:30).

The Church is organized in the spirit world, with each prophet standing at the head of his own generation (see Joseph Smith, *History of the Church*, 4:209). Priesthood holders continue their responsibilities in the spirit world. President Wilford Woodruff taught: "The same Priesthood exists on the other side of the veil. . . . Every Apostle, every Seventy, every Elder, etc., who has died in the faith as soon as he passes to the other side of the veil, enters into the work of the ministry" (in *Journal of Discourses*, 22:333–34).

Family relationships are also important. President Jedediah M. Grant, a counselor to Brigham Young, saw the spirit world and described to Heber C. Kimball the organization that exists there: "He said that the people he there saw were organized in family capacities. . . . He said, 'When I looked at families, there was a deficiency in some, . . . for I saw families that would not be permitted to come and dwell together, because they had not honored their calling here' " (Heber C. Kimball, in *Journal of Discourses*, 4:135–36).

Discussion
• What do the spirits in paradise do?
• Why are some families incomplete in paradise?

Spirit Prison
The Apostle Peter referred to the spirit world as a prison, which it is for some (see 1 Peter 3:18–20). In the spirit prison are the spirits of those who have not yet received the gospel of Jesus Christ. These spirits have agency and may be enticed by both good and evil. If they accept the gospel and the ordinances performed for them in the temples, they may prepare themselves to leave the spirit prison and dwell in paradise.

Also in the spirit prison are those who rejected the gospel after it was preached to them on earth or in the spirit prison. These spirits suffer in a condition known as hell. They have removed themselves from the mercy of Jesus Christ, who said, "Behold, I, God, have suffered these things for all, that they might not suffer if they would repent; but if they would not repent they must suffer even as I; which suffering caused myself, even God, the greatest of all, to tremble because of pain, and to bleed at every pore, and to suffer both body and spirit" (D&C 19:16–18). After suffering in full for their sins, they will be allowed to inherit the lowest degree of glory, which is the telestial kingdom.

The hell in the spirit world will not continue forever. Even the spirits who have committed the greatest sins will have suffered sufficiently by the end of the Millennium (see Acts 2:25–27). They will then be resurrected.

Discussion

• What are some of the activities that go on in the spirit world?

Additional Scriptures

• 1 Peter 4:6 (gospel preached to the dead)
• Moses 7:37–39 (spirit prison prepared for the wicked)
• D&C 76 (revelation about the three kingdoms of glory)
• Luke 16:19–31 (fate of beggar and rich man in the spirit world)

THE LAST JUDGMENT

Chapter 46

Judgments of God

We are often told in the scriptures that the day will come when we will stand before God and be judged. We need to understand how judgment takes place so we can be better prepared for this important event.

The scriptures teach that all of us will be judged according to our works: *And I saw the dead, small and great, stand before God; and the books were opened: and another book was opened, which is the book of life: and the dead were judged out of those things which were written in the books, according to their works* (Revelation 20:12; see also D&C 76:111; 1 Nephi 15:32; Abraham 3:25–28).

In this scripture, John the Revelator is referring to the Final Judgment. This judgment is the last in a long series of judgments. In the premortal life all spirits who were judged worthy were allowed to receive a body and come to earth. Here on earth we are often judged as to our worthiness to receive opportunities within the kingdom of God. When we are baptized we are judged worthy to receive this ordinance. When we are called to serve in the Church or interviewed for a priesthood advancement or a temple recommend, we are judged.

Alma taught that when we die our spirits are assigned to a state of happiness or of misery (see Alma 40:11–15). This is a partial judgment.

Discussion

• Name some of the judgments we have received and will receive.

Our Words, Works, and Thoughts Are Used to Judge Us

The prophet Alma testified, "Our words will condemn us, yea, all our works will condemn us; . . . and our thoughts will also condemn us" (Alma 12:14).

The Lord said: "Every idle word that men shall speak, they shall give account thereof in the day of judgment. For by thy words thou shalt be justified, and by thy words thou shalt be condemned" (Matthew 12:36–37).

Only through faith in Jesus Christ can we be prepared for the Final Judgment. Through faithful discipleship to him and repentance of all our sins, we can be forgiven for our sins and become pure and holy so that we can dwell in the presence of God. As we repent of our sins, giving up every impure thought and act, the Holy Ghost will change our hearts so we no longer have even the desire to sin. Then when we are judged, we will be found ready to enter into God's presence.

Discussion

• Ask each person to imagine hearing all his thoughts, words, and actions revealed at the Judgment. Then have each silently think about what he can do to improve his thoughts, words, and actions.

We Will Be Judged by Records

The Prophet Joseph Smith said that the dead will be judged out of records kept on earth. We will also be judged out of the "book of life," which is kept in heaven (see D&C 128:6–8).

"We are going to be judged out of the things written in books, out of the revelations of God, out of the temple records, out of

those things which the Lord has commanded us to keep. . . .
There will be the record in heaven which is a perfect record"
(Joseph Fielding Smith, *Doctrines of Salvation,* 2:200).

There is another record that will be used to judge us. The
Apostle Paul taught that man himself is the most complete
record of his life (see Romans 2:15; 2 Corinthians 3:1–3).
Stored in our body and mind is a complete history of everything we have done. President John Taylor taught this truth:
"[The individual] tells the story himself, and bears witness
against himself. . . . That record that is written by the man
himself in the tablets of his own mind—that record that cannot lie—will in that day be unfolded before God and angels,
and those who sit as judges" (Daniel H. Ludlow, ed., *Latter-
day Prophets Speak,* pp. 56–57).

Discussion
• What are three records from which we will be judged?
• How do our daily thoughts and actions influence these
  records?

Those Who Will Judge
The Apostle John taught that "the Father judgeth no man, but
hath committed all judgment unto the Son" (John 5:22). The
Son, in turn, will call upon others to assist in the Judgment.
The Twelve who were with him in his ministry will judge the
twelve tribes of Israel (see Matthew 19:28; Luke 22:30). The
Nephite Twelve will judge the Nephite and Lamanite people
(see 1 Nephi 12:9–10; Mormon 3:18–19). President John
Taylor said the First Presidency and the Twelve Apostles in
our own dispensation will also judge us (see *The Mediation and
Atonement,* p. 157).

Discussion
• Read John 5:22.
• Who is at the head of the Judgment of all people?
• Who will help to judge the people living in our day?

Assignment to Glories

At the Final Judgment we will be assigned to the kingdom for which we are prepared. We will be sent to one of four places: the celestial kingdom (the highest degree of glory), the terrestrial kingdom (the second degree), the telestial kingdom (the lowest degree), or outer darkness (the kingdom of the devil—not a degree of glory).

In Doctrine and Covenants 76, the Lord described the ways we can choose to live our mortal lives. He explained that our choices will determine which of the four kingdoms we are prepared for. We learn from this revelation that even members of the Church will inherit different kingdoms because they will not be equally faithful and valiant in their obedience to Christ.

The following are the kinds of lives we can choose to live and the kingdoms our choices will obtain for us.

Celestial

"They are they who received the testimony of Jesus, and believed on his name and were baptized, . . . that by keeping the commandments they might be washed and cleansed from all their sins, and receive the Holy Spirit." These are they who overcome the world by their faith. They are just and true so that the Holy Ghost can seal their blessings upon them. (See D&C 76:51–53.) Those who inherit the highest degree of the celestial kingdom, who become gods, must also have been married for eternity in the temple (see D&C 131:1–4). All who inherit the celestial kingdom will live with Heavenly Father and Jesus Christ forever (see D&C 76:62).

Terrestrial

These are they who rejected the gospel on earth but afterward received it in the spirit world. These are the honorable people on the earth who were blinded to the gospel of Jesus Christ by the craftiness of men. These are also they who received the gospel and a testimony of Jesus but then were not valiant.

They will be visited by Jesus Christ but not by our Heavenly Father. (See D&C 76:73–79.) They will not be part of eternal families; they will live separately and singly forever (see D&C 131:1–4).

Telestial

These people did not receive the gospel or the testimony of Jesus either on earth or in the spirit world. They will suffer for their own sins in hell until after the Millennium, when they will be resurrected. "These are they who are liars, and sorcerers, and adulterers, and whoremongers, and whosoever loves and makes a lie." These people are as numerous as the stars in heaven and the sand on the seashore. They will be visited by the Holy Ghost but not by the Father or the Son. (See D&C 76:81–86, 103–6.)

Outer Darkness

These are they who had testimonies of Jesus through the Holy Ghost and knew the power of the Lord but allowed Satan to overcome them. They denied the truth and defied the power of the Lord. There is no forgiveness for them, for they denied the Holy Spirit after having received it. They will not have a kingdom of glory. They will live in eternal darkness, torment, and misery with Satan and his angels forever. (See D&C 76:28–35, 44–48.)

Discussion

• Have someone tell about the three degrees of glory and outer darkness and describe who will go to each (see D&C 76:50–88).

We Should Prepare Now for Judgment

In reality, every day is a day of judgment. We speak, think, and act according to celestial, terrestrial, or telestial law. Our faith in Jesus Christ, as shown by our daily actions, determines which kingdom we will inherit.

We have the restored gospel of Jesus Christ in its fulness. The gospel is the law of the celestial kingdom. All the priesthood ordinances necessary for our progression have been revealed. We have entered the waters of baptism and have made a covenant to live Christlike lives. If we are faithful and keep the covenants we have made, the Lord has told us what our judgment will be. He will say unto us: "Come, ye blessed of my Father, inherit the kingdom prepared for you from the foundation of the world" (Matthew 25:34).

Discussion

• What must we do to be ready for the Final Judgment?

• Ask class members to think how they would feel about hearing the words recorded in Matthew 25:34 spoken to them.

Additional Scriptures

• D&C 88:98–102 (sounding of the trumps of judgment)

• Alma 11:41, 45; Mormon 7:6; 9:13–14 (we are judged in a resurrected state)

• 2 Nephi 29:11; 3 Nephi 27:23–26 (books used in the Judgment)

• (Alma 41:2–7 (our judgment is determined by our works, the desires of our hearts, repentance, enduring to the end)

• Mormon 3:22 (repent and prepare to stand before the judgment seat)

• Luke 12:47–48; D&C 82:3 (of whom much is given, much is required)

• D&C 88:16–33 (we each receive that for which we are worthy)

Those who are faithful to the end will be exalted with Heavenly Father and Jesus Christ.

EXALTATION

Chapter 47

When we lived with our Heavenly Father, he explained a plan for our progression. We could become like him, an exalted being. The plan required that we be separated from him and come to earth. This separation was necessary to prove whether we would obey our Father's commandments even though we were no longer in his presence. The plan provided that when earth life ended, we would be judged and rewarded according to the degree of our faith and obedience. We would then be assigned to the place for which we had prepared.

Jesus taught, "In my Father's house are many mansions" (John 14:2). From the scriptures we learn that there are three kingdoms of glory in heaven. The Apostle Paul mentioned that he knew a man who was "caught up to the third heaven" (2 Corinthians 12:2). Paul named two of the kingdoms in heaven: the celestial and the terrestrial (see 1 Corinthians 15:40–42). The celestial is the highest, and the terrestrial is second. Through latter-day revelation we learn that the third kingdom is the telestial kingdom (see D&C 76:81). We also learn that there are three heavens or degrees within the celestial kingdom (see D&C 131:1).

Discussion

• Have someone tell about our Heavenly Father's plan for our exaltation.

What Is Exaltation?

Exaltation is eternal life, the kind of life God lives. He lives in great glory. He is perfect. He possesses all knowledge and all wisdom. He is the Father of spirit children. He is a creator. We can become like our Heavenly Father. This is exaltation.

If we prove faithful to the Lord, we will live in the highest degree of the celestial kingdom of heaven. We will become exalted, just like our Heavenly Father. Exaltation is the greatest gift that Heavenly Father can give his children (see D&C 14:7).

Discussion

• What is exaltation?

Blessings of Exaltation

Our Heavenly Father is perfect. However, he is not jealous of his wisdom and perfection. He glories in the fact that it is possible for his children to become like him. He has said, "This is my work and my glory—to bring to pass the immortality and eternal life of man" (Moses 1:39).

Those who receive exaltation in the celestial kingdom through faith in Jesus Christ will receive special blessings. The Lord has promised, "All things are theirs" (D&C 76:59). These are some of the blessings given to exalted people:

1. They will live eternally in the presence of Heavenly Father and Jesus Christ (see D&C 76).
2. They will become gods.
3. They will have their righteous family members with them and will be able to have spirit children also. These spirit children will have the same relationship to them as we do to our Heavenly Father. They will be an eternal family.
4. They will receive a fulness of joy.
5. They will have everything that our Heavenly Father and Jesus Christ have—all power, glory, dominion, and knowledge. President Joseph Fielding Smith wrote: "The Father has promised through the Son that all that he has shall be given to those who are obedient to his commandments.

They shall increase in knowledge, wisdom, and power, going from grace to grace, until the fulness of the perfect day shall burst upon them" (*Doctrines of Salvation*, 2:36).

Discussion

• List some of the blessings that will be given to those who are exalted.

Requirements for Exaltation

The time to fulfill the requirements for exaltation is now (see Alma 34:32–34). President Joseph Fielding Smith said, "In order to obtain the exaltation we must accept the gospel and all its covenants; and take upon us the obligations which the Lord has offered; and walk in the light and understanding of the truth; and 'live by every word that proceedeth forth from the mouth of God'" (*Doctrines of Salvation*, 2:43).

To be exalted, we first must place our faith in Jesus Christ and then endure in that faith to the end of our lives. Our faith in him must be such that we repent of our sins and obey his commandments.

He commands us all to receive certain ordinances:

1. We must be baptized and confirmed a member of the Church of Jesus Christ.
2. We must receive the laying on of hands for the gift of the Holy Ghost.
3. We must receive the temple endowment.
4. We must be married for time and eternity.

In addition to receiving the required ordinances, the Lord commands all of us to—

1. Love and worship God.
2. Love our neighbor.
3. Repent of our wrongdoings.
4. Live the law of chastity.
5. Pay honest tithes and offerings.
6. Be honest in our dealings with others and with the Lord.

7. Speak the truth always.
8. Obey the Word of Wisdom.
9. Search out our kindred dead and perform the saving ordinances of the gospel for them.
10. Keep the Sabbath day holy.
11. Attend our Church meetings as regularly as possible so we can renew our baptismal covenants by partaking of the sacrament.
12. Love our family members and strengthen them in the ways of the Lord.
13. Have family and individual prayers every day.
14. Honor our parents.
15. Teach the gospel to others by word and example.
16. Study the scriptures.
17. Listen to and obey the inspired words of the prophets of the Lord.

Finally, each of us needs to receive the Holy Ghost and learn to follow his direction in our individual lives.

Discussion
• Why are faith in and obedience to Jesus Christ necessary to become exalted?
• What ordinances must we accept in order to become exalted?
• What laws does the Lord give us that we must obey to become exalted?
• Why must we learn to follow the direction of the Holy Ghost to become exalted?

After We Have Endured to the End
What happens when we have endured to the end in faithful discipleship to Christ? The Lord has said, "If you keep my commandments and endure to the end you shall have eternal life, which gift is the greatest of all the gifts of God" (D&C 14:7). President Joseph Fielding Smith said, "If we will continue in God; that is, keep his commandments, worship him and live his truth; then the time will come when we shall be

bathed in the fulness of truth, which shall grow brighter and brighter until the perfect day*" (*Doctrines of Salvation,* 2:36).

The Prophet Joseph Smith taught: "*When you climb up a ladder, you must begin at the bottom, and ascend step by step, until you arrive at the top; and so it is with the principles of the Gospel — you must begin with the first, and go on until you learn all the principles of exaltation. But it will be a great while after you have passed through the veil [died] before you will have learned them. It is not all to be comprehended in this world; it will be a great work to learn our salvation and exaltation even beyond the grave*" (*Teachings of the Prophet Joseph Smith,* p. 348).

This is the way our Heavenly Father became God. Joseph Smith taught: "*It is the first principle of the Gospel to know for a certainty the character of God. . . . He was once a man like us; . . . God himself, the Father of us all, dwelt on an earth, the same as Jesus Christ himself did*" (*Teachings of the Prophet Joseph Smith,* pp. 345–46).

Our Heavenly Father knows our trials, our weaknesses, and our sins. He has compassion and mercy on us. He wants us to succeed even as he did.

Imagine what joy each of us will have when we return to our Heavenly Father if we can say: "Father, I did what you wanted me to do. I have been faithful and have kept your commandments. I am happy to be home again." Then we will hear him say, "*Well done; . . . thou hast been faithful over a few things, I will make thee ruler over many things: enter thou into the joy of thy lord*" (Matthew 25:23).

Discussion

• Describe how you might feel to hear the Savior's words in Matthew 25:23.
• What must we do to endure to the end?

Additional Scriptures

• D&C 132:3–4, 16–26, 37 (pertaining to exaltation)
• D&C 131:1–4 (eternal marriage is key to exaltation)
• D&C 76:59–70 (blessings of celestial glory explained)

THE ARTICLES OF FAITH

In the spring of 1842, the Prophet Joseph Smith sent a letter to John Wentworth, who was editor of a newspaper called the *Chicago Democrat*. This letter contained an account of many of the events of early Church history. The document also contained thirteen statements outlining Latter-day Saint beliefs. These have come to be known as the Articles of Faith, which are given below.

The Articles of Faith are official doctrine of the Church and have been canonized as a part of Latter-day scripture. They are clear statements of belief that help members understand the basic beliefs of the Church and explain these beliefs to others. They are not, however, a complete summary of Church doctrine. Through living prophets, the Church is guided by continuous revelation and inspiration.

1 We believe in God, the Eternal Father, and in His Son, Jesus Christ, and in the Holy Ghost.

2 We believe that men will be punished for their own sins, and not for Adam's transgression.

3 We believe that through the Atonement of Christ, all mankind may be saved, by obedience to the laws and ordinances of the Gospel.

4 We believe that the first principles and ordinances of the Gospel are: first, Faith in the Lord Jesus Christ; second, Repentance; third, Baptism by immersion for the remission of sins; fourth, Laying on of hands for the gift of the Holy Ghost.

5 We believe that a man must be called of God, by prophecy, and by the laying on of hands by those who are in authority, to preach the Gospel and administer in the ordinances thereof.

6 We believe in the same organization that existed in the Primitive Church, namely, apostles, prophets, pastors, teachers, evangelists, and so forth.

7 We believe in the gift of tongues, prophecy, revelation, visions, healing, interpretation of tongues, and so forth.

8 We believe the Bible to be the word of God as far as it is translated correctly; we also believe the Book of Mormon to be the word of God.

9 We believe all that God has revealed, all that He does now reveal, and we believe that He will yet reveal many great and important things pertaining to the Kingdom of God.

10 We believe in the literal gathering of Israel and in the restoration of the Ten Tribes; that Zion (the New Jerusalem) will be built upon the American continent; that Christ will reign personally upon the earth; and, that the earth will be renewed and receive its paradisiacal glory.

11 We claim the privilege of worshiping Almighty God according to the dictates of our own conscience, and allow all men the same privilege, let them worship how, where, or what they may.

12 We believe in being subject to kings, presidents, rulers, and magistrates, in obeying, honoring, and sustaining the law.

13 We believe in being honest, true, chaste, benevolent, virtuous, and in doing good to all men; indeed, we may say that we follow the admonition of Paul–We believe all things, we hope all things, we have endured many things, and hope to be able to endure all things. If there is anything virtuous, lovely, or of good report or praiseworthy, we seek after these things.

Joseph Smith

HYMNS

Music

Come, Come, Ye Saints

With conviction ♩ = 66–84

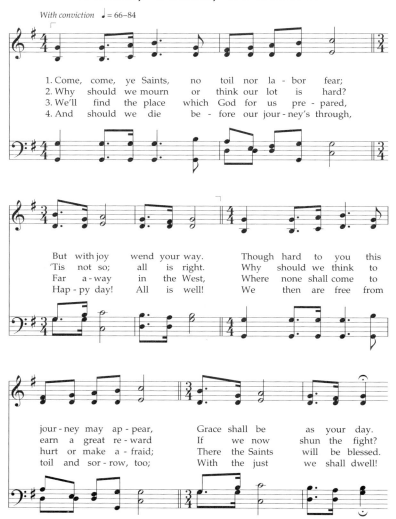

1. Come, come, ye Saints, no toil nor la - bor fear;
2. Why should we mourn or think our lot is hard?
3. We'll find the place which God for us pre - pared,
4. And should we die be - fore our jour - ney's through,

But with joy wend your way. Though hard to you this
'Tis not so; all is right. Why should we think to
Far a - way in the West, Where none shall come to
Hap - py day! All is well! We then are free from

jour - ney may ap - pear, Grace shall be as your day.
earn a great re - ward If we now shun the fight?
hurt or make a - fraid; There the Saints will be blessed.
toil and sor - row, too; With the just we shall dwell!

'Tis bet - ter far for us to strive Our
Gird up your loins; fresh cour - age take. Our
We'll make the air with mu - sic ring, Shout
But if our lives are spared a - gain To

use - less cares from us to drive; Do this, and joy
God will nev - er us for - sake; And soon we'll have
prais - es to our God and King; A - bove the rest
see the Saints their rest ob - tain, Oh, how we'll make

your hearts will swell— All is well! All is well!
this tale to tell— All is well! All is well!
these words we'll tell— All is well! All is well!
this cho - rus swell— All is well! All is well!

Text: William Clayton, 1814–1879

Music: English folk song

Doctrine and Covenants 61:36–39
Doctrine and Covenants 59:1–4

311

Come, Ye Children of the Lord

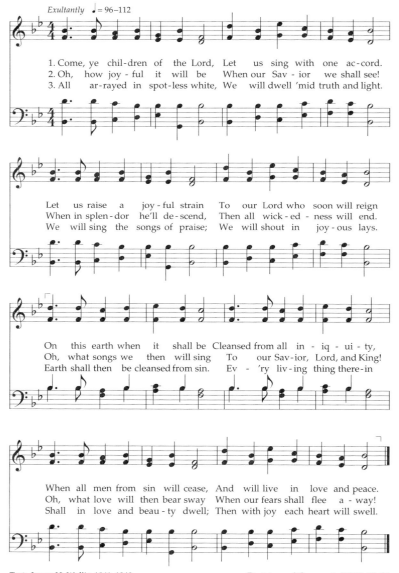

Exultantly ♩ = 96–112

1. Come, ye chil-dren of the Lord, Let us sing with one ac-cord.
2. Oh, how joy-ful it will be When our Sav-ior we shall see!
3. All ar-rayed in spot-less white, We will dwell 'mid truth and light.

Let us raise a joy-ful strain To our Lord who soon will reign
When in splen-dor he'll de-scend, Then all wick-ed-ness will end.
We will sing the songs of praise; We will shout in joy-ous lays.

On this earth when it shall be Cleansed from all in-iq-ui-ty,
Oh, what songs we then will sing To our Sav-ior, Lord, and King!
Earth shall then be cleansed from sin. Ev-'ry liv-ing thing there-in

When all men from sin will cease, And will live in love and peace.
Oh, what love will then bear sway When our fears shall flee a-way!
Shall in love and beau-ty dwell; Then with joy each heart will swell.

Text: James H. Wallis, 1861–1940
Music: Spanish melody; arr. by Benjamin Carr, 1768–1831

Doctrine and Covenants 133:25, 33, 56
Revelation 7:9–17

Redeemer of Israel

Confidently ♩ = 84–100

1. Re - deem - er of Is - rael, Our on - ly de - light, On
2. We know he is com - ing To gath - er his sheep And
3. How long we have wan - dered As strang - ers in sin, And
4. As chil - dren of Zi - on, Good tid - ings for us. The

whom for a bless - ing we call, Our shad - ow by day And our
lead them to Zi - on in love, For why in the val - ley Of
cried in the des - ert for thee! Our foes have re - joiced When our
to - kens al - read - y ap - pear. Fear not, and be just, For the

pil - lar by night, Our King, our De - liv - 'rer, our all!
death should they weep Or in the lone wil - der-ness rove?
sor - rows they've seen, But Is - rael will short - ly be free.
king - dom is ours. The hour of re - demp - tion is near.

5. Restore, my dear Savior,
   The light of thy face;
   Thy soul-cheering comfort impart;
   And let the sweet longing
   For thy holy place
   Bring hope to my desolate heart.

6. He looks! and ten thousands
   Of angels rejoice,
   And myriads wait for his word;
   He speaks! and eternity,
   Filled with his voice,
   Re-echoes the praise of the Lord.

Text: William W. Phelps, 1792–1872; adapted from Joseph Swain, 1761–1796.
Included in the first LDS hymnbook , 1835.
Music: Freeman Lewis, 1780–1859

Exodus 13:21–22
1 Nephi 22:12

How Firm a Foundation

With dignity ♩ = 100–112

1. How firm a foun - da - tion, ye Saints of the Lord,
2. In ev - 'ry con - di - tion— in sick - ness, in health,
3. Fear not, I am with thee; oh, be not dis - mayed,

Is laid for your faith in his ex - cel - lent word!
In pov - er - ty's vale or a - bound - ing in wealth,
For I am thy God and will still give thee aid.

What more can he say than to you he hath said, Who
At home or a - broad, on the land or the sea— As thy
I'll strength - en thee, help thee, and cause thee to stand, Up-

un - to the Sav - ior, who un - to the Sav - ior, Who
days may de - mand, as thy days may de - mand, As thy
held by my righ - teous, up - held by my righ - teous, Up-

un - to the Sav - ior for ref - uge have fled?
days may de - mand, so thy suc - cor shall be.
held by my righ - teous, om - nip - o - tent hand.

4. When through the deep waters I call thee to go,
   The rivers of sorrow shall not thee o'erflow,
   For I will be with thee, thy troubles to bless,
   And sanctify to thee, And sanctify to thee,
   And sanctify to thee thy deepest distress.

5. When through fiery trials thy pathway shall lie,
   My grace, all sufficient, shall be thy supply.
   The flame shall not hurt thee; I only design
   Thy dross to consume, Thy dross to consume,
   Thy dross to consume and thy gold to refine.

6. E'en down to old age, all my people shall prove
   My sov'reign, eternal, unchangeable love;
   And then, when gray hair shall their temples adorn,
   Like lambs shall they still, Like lambs shall they still,
   Like lambs shall they still in my bosom be borne.

7. The soul that on Jesus hath leaned for repose
   I will not, I cannot, desert to his foes;
   That soul, though all hell should endeavor to shake,
   I'll never, no never, I'll never, no never,
   I'll never, no never, no never forsake!

Text: Attr. to Robert Keen, ca. 1787. Included in the first
  LDS hymnbook, 1835.
Music: Attr. to J. Ellis, ca. 1889

Isaiah 41:10; 43:2–5
Helaman 5:12

Count Your Blessings

Brightly ♩ = 80–96

1. When up - on life's bil - lows you are tem - pest - tossed,
2. Are you ev - er bur - dened with a load of care?
3. When you look at oth - ers with their lands and gold,
4. So a - mid the con - flict, wheth - er great or small,

When you are dis - cour - aged, think - ing all is lost,
Does the cross seem heav - y you are called to bear?
Think that Christ has prom - ised you his wealth un - told.
Do not be dis - cour - aged; God is o - ver all.

Count your man - y bless - ings; name them one by one,
Count your man - y bless - ings; ev - 'ry doubt will fly,
Count your man - y bless - ings; mon - ey can - not buy
Count your man - y bless - ings; an - gels will at - tend,

And it will sur - prise you what the Lord has done.
And you will be sing - ing as the days go by.
Your re - ward in heav - en nor your home on high.
Help and com - fort give you to your jour - ney's end.

Text: Johnson Oatman, Jr., 1856–1922
Music: Edwin O. Excell, 1851–1921

Doctrine and Covenants 78:17–19
Alma 34:38

317

Let Us All Press On

With vigor ♩ = 92–108

1. Let us all press on in the work of the Lord,
2. We will not re - treat, though our num - bers may be few
3. If we do what's right we have no need to fear,

That when life is o'er we may gain a re - ward;
When com - pared with the op - po - site host in view;
For the Lord, our help - er, will ev - er be near;

In the fight for right let us wield a sword,
But an un - seen pow'r will aid me and you
In the days of trial his Saints he will cheer,

The might - y sword of truth.
In the glo - rious cause of truth.
And pros - per the cause of truth.

Fear not, though the en-e-my de-ride;
Fear not, cour-age, though the en-e-my de-ride; We must

Cour - age, for the Lord is on our side. We will
be vic - to - rious, for the Lord is on our side. We'll not

heed not what the wick - ed may say, But the
fear the wick - ed nor give heed to what they say, But the

Lord a - lone we will o - bey.
Lord, our Heav'n - ly Fa - ther, him a - lone we will o - bey.

Text and music: Evan Stephens, 1854–1930

Doctrine and Covenants 6:33–37
1 Nephi 22:15–17

I Need Thee Every Hour

1. I need thee ev-ery hour, Most gra - cious Lord.
2. I need thee ev-ery hour; Stay thou near - by.
3. I need thee ev-ery hour, In joy or pain.
4. I need thee ev-ery hour, Most ho - ly One.

No ten - der voice like thine Can peace af - ford.
Temp - ta - tions lose their pow'r When thou art nigh.
Come quick - ly and a - bide, Or life is vain.
Oh, make me thine in - deed, Thou bless - ed Son!

I need thee, oh, I need thee; Ev - ery hour I need thee!

Oh, bless me now, my Sav - ior; I come to thee!

Text: Annie S. Hawkes, 1835–1918
Music: Robert Lowry, 1826–1899

2 Nephi 4:16–35
Psalm 143:1

320

Sweet Is the Work

Fervently ♩ = 84–96

1. Sweet is the work, my God, my King, To praise thy
2. Sweet is the day of sa - cred rest. No mor - tal
3. My heart shall tri - umph in my Lord And bless his
4. But, oh, what tri - umph shall I raise To thy dear

name, give thanks and sing, To show thy love by
care shall seize my breast. Oh, may my heart in
works and bless his word. Thy works of grace, how
name through end - less days, When in the realms of

morn - ing light, And talk of all thy truths at night.
tune be found, Like Da - vid's harp of sol - emn sound!
bright they shine! How deep thy coun - sels, how di - vine!
joy I see Thy face in full fe - lic - i - ty!

5. Sin, my worst enemy before,
Shall vex my eyes and ears no more.
My inward foes shall all be slain,
Nor Satan break my peace again.

6. Then shall I see and hear and know
All I desired and wished below,
And every pow'r find sweet employ
In that eternal world of joy.

Text: Isaac Watts, 1674–1748
Music: John J. McClellan, 1874–1925

Psalm 92:1–5
Enos 1:27

321

Joseph Smith's First Prayer

With dignity ♩ = 84–92

1. Oh, how love - ly was the morn - ing! Ra - diant
2. Hum - bly kneel - ing, sweet ap - peal - ing— 'Twas the
3. Sud - den - ly a light de - scend - ed, Bright - er
4. "Jo - seph, this is my Be - lov - ed; Hear him!"

beamed the sun a - bove. Bees were hum - ming, sweet birds
boy's first ut - tered prayer— When the pow'rs of sin as -
far than noon - day sun, And a shin - ing glo - rious
Oh, how sweet the word! Jo - seph's hum - ble prayer was

sing - ing, Mu - sic ring - ing thru the grove,
sail - ing Filled his soul with deep de - spair;
pil - lar O'er him fell, a - round him shone,
an - swered, And he lis - tened to the Lord.

322

Text: George Manwaring, 1854–1889
Music: Sylvanus Billings Pond, 1792–1871; adapted by
    A. C. Smyth, 1840–1909

Joseph Smith—History 1:14–20, 25
James 1:5

Behold the Great Redeemer Die

Reverently ♩ = 69–84

1. Be - hold the great Re - deem - er die,
2. While guilt - y men his pains de - ride,
3. Al - though in ag - o - ny he hung,
4. "Fa - ther, from me re - move this cup.

A bro - ken law to sat - is - fy.
They pierce his hands and feet and side;
No mur - m'ring word es - caped his tongue.
Yet, if thou wilt, I'll drink it up.

He dies a sac - ri - fice for sin,
And with in - sult - ing scoffs and scorns,
His high com - mis - sion to ful - fill,
I've done the work thou gav - est me,

He dies a sac - ri - fice for sin,
And with in - sult - ing scoffs and scorns,
His high com - mis - sion to ful - fill,
I've done the work thou gav - est me;

That man may live and glo - ry win.
They crown his head with plait - ed thorns.
He mag - ni - fied his Fa - ther's will.
Re - ceive my spir - it un - to thee."

5. He died, and at the awful sight
   The sun in shame withdrew its light!
   Earth trembled, and all nature sighed
   Earth trembled, and all nature sighed
   In dread response, "A God has died!"

6. He lives — he lives. We humbly now
   Around these sacred symbols bow,
   And seek, as Saints of latter days,
   And seek, as Saints of latter days,
   To do his will and live his praise.

Text: Eliza R. Snow, 1804–1887
Music: George Careless, 1839–1932

Doctrine and Covenants 18:11
Luke 22:42; 23:46

O God, the Eternal Father

1. O God, th'E-ter-nal Fa-ther, Who dwells a-mid the sky,
2. That sa-cred, ho-ly of-f'ring, By man least un-der-stood,
3. When Je-sus, the A-noint-ed, De-scend-ed from a-bove
4. How in-fi-nite that wis-dom, The plan of ho-li-ness,

In Je-sus' name we ask thee To bless and sanc-ti-fy,
To have our sins re-mit-ted And take his flesh and blood,
And gave him-self a ran-som To win our souls with love—
That made sal-va-tion per-fect And veiled the Lord in flesh,

If we are pure be-fore thee, This bread and cup of wine,
That we may ev-er wit-ness The suf-f'ring of thy Son,
With no ap-par-ent beau-ty, That man should him de-sire—
To walk up-on his foot-stool And be like man, al-most,

That we may all re-mem-ber That of-fer-ing di-vine—
And al-ways have his Spir-it To make our hearts as one.
He was the prom-ised Sav-ior, To pu-ri-fy with fire.
In his ex-alt-ed sta-tion, And die, or all was lost.

Text: William W. Phelps, 1792–1872. Included in the first
LDS hymnbook, 1835.
Music: Felix Mendelssohn, 1809–1847

Doctrine and Covenants 20:77, 79
Isaiah 53:2–5

How Great the Wisdom and the Love

Calmly ♩ = 66–76

1. How great the wis - dom and the love That filled the courts on high And sent the Sav - ior from a - bove To suf - fer, bleed, and die!
2. His pre - cious blood he free - ly spilt; His life he free - ly gave, A sin - less sac - ri - fice for guilt, A dy - ing world to save.
3. By strict o - be - dience Je - sus won The prize with glo - ry rife: "Thy will, O God, not mine be done," A - dorned his mor - tal life.
4. He marked the path and led the way, And ev - 'ry point de - fines To light and life and end - less day Where God's full pres - ence shines.

5. In mem'ry of the broken flesh
We eat the broken bread,
And witness with the cup, afresh,
Our faith in Christ, our Head.

6. How great, how glorious, how complete,
Redemption's grand design,
Where justice, love, and mercy meet
In harmony divine!

Text: Eliza R. Snow, 1804–1887
Music: Thomas McIntyre, 1833–1914

Moses 4:1–2
Alma 42:14–15

Verses 1, 2, 5, and 6 are especially appropriate for the sacrament.

Jesus, Once of Humble Birth

1. Jesus, once of humble birth, Now in glory
2. Once a meek and lowly Lamb, Now the Lord, the
3. Once he groaned in blood and tears; Now in glory
4. Once forsaken, left alone, Now exalted

comes to earth. Once he suffered grief and pain; Now he
great I Am. Once upon the cross he bowed; Now his
he appears. Once rejected by his own, Now their
to a throne. Once all things he meekly bore, But he

comes on earth to reign. Now he comes on earth to reign.
chariot is the cloud. Now his chariot is the cloud.
King he shall be known. Now their King he shall be known.
now will bear no more. But he now will bear no more.

Text: Parley P. Pratt, 1807–1857
Music: Giacomo Meyerbeer, 1791–1864, adapted

Luke 2:7
Matthew 25:31

God, Our Father, Hear Us Pray

Worshipfully ♩ = 69–84

1. God, our Fa - ther, hear us pray; Send thy
2. Grant us, Fa - ther, grace di - vine; May thy
3. As we drink the wa - ter clear, Let thy

grace this ho - ly day. As we take of
smile up - on us shine. As we eat the
Spir - it lin - ger near. Par - don faults, O

em - blems blest, On our Sav - ior's love we rest.
bro - ken bread, Thine ap - prov - al on us shed.
Lord, we pray; Bless our ef - forts day by day.

Text: Annie Pinnock Malin, 1863–1935
Music: Louis M. Gottschalk, 1829–1869;
  adapted by Edwin P. Parker, 1836–1925

Doctrine and Covenants 59:9–12
2 Nephi 10:24–25

I Stand All Amazed

Thoughtfully ♩ = 66–84

1. I stand all a-mazed at the love Je-sus of-fers me,
2. I mar-vel that he would de-scend from his throne di-vine
3. I think of his hands pierced and bleed-ing to pay the debt!

Con-fused at the grace that so ful-ly he prof-fers me.
To res-cue a soul so re-bel-lious and proud as mine,
Such mer-cy, such love, and de-vo-tion can I for-get?

I trem-ble to know that for me he was cru-ci-fied,
That he should ex-tend his great love un-to such as I,
No, no, I will praise and a-dore at the mer-cy seat,

That for me, a sin-ner, he suf-fered, he bled and died.
Suf-fi-cient to own, to re-deem, and to jus-ti-fy.
Un-til at the glo-ri-fied throne I kneel at his feet.

Oh, it is won-der-ful that he should care for me E-nough to

die for me! Oh, it is won-der-ful, won-der-ful to me!

Text and music: Charles H. Gabriel, 1856–1932

Mosiah 3:5–8
John 15:13

There Is a Green Hill Far Away

1. There is a green hill far a-way, Without a cit-y wall, Where the dear Lord was
cru-ci-fied, Who died to save us all.

2. We may not know, we can-not tell, What
pains he had to bear, But we be-lieve it
was for us He hung and suf-fered there.

3. There was no oth-er good e-nough To
pay the price of sin. He on-ly could un-
lock the gate Of heav'n and let us in.

4. Oh, dear-ly, dear-ly has he loved! And
we must love him too, And trust in his re-
deem-ing blood, And try his works to do.

Text: Cecil Frances Alexander, 1818–1895
Music: John H. Gower, 1855–1922

John 19:16–20
Hebrews 13:12

We'll Sing All Hail to Jesus' Name

Fervently ♩ = 76–88

1. We'll sing all hail to Jesus' name, And praise and hon - or give To him who bled on Cal - vary's hill And died that we might live.
2. He passed the por - tals of the grave; Sal - va - tion was his song; He called up - on the sin - bound soul To join the heav'n - ly throng.
3. He seized the keys of death and hell And bruised the ser - pent's head; He bid the pris - on doors un - fold, The grave yield up her dead.
4. The bread and wa - ter rep - re - sent His sac - ri - fice for sin; Ye Saints, par - take and tes - ti - fy Ye do re - mem - ber him.

Text: Richard Alldridge, 1815–1896
Music: Joseph Coslett, 1850–1910

2 Nephi 9:5, 10–12
Moses 4:20–21

In Humility, Our Savior

Meekly ♩ = 72–84

1. In hu - mil - i - ty, our Sav - ior, Grant thy
2. Fill our hearts with sweet for - giv - ing; Teach us

Spir - it here, we pray, As we bless the
tol - er - ance and love. Let our prayers find

bread and wa - ter In thy name this ho - ly day.
ac - cess to thee In thy ho - ly courts a - bove.

Let me not for - get, O Sav - ior, Thou didst
Then, when we have prov - en wor - thy Of thy

bleed and die for me When thy heart was
sac - ri - fice di - vine, Lord, let us re -

stilled and bro - ken On the cross at Cal - va - ry.
gain thy pres - ence; Let thy glo - ry round us shine.

Text: Mabel Jones Gabbott, b. 1910. © 1948 LDS

Music: Rowland H. Prichard, 1811–1887

2 Nephi 2:7
Doctrine and Covenants 59:9

335

The Spirit of God

Exultantly ♩ = 96–112

1. The Spir - it of God like a fire is burn - ing!
2. The Lord is ex - tend - ing the Saints' un - der - stand - ing,
3. We'll call in our sol - emn as - sem - blies in spir - it,
4. How bless - ed the day when the lamb and the li - on

The lat - ter - day glo - ry be - gins to come forth;
Re - stor - ing their judg - es and all as at first.
To spread forth the king - dom of heav - en a - broad,
Shall lie down to - geth - er with - out an - y ire,

The vi - sions and bless - ings of old are re - turn - ing,
The knowl - edge and pow - er of God are ex - pand - ing;
That we through our faith may be - gin to in - her - it
And E - phraim be crowned with his bless - ing in Zi - on,

And an - gels are com - ing to vis - it the earth.
The veil o'er the earth is be - gin - ning to burst.
The vi - sions and bless - ings and glo - ries of God.
As Je - sus de - scends with his char - iot of fire!

We'll sing and we'll shout with the ar - mies of heav - en,

Ho - san - na, ho - san - na to God and the Lamb!

Let glo - ry to them in the high - est be giv - en,

Hence - forth and for - ev - er, A - men and a - men!

Text: William W. Phelps, 1792–1872. Included in the first LDS
hymnbook, 1835. Sung at the Kirtland Temple dedication in 1836.
Music: Anon., ca. 1844

Doctrine and Covenants
109:79–80
Doctrine and Covenants 110

337

High on the Mountain Top

Resolutely ♩ = 56–72

1. High on the moun-tain top A ban-ner is un-furled.
2. For God re-mem-bers still His prom-ise made of old
3. His house shall there be reared, His glo-ry to dis-play,
4. For there we shall be taught The law that will go forth,

Ye na-tions, now look up; It waves to all the world.
That he on Zi-on's hill Truth's stan-dard would un-fold!
And peo-ple shall be heard In dis-tant lands to say:
With truth and wis-dom fraught, To gov-ern all the earth.

In Des-er-et's sweet, peace-ful land, On Zi-on's mount be-hold it stand!
Her light should there at-tract the gaze Of all the world in lat-ter days.
We'll now go up and serve the Lord, O-bey his truth and learn his word.
For-ev-er there his ways we'll tread, And save our-selves with all our dead.

Text: Joel H. Johnson, 1802–1882
Music: Ebenezer Beesley, 1840–1906

Isaiah 2:2–3
Isaiah 5:26

Oh Say, What Is Truth?

Firmly ♩ = 72–96

1. Oh say, what is truth? 'Tis the fair - est gem That the
2. Yes, say, what is truth? 'Tis the bright - est prize To which
3. The scep - tre may fall from the des - pot's grasp When with
4. Then say, what is truth? 'Tis the last and the first, For the

rich - es of worlds can pro - duce, And price - less the val - ue of
mor - tals or Gods can as - pire. Go search in the depths where it
winds of stern jus - tice he copes. But the pil - lar of truth will en-
lim - its of time it steps o'er. Tho the heav - ens de - part and the

truth will be when The proud mon - arch's cost - li - est
glit - ter - ing lies, Or as - cend in pur - suit to the
dure to the last, And its firm - root - ed bul - warks out-
earth's foun - tains burst, Truth, the sum of ex - is - tence, will

di - a - dem Is count - ed but dross and ref - use.
loft - i - est skies: 'Tis an aim for the no - blest de - sire.
stand the rude blast And the wreck of the fell ty - rant's hopes.
weath - er the worst, E - ter - nal, un-changed, ev - er - more.

Text: John Jaques, 1827–1900
Music: Ellen Knowles Melling, 1820–1905

Doctrine and Covenants 93:23–28
John 18:37–38

Now Let Us Rejoice

Cheerfully ♩ = 100–120

1. Now let us re - joice in the day of sal - va - tion.
2. We'll love one an - oth - er and nev - er dis - sem - ble,
3. In faith we'll re - ly on the arm of Je - ho - vah

No lon - ger as strang - ers on earth need we roam.
But cease to do e - vil and ev - er be one.
To guide thru these last days of trou - ble and gloom,

Good tid - ings are sound - ing to us and each na - tion,
And when the un - god - ly are fear - ing and trem - ble,
And af - ter the scourg - es and har - vest are o - ver,

And short - ly the hour of re - demp - tion will come,
We'll watch for the day when the Sav - ior will come,
We'll rise with the just when the Sav - ior doth come.

When all   that was prom - ised   the Saints   will be giv - en,
When all   that was prom - ised   the Saints   will be giv - en,
Then all   that was prom - ised   the Saints   will be giv - en,

And none will   mo - lest   them from   morn un - til   ev'n,
And none will   mo - lest   them from   morn un - til   ev'n,
And they will   be   crown'd with   the   an - gels of   heav'n,

And   earth will   ap - pear   as   the   Gar - den of   E - den,
And   earth will   ap - pear   as   the   Gar - den of   E - den,
And   earth will   ap - pear   as   the   Gar - den of   E - den,

And   Je - sus will say   to   all   Is - rael, "Come   home."
And   Je - sus will say   to   all   Is - rael, "Come   home."
And   Christ   and his peo - ple will ev - er   be   one.

Text: William W. Phelps, 1792–1872. Included in the
  first LDS hymnbook, 1835.
Music: Henry Tucker, ca. 1863

Moses 7:61–67
Tenth Article of Faith

341

Do What Is Right

Resolutely ♩ = 96–116

1. Do what is right; the day - dawn is break - ing,
2. Do what is right; the shack - les are fall - ing.
3. Do what is right; be faith - ful and fear - less.

Hail - ing a fu - ture of free - dom and light.
Chains of the bonds - men no lon - ger are bright;
On - ward, press on - ward, the goal is in sight.

An - gels a - bove us are si - lent notes tak - ing
Light - ened by hope, soon they'll cease to be gall - ing.
Eyes that are wet now, ere long will be tear - less.

Of ev - 'ry ac - tion; then do what is right!
Truth go - eth on - ward; then do what is right!
Bless - ings a - wait you in do - ing what's right!

Do what is right; let the con - se - quence fol - low.

Bat - tle for free - dom in spir - it and might;

And with stout hearts look ye forth till to - mor - row.

God will pro - tect you; then do what is right!

Text: Anon., *The Psalms of Life*, Boston, 1857
Music: George Kaillmark, 1781–1835

Deuteronomy 6:17–18
Helaman 10:4–5

343

We Thank Thee, O God, for a Prophet

Brightly ♩ = 76–92

1. We thank thee, O God, for a proph - et To
2. When dark clouds of trou - ble hang o'er us And
3. We'll sing of his good - ness and mer - cy. We'll

guide us in these lat - ter days.
threat - en our peace to de - stroy,
praise him by day and by night,

We thank thee for
There is hope smil - ing
Re - joice in his

send - ing the gos - pel To light - en our minds with its
bright - ly be - fore us, And we know that de - liv - 'rance is
glo - ri - ous gos - pel, And bask in its life - giv - ing

rays. We thank thee for ev - e - ry bless - ing Be -
nigh. We doubt not the Lord nor his good - ness. We've
light. Thus on to e - ter - nal per - fec - tion The

stowed by thy boun - te - ous hand. We feel it a
proved him in days that are past. The wick - ed who
hon - est and faith - ful will go, While they who re-

plea - sure to serve thee, And love to o - bey thy com - mand.
fight a - gainst Zi - on Will sure - ly be smit - ten at last.
ject this glad mes - sage Shall nev - er such hap - pi - ness know.

Text: William Fowler, 1830–1865   Doctrine and Covenants 21:1–5
Music: Caroline Sheridan Norton, 1808–ca. 1877   Mosiah 2:41

345

I Know That My Redeemer Lives

Peacefully ♩ = 72–84

Unison

1. I know that my Re - deem - er lives. What com - fort this
2. He lives to grant me rich sup - ply. He lives to guide
3. He lives, my kind, wise heav'n - ly Friend. He lives and loves
4. He lives! All glo - ry to his name! He lives, my Sav -

sweet sen - tence gives! He lives, he lives, who once was
me with his eye. He lives to com - fort me when
me to the end. He lives, and while he lives, I'll
ior, still the same. Oh, sweet the joy this sen - tence

dead. He lives, my ev - er - liv - ing Head.
faint. He lives to hear my soul's com - plaint.
sing. He lives, my Proph - et, Priest, and King.
gives: "I know that my Re - deem - er lives!"

He lives to bless me with his love. He lives to
He lives to si - lence all my fears. He lives to
He lives and grants me dai - ly breath. He lives, and
He lives! All glo - ry to his name! He lives, my

plead for me a - bove. He lives my hun - gry soul to
wipe a - way my tears. He lives to calm my trou - bled
I shall con - quer death. He lives my man - sion to pre -
Sav - ior, still the same. Oh, sweet the joy this sen - tence

feed. He lives to bless in time of need.
heart. He lives all bless - ings to im - part.
pare. He lives to bring me safe - ly there.
gives: "I know that my Re - deem - er lives!"

Text: Samuel Medley, 1738–1799. Included in the first
   LDS hymnbook, 1835.
Music: Lewis D. Edwards, 1858–1921

Job 19:25
Psalm 104:33–34

God Be with You Till We Meet Again

Reverently ♩ = 66–80

1. God be with you till we meet a - gain; By his
2. God be with you till we meet a - gain; When life's
3. God be with you till we meet a - gain; Keep love's

coun-sels guide, up - hold you; With his sheep se - cure - ly
per - ils thick con - found you, Put his arms un - fail - ing
ban - ner float - ing o'er you; Smite death's threat-'ning wave be -

fold you. God be with you till we meet a - gain.
round you. God be with you till we meet a - gain.
fore you. God be with you till we meet a - gain.

Till we meet, till we meet, Till we
Till we meet, till we meet, till we meet,

meet at Je - sus' feet, Till we meet, till we
till we meet, Till we meet, till we

meet, God be with you till we meet a - gain.
meet, till we meet,

Text: Jeremiah E. Rankin, 1828–1904
Music: William G. Tomer, 1833–1896

2 Thessalonians 3:16
Numbers 6:24–26

O My Father

Fervently ♩ = 42–56

1. O my Fa - ther, thou that dwell - est In the
2. For a wise and glo - rious pur - pose Thou hast
3. I had learned to call thee Fa - ther, Thru thy
4. When I leave this frail ex - is - tence, When I

high and glo - rious place, When shall I re - gain thy
placed me here on earth And with - held the rec - ol -
Spir - it from on high, But, un - til the key of
lay this mor - tal by, Fa - ther, Moth - er, may I

pres - ence And a - gain be - hold thy face?
lec - tion Of my for - mer friends and birth;
knowl - edge Was re - stored, I knew not why.
meet you In your roy - al courts on high?

In thy ho - ly hab - i - ta - tion, Did my
Yet oft - times a se - cret some - thing Whis - pered,
In the heav'ns are par - ents sin - gle? No, the
Then, at length, when I've com - plet - ed All you

spir - it once re - side? In my first pri - me - val
"You're a strang - er here," And I felt that I had
thought makes rea - son stare! Truth is rea - son; truth e -
sent me forth to do, With your mu - tual ap - pro-

child - hood, Was I nur - tured near thy side?
wan - dered From a more ex - alt - ed sphere.
ter - nal Tells me I've a moth - er there.
ba - tion Let me come and dwell with you.

Text: Eliza R. Snow, 1804–1887
Music: James McGranahan, 1840–1907

Romans 8:16–17
Acts 17:28–29 (22–31)

351

Love at Home

Fervently ♩ = 88–108

1. There is beau - ty all a - round When there's love at home;
2. In the cot - tage there is joy When there's love at home;
3. Kind - ly heav - en smiles a - bove When there's love at home;

There is joy in ev - 'ry sound When there's love at home.
Hate and en - vy ne'er an - noy When there's love at home.
All the world is filled with love When there's love at home.

Peace and plen - ty here a - bide, Smil - ing sweet on ev - 'ry side.
Ros - es bloom be - neath our feet; All the earth's a gar - den sweet,
Sweet - er sings the brook - let by; Bright - er beams the az - ure sky.

Time doth soft-ly, sweet-ly glide When there's love at home.
Mak-ing life a bliss com-plete When there's love at home.
Oh, there's One who smiles on high When there's love at home.

Love at home, love at home;
Love at home, love at home;
Love at home, love at home;

Time doth soft-ly, sweet-ly glide When there's love at home.
Mak-ing life a bliss com-plete When there's love at home.
Oh, there's One who smiles on high When there's love at home.

Text and music: John Hugh McNaughton, 1829–1891

Mosiah 4:14–15
Ecclesiastes 9:9

353

I'll Go Where You Want Me to Go

Resolutely ♩. = 48–58

1. It may not be on the moun - tain height Or
2. Per - haps to - day there are lov - ing words Which
3. There's sure - ly some - where a low - ly place In

o - ver the storm - y sea, It may not be at the
Je - sus would have me speak; There may be now in the
earth's har - vest fields so wide Where I may la - bor thru

bat - tle's front My Lord will have need of me.
paths of sin Some wan - d'rer whom I should seek.
life's short day For Je - sus, the Cru - ci - fied.

But if, by a still, small voice he calls To
O Sav - ior, if thou wilt be my guide, Tho
So trust - ing my all to thy ten - der care, And

paths that I do not know, I'll an - swer, dear Lord, with my
dark and rug - ged the way, My voice shall ech - o the
know - ing thou lov - est me, I'll do thy will with a

hand in thine: I'll go where you want me to go.
mes - sage sweet: I'll say what you want me to say.
heart sin - cere: I'll be what you want me to be.

I'll go where you want me to go, dear Lord, O - ver

moun - tain or plain or sea; I'll say what you want me to

say, dear Lord; I'll be what you want me to be.

Text: Mary Brown, 1856–1918
Music: Carrie E. Rounsefell, 1861–1930

1 Nephi 3:7
Doctrine and Covenants 4:2

Did You Think to Pray?

Thoughtfully ♩ = 72–88

1. Ere you left your room this morn - ing, Did you think to
2. When your heart was filled with an - ger, Did you think to
3. When sore tri - als came up - on you, Did you think to

pray? In the name of Christ, our Sav - ior,
pray? Did you plead for grace, my broth - er,
pray? When your soul was full of sor - row,

Did you sue for lov - ing fa - vor As a shield to -
That you might for - give an - oth - er Who had crossed your
Balm of Gil - ead did you bor - row At the gates of

day?
way?   Oh,   how pray-ing rests the wea - ry!
day?

Prayer will change the night to day.   So, when life gets dark and

drea - ry,   Don't for-get to pray.

Text: Mary A. Pepper Kidder, 1820–1905   Psalm 5:3, 12
Music: William O. Perkins, 1831–1902   Mark 11:24–25

357

Praise to the Man

Vigorously ♩ = 76–96

1. Praise to the man who com-muned with Je - ho - vah!
2. Praise to his mem - 'ry, he died as a mar - tyr;
3. Great is his glo - ry and end - less his priest - hood.
4. Sac - ri - fice brings forth the bless - ings of heav - en;

Je - sus a - noint - ed that Proph - et and Seer.
Hon - ored and blest be his ev - er great name!
Ev - er and ev - er the keys he will hold.
Earth must a - tone for the blood of that man.

Bless - ed to o - pen the last dis - pen - sa - tion,
Long shall his blood, which was shed by as - sas - sins,
Faith - ful and true, he will en - ter his king - dom,
Wake up the world for the con - flict of jus - tice.

Kings shall ex - tol him, and na - tions re - vere.
Plead un - to heav'n while the earth lauds his fame.
Crowned in the midst of the proph - ets of old.
Mil - lions shall know "Broth - er Jo - seph" a - gain.

358

Hail to the Proph - et, as - cend - ed to heav - en!
Trai - tors and ty - rants now fight him in vain.
Min - gling with Gods, he can plan for his breth - ren;
Death can - not con - quer the he - ro a - gain.

Text: William W. Phelps, 1792–1872

Doctrine and Covenants 135

Music: Scottish folk song

Far, Far Away on Judea's Plains

Text and music: John Menzies Macfarlane, 1833–1892

Luke 2:8–20
Doctrine and Covenants 45:71

360

Silent Night

1. Si - lent night! Ho - ly night! All is calm,
2. Si - lent night! Ho - ly night! Shep - herds quake
3. Si - lent night! Ho - ly night! Son of God,

all is bright Round yon vir - gin moth - er and Child.
at the sight! Glo - ries stream from heav - en a - far;
love's pure light Ra - diant beams from thy ho - ly face,

Ho - ly In - fant, so ten - der and mild, Sleep in heav - en-ly
Heav'n - ly hosts sing Al - le - lu - ia! Christ, the Sav - ior, is
With the dawn of re - deem - ing grace, Je - sus, Lord, at thy

peace; Sleep in heav - en - ly peace.
born! Christ, the Sav - ior, is born!
birth; Je - sus, Lord, at thy birth.

Text: Joseph Mohr, 1792–1848; trans. by John F. Young, 1820–1885
Music: Franz Gruber, 1787–1863

Luke 2:7–14
Alma 7:10–12

361

Christ the Lord Is Risen Today

With exultation ♩ = 96–108

1. Christ the Lord is ris'n to-day,
2. Love's re-deem-ing work is done, Al - le - lu - ia!
3. Lives a - gain our glo-rious King,

Sons of men and an-gels say,
Fought the fight, the vic-t'ry won, Al - le - lu - ia!
Where, O death, is now thy sting?

Raise your joys and tri-umphs high,
Je - sus' ag - o - ny is o'er, Al - le - lu - ia!
Once he died our souls to save,

Sing, ye heav'ns, and earth re - ply,
Dark - ness veils the earth no more, Al - le - lu - ia!
Where thy vic - to - ry, O grave?

Text: Charles Wesley, 1707–1788
Music: Anon., *Lyra Davidica*, 1708

Matthew 28:5–6
1 Corinthians 15:20, 53–57

He Is Risen

With dignity ♩ = 92–104

1. He is ris - en! He is ris - en! Tell it out with
2. Come with high and ho - ly hymn - ing; Chant our Lord's tri -
3. He is ris - en! He is ris - en! He hath o - pened

joy - ful voice. He has burst his three days' pris - on;
um - phant lay. Not one dark - some cloud is dim - ming
heav - en's gate. We are free from sin's dark pris - on,

Let the whole wide earth re - joice. Death is con - quered,
Yon - der glo - rious morn - ing ray, Break - ing o'er the
Ris - en to a ho - lier state. And a bright - er

man is free. Christ has won the vic - to - ry.
pur - ple east, Sym - bol of our Eas - ter feast.
Eas - ter beam On our long - ing eyes shall stream.

Text: Cecil Frances Alexander, 1818–1895
Music: Joachim Neander, 1650–1680

Mark 16:6–7
Mosiah 16:7–9

I Am a Child of God

Fervently ♩ = 80–96

1. I am a child of God, And he has sent me here,
2. I am a child of God, And so my needs are great;
3. I am a child of God. Rich bless-ings are in store;

Has giv-en me an earth-ly home With par-ents kind and dear.
Help me to un-der-stand his words Be-fore it grows too late.
If I but learn to do his will I'll live with him once more.

Lead me, guide me, walk be-side me, Help me find the way.

Teach me all that I must do To live with him some-day.

Text: Naomi W. Randall, b. 1908. © 1957 LDS
Music: Mildred T. Pettit, 1895–1977. © 1957 LDS

Psalm 82:6; Mosiah 4:15
Doctrine and Covenants 14:7

I Know My Father Lives

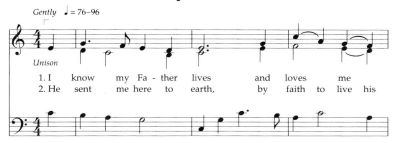

1. I know my Fa - ther lives and loves me too.
2. He sent me here to earth, by faith to live his plan.

The Spir - it whis - pers this to me and tells me it is true,
The Spir - it whis - pers this to me and tells me that I can,

And tells me it is true.
And tells me that I can.

Text and music: Reid N. Nibley, b. 1923. © 1969 LDS
When played on organ, use manuals only (no pedals).

Moroni 10:5
Abraham 3:22–28

I Think When I Read That Sweet Story

Lovingly ♩. = 42–46

1. I think when I read that sweet story of old, When Jesus was here among men, How he called little children like lambs to his fold; I should like to have been with him then.

2. I wish that his hands had been placed on my head, That his arms had been thrown around me, That I might have seen his kind look when he said, "Let the little ones come unto me."

3. Yet still to his footstool in prayer I may go, And ask for a share in his love; And if I thus earnestly seek him below, I shall see him and hear him above.

Text: Jemima Luke, 1813–1906
Music: Leah Ashton Lloyd, 1894–1965

3 Nephi 17:21–23
Luke 18:16

I Thank Thee, Dear Father

Smoothly ♩ = 52–58

1. I thank thee, dear Father in heaven above, For thy
2. Help me to be good, kind, and gentle today, And

good - ness and mer - cy, thy kind - ness and love. I
mind what my fa - ther and moth - er shall say. In the

thank thee for home, friends, and par - ents so dear, And
dear name of Je - sus, so lov - ing and mild, I

for ev - 'ry bless - ing that I en - joy here.
ask thee to bless me and keep me thy child.

Text: Anon.
Music: George Careless, 1839–1932

Ephesians 5:20
Alma 37:36–37

The Lord Gave Me a Temple

Text: Donnell Hunter, b. 1930. © 1969 LDS
Music: Darwin Wolford, b. 1936. © 1969 LDS

1 Corinthians 3:16–17
Doctrine and Covenants 88:27–29

Kindness Begins with Me

Text and music: Clara W. McMaster, b. 1904. © 1969 LDS

Luke 6:31, 10:30–37
Ephesians 4:32

Dare to Do Right

Boldly ♩. = 44–54

1. Dare to do right! Dare to be true! You have a work that no
2. Dare to do right! Dare to be true! Oth - er men's fail - ures can

oth - er can do; Do it so brave - ly, so
nev - er save you. Stand by your con - science, your

kind - ly, so well, An - gels will has - ten the sto - ry to tell.
hon - or, your faith; Stand like a he - ro and bat - tle till death.

Chorus

Dare, dare, dare to do right; Dare, dare,

Text: Anon.
Music: Arr. by A. C. Smyth, 1840–1909

Matthew 4:1–11
Ephesians 6:1

The Golden Plates

Text: Rose Thomas Graham, 1875–1967
Music: J. Spencer Cornwall, 1888–1983. Arr. © 1989 LDS

Joseph Smith—History 1:51–53, 59

Teach Me to Walk in the Light

Prayerfully ♩ = 84–100

1. Teach me to walk in the light of his love; Teach me to
2. Come, lit - tle child, and to - geth - er we'll learn Of his com-
3. Fa - ther in Heav - en, we thank thee this day For lov - ing

pray to my Fa -ther a - bove; Teach me to know of the
mand-ments, that we may re - turn Home to his pres - ence, to
guid - ance to show us the way. Grate -ful, we praise thee with

things that are right; Teach me, teach me to walk in the light.
live in his sight— Al - ways, al -ways to walk in the light.
songs of de - light! Glad - ly, glad - ly we'll walk in the light.

Text and music: Clara W. McMaster, b. 1904. © 1958 LDS

Isaiah 2:5
Ephesians 5:8

Family Prayer

Reverently ♩ = 96–104

1. Let us gath - er in a cir - cle And
2. Let us thank him for our meal - time, For
3. Oh, may we al - ways serve him, In

kneel in fam - 'ly prayer To thank our Heav'n - ly
clothes we dai - ly wear, For par - ents, home, and
thought and ac - tion too, And hum - bly kneel at

Fa - ther For the bless - ings we all share.
fam - 'ly, For his kind and lov - ing care.
prayer - time As so man - y fam - 'lies do.

Text and music: DeVota Mifflin Peterson b. 1910.
© 1969 LDS

Doctrine and Covenants 59:7
3 Nephi 18:21

GLOSSARY

Aaronic Priesthood: The lesser of the two divisions of the priesthood in the Church. It includes the offices of deacon, teacher, priest, and bishop.

Adam: The first man; the father of the human race. Before his earth life, he was known as Michael. He led the righteous in the War in Heaven. He helped to create the earth.

Administer the sacrament: To bless the sacrament.

Administer to the sick: To anoint and bless the sick by the power of the priesthood.

Adultery: Sexual intercourse between a married person and someone other than his or her wife or husband.

Adversary: One of Satan's names.

Affliction: Anything causing pain or suffering.

Agency: The ability and freedom to choose good or evil.

Age of accountability: The age at which a person becomes responsible for his actions and may be baptized. In most cases a person begins to be responsible for his actions when he is eight years old.

Altar: Anciently, a raised place on which sacrifices were offered. In Latter-day Saint temples today, a place where covenants are made and couples or families are sealed together for time and eternity.

Angel: A messenger sent from God.

Anoint: To place a few drops of oil on the head, usually as part of a priesthood blessing.

Apostasy: Turning away from or leaving the teachings of the gospel.

Apostle: A person called and appointed to be a special witness for Christ. An office in the Melchizedek Priesthood.

Articles of Faith: Thirteen statements written by the Prophet Joseph Smith describing some of the basic teachings and ordinances of The Church of Jesus Christ of Latter-day Saints.

Atonement: The suffering and death of Jesus Christ, through which resurrection is provided to all mortals and eternal life is offered to those who have faith in Christ and repent of their sins.

Authority: The right to function in certain capacities in the Church.

Baptism by immersion: An ordinance in which a person is immersed in water and brought up out of the water. It is necessary to become a member of The Church of Jesus Christ of Latter-day Saints.

Baptism for the dead: Baptism by immersion performed by a living person for one who is dead. This ordinance is performed in temples.

Bible: One of the standard works of the Church. It includes the Old and New Testaments.

Bishop: A man who has been ordained and set apart as the presiding high priest for a ward. He has responsibility for the temporal and spiritual well-being of all his ward members. He also presides over the Aaronic Priesthood.

Book of Mormon: One of the standard works of the Church. An account of God's dealings with the people of the American continents from about 2,200 years before the birth of Jesus Christ to 421 years after the death of Jesus Christ. It was translated from gold plates by Joseph Smith and contains the fulness of the gospel.

Born in the covenant: Born to parents who have been sealed in the temple.

Broken heart and contrite spirit: A deep, godly sorrow for our sins; humility.

Called: To be assigned a duty or position in the Church.

Celestial kingdom: The highest kingdom of glory, where one is in the presence of Heavenly Father and Jesus Christ.

Charity: Love and compassion; the pure love of Christ.

Chastity: Avoiding sexual relations with anyone except one's spouse.

Comforter: The Holy Ghost.

Commandments: Directions given by God to his children to prepare them for eternal life in the world to come.

Confirmation: An ordinance in which a person is confirmed a member of The Church of Jesus Christ of Latter-day Saints by the laying on of hands and given the gift of the Holy Ghost. The ordinance is performed after baptism.

Convert: One who has accepted the gospel of Jesus Christ and been baptized and confirmed. Usually applied to those who join the Church after eight years of age.

Council in Heaven: The meeting in heaven in which Heavenly Father announced the plan of salvation and chose Jesus Christ as our Redeemer.

Covenant: A binding agreement or promise between God and a person or group of people.

Create: To organize elements that already exist into a new form.

Crucifixion: A method of execution used in the days of the Savior. A person's hands and feet were nailed or tied to a cross.

Death: Separation of a person's spirit from his physical body.

Devil: A spirit son of God who rebelled against the Father and tried to destroy the agency of man. He is also known as Lucifer or Satan and is the author of sin.

Discernment: A spiritual gift that allows a person to understand or know something.

Disciple: A follower, especially a follower of Christ.

Dispensation: A period of time in which truth from heaven is given to men on earth through prophets.

Doctrine and Covenants: One of the standard works of the Church containing revelations given to Joseph Smith and other latter-day Presidents of the Church.

Endowment: A gift of power given through ordinances in the temple to worthy members of the Church. The endowment includes instructions about the plan of salvation.

Enduring to the end: Obedience to God's laws to the end of mortal life.

Eternal: Everlasting, without beginning or end.

Eternity: Time without end.

Eve: Adam's wife, the mother of the human race.

Exaltation: The highest state of happiness and glory in the celestial kingdom; the continuation of the family unit in eternity; "all that [the] Father hath" (D&C 84:38).

Fall of Adam: The change to mortality that occurred when Adam and Eve ate the forbidden fruit in the Garden of Eden.

Family history: Research to identify ancestors.

Fast: To abstain from food and drink for the purpose of drawing closer to the Lord.

Fast offering: Contribution to the Church of the money or commodities saved by fasting for two consecutive meals.

First Presidency: A quorum that presides over the entire Church; made up of the President of the Church and his Counselors.

Foreordination: Callings given by Heavenly Father to his children to come to earth at a specific time and place to help with his work in a particular way.

Fornication: Sexual intercourse between unmarried people.

Full-tithe payer: A person who pays one-tenth of his annual increase to the Lord.

Gathering of Israel: The spiritual and physical gathering of all the house of Israel in the latter days.

Gentile: A person who does not belong to the chosen people. The scriptures use the word to mean (1) non-Israelites, and (2) nonmembers of The Church of Jesus Christ of Latter-day Saints.

Gift of the Holy Ghost: The right, received by the laying on of hands, to enjoy the constant companionship of the Holy Ghost when we are worthy.

Gifts of the Spirit: Spiritual blessings given by God to those who are faithful to Jesus Christ.

God: Our Father in Heaven, the Father of Jesus Christ in the flesh and of the spirits of all mortals.

Godhead: Our Father in Heaven; his Son, Jesus Christ; and the Holy Ghost.

Gospel: The plan of salvation, which embraces all that is necessary to save and exalt mankind; the good news that Jesus is the Christ.

Hell: The part of the spirit world where wicked spirits await the day of their resurrection; also the place where Satan and his followers dwell.

Holy Ghost: The third member of the Godhead; a personage of spirit.

House of Israel: Natural or adopted descendants of the sons of Jacob, who was given the name of Israel by the Lord.

Humble: Willing to learn, teachable.

Immerse: To put completely under water.

Immortal: Beyond the power of death. If a person is immortal he cannot die.

Inspiration: Divine guidance that comes through the promptings of the Holy Ghost.

Israel: (1) The name given to Jacob of the Old Testament. (2) The name given to the descendants of Jacob's twelve sons.

(3) The modern nation to which many Jews have gathered today.

Jesus Christ: The Only Begotten Son of the Father in the flesh and the Firstborn Son in the spirit; our Redeemer and Savior.

Jew: Someone who belongs to the tribe of Judah, to the ancient kingdom of Judah, or to the Jewish religion.

Kingdom of God: The Church of Jesus Christ of Latter-day Saints on earth; also the celestial kingdom.

Last days: The time near the end of the world and the second coming of the Savior.

Latter-day Saints: Members of The Church of Jesus Christ of Latter-day Saints.

Laying on of hands: The placing of hands on a person's head by a priesthood holder to bless, anoint, confirm, ordain, or heal the person.

Lord: God, master; often refers to Jesus.

Lucifer: Satan, the devil.

Mercy: Love and forgiveness.

Millennium: One thousand years of peace when Jesus Christ will reign personally on the earth.

Messiah: Jesus Christ, the Anointed One.

Mission: A period of time during which a person who has been called and set apart preaches the gospel; a task or assignment.

Missionary: A member of the Church who is called to preach the gospel to the people of the world.

Mortal: Able to die; pertaining to this life.

Mortality: Earthly existence in a body that is subject to death.

Nonmember: Used to refer to people who are not members of The Church of Jesus Christ of Latter-day Saints.

Only Begotten Son: Jesus Christ, the only person who had God the Father as the father of his mortal body.

Ordain: To give a man a priesthood office by the laying on of hands.

Ordinances: Sacred rites and ceremonies that are necessary for eternal progression. God's laws and commandments.

Outer darkness: The dwelling place of the devil and his followers.

Paradise: The part of the spirit world where righteous spirits await the day of their resurrection.

Patriarchal blessing: An inspired blessing declaring a person's lineage and giving inspired counsel and insight about his life.

Pearl of Great Price: One of the standard works of the Church, including ancient and modern scripture.

Plan of salvation: Our Heavenly Father's plan for his children by which they can overcome sin and death and gain eternal life.

Prayer: Communication with the Lord.

Premortal existence: The period between the birth of spirit children of God and their birth into mortal life.

Preside: To take charge of; to be in authority.

Priesthood: The power and authority of God given to men on earth to act in all things for the salvation of men.

Prophecy: Inspired words of a prophet about a future event.

Prophesy: To tell something before it happens.

Prophet: One who has been called of the Lord to be a special witness of the divinity of Jesus Christ. *The prophet* refers to the President of The Church of Jesus Christ of Latter-day Saints.

Quorum: An organized unit of the priesthood.

Recommend: A certificate to identify people as members of the Church and to certify their worthiness to receive certain ordinances or blessings.

Redeem: To free someone from the results of sins he has repented of. To free from the effects of physical death.

Redeemer: The Savior, Jesus Christ.

Remission: Forgiveness.

Repentance: Turning from sin and changing the course of one's life to follow the Savior's teachings.

Restitution: Giving repayment for a sin.

Restoration: To make something as it was; to reestablish; to bring back.

Resurrection: Reuniting of body and spirit, never to be separated again.

Revelation: Divine truths communicated from God to mankind.

Sabbath day: A day of worship and rest from daily work and activities; observed by members of the Church on Sunday, the first day of the week.

Sacrament: An ordinance in which bread and water are blessed and passed to members of the Church. The bread and water are emblems of the body and blood sacrificed by the Savior.

Sacrifice: To offer to God something precious; to forsake all things for the gospel of Jesus Christ.

Salvation: Inseparable connection of body and spirit brought about through the Savior's atonement and resurrection; eternal life.

Sanctify: To make clean, pure, and spotless; to make free from the blood and sins of this world.

Satan: A name of the devil, who opposes the plan of salvation.

Savior: Jesus Christ, who has saved us from physical death and made it possible for us to be saved from spiritual death.

Scriptures: Words written and spoken by holy men of God when moved upon by the Holy Ghost.

Sealing: An ordinance performed in the temple, eternally uniting a husband and wife or children and their parents.

Second death: Spiritual death; death as to things of righteousness.

Seed: In one sense, children or descendants.

Set apart: To authorize someone, by the laying on of hands, to act in a specific calling.

Sin: Breaking the laws of God.

Son of God: The Savior, Jesus Christ.

Sons of perdition: The spirit hosts of heaven who followed Lucifer. Also, those who gain a perfect knowledge of the divinity of the Savior and then turn from him and follow Satan.

Spiritual death: Separation from the Spirit of God and from his presence.

Standard works: The volumes of scripture officially accepted by the Church: Bible, Book of Mormon, Doctrine and Covenants, and Pearl of Great Price.

Sustain: To support and accept.

Telestial kingdom: The lowest kingdom of glory.

Temple: A place of worship and prayer; the house of the Lord prepared and dedicated for sacred gospel ordinances.

Temple ordinance work: Sacred gospel ordinances performed in temples by the living for themselves and for those who are dead. These ordinances include baptisms, endowments, marriages, and sealings.

Terrestrial kingdom: The middle kingdom of glory.

Testify: To declare what one knows; to bear witness.

Testimony: Knowledge revealed by the Holy Ghost, of the divinity of the Savior and of gospel truths.

Tithe: Payment to the Lord of one-tenth of one's annual increase.

Transgression: Violation or breaking of a commandment or law; sin.

Word of Wisdom: A revelation concerning health practices given to Joseph Smith in 1833; section 89 of the Doctrine and Covenants.

Worship: Reverence, honor, or devotion given to God.

Zion: The name given by the Lord to those who obey his laws. The name of the place where the righteous live.

BOOKS CITED

Grant, Heber J. *Gospel Standards.* Compiled by G. Homer Durham. Salt Lake City: Improvement Era, 1941.

Hinckley, Bryant S. *The Faith of Our Pioneer Fathers.* Salt Lake City: Bookcraft, 1956.

Journal of Discourses. 26 vols. London: Latter-day Saints' Book Depot, 1854–86.

Kimball, Spencer W. *Faith Precedes the Miracle.* Salt Lake City: Deseret Book Co., 1972.

———. *The Miracle of Forgiveness.* Salt Lake City: Bookcraft, 1969.

———, et. al. *Priesthood.* Salt Lake City: Deseret Book Co., 1981.

Lee, Harold B. *Stand Ye in Holy Places.* Salt Lake City: Deseret Book Co., 1974.

Ludlow, Daniel, ed. *Latter-day Prophets Speak,* Salt Lake City: Bookcraft, 1948.

McConkie, Bruce R. *Mormon Doctrine.* 2nd ed. Salt Lake City: Bookcraft, 1966.

McKay, David O. *Gospel Ideals.* 2nd printing. Salt Lake City: Improvement Era, 1954.

————. Treasures of Life. Compiled by Clare Middlemiss. Salt Lake City: Deseret Book., 1962.

————. *True to the Faith.* Compiled by Llewelyn R. McKay. Salt Lake City: Bookcraft, 1966.

Packer, Boyd K. *Mothers.* Salt Lake City: Deseret Book Co., 1977.

Principles of the Gospel. Salt Lake City: The Church of Jesus Christ of Latter-day Saints, 1976.

Smith, Joseph. *History of The Church of Jesus Christ of Latter-day Saints.* 7 vols. 2nd ed. rev. Edited by B. H. Roberts. Salt Lake City: The Church of Jesus Christ of Latter-day Saints, 1932–51.

————. *Lectures on Faith.* Compiled by N. B. Lundwall. Salt Lake City: N. B. Lundwall, n. d.

————. *Teachings of the Prophet Joseph Smith.* Selected by Joseph Fielding Smith. Salt Lake City: Deseret Book Co., 1938.

Smith, Joseph F. *Gospel Doctrine.* 5th ed. Salt Lake City: Deseret Book Co., 1939.

Smith, Joseph Fielding. *Answers to Gospel Questions.* 5 vols. Compiled by Joseph Fielding Smith, Jr. Salt Lake City: Deseret Book Co., 1957–66.

————. *Doctrines of Salvation.* 3 vols. Compiled by Bruce R. McConkie. Salt Lake City: Bookcraft, 1954–56.

Talmage, James E. *Jesus the Christ.* 3rd ed. Salt Lake City: The Church of Jesus Christ of Latter-day Saints, 1916.

Taylor, John. *The Mediation and Atonement.* Photolithographic reprint of 1st ed., 1882. Salt Lake City: Deseret News Co., 1964.

Young, Brigham. *Discourses of Brigham Young.* Selected by John A. Widtsoe. Salt Lake City: Deseret Book Co., 1941.

INDEX

High priest, office and duties of, 90

Holy Ghost, 36–39
  baptism necessary to receive gift of, 131
  gift of. *See* Gift of Holy ghost
  mission of, 37
    statements on, by Joseph Fielding Smith, 38
  who is the, 37

Honesty, 203–6
  statement on, by Joseph F. Smith, 206
  statements on, by Mark E. Petersen, 203, 204
  statement on, by Spencer W. Kimball, 205

Hot drinks, 193

I

Idleness, 182

Interpretation of tongues, gift of, 143

Isaac, God's covenant with, 97

Israel
  name of Jacob changed to, 97, 271
  gathering of House of, 271–75
    statement on, by Bruce R. McConkie, 274
    statement on, by Joseph Fielding Smith, 273
  scattering, 271–72

Israelites, 97, 271

J

Jacob
  God's covenant with, 97
  name changed to Israel, 97, 271

Jesus Christ
  Atonement of. *See* Atonement
  creator, 27
  example of charity, 200
  example of service, 191
  faith in. *See* Faith in Jesus Christ
  introduced sacrament, 151–53
  life of, 61–69
    meaning of, for us, 69
    predicted before birth, 61–63
  obeyed the Father, 226–27
  Only Begotten Son of the Father, 63–64
  organized Church, 67
  perfect life of, 64–65
  redemption by, 67–68
    witness of, by Orson F. Whitney, 67
  Savior and leader in earth life, 18
  second coming of. *See* Second coming of Jesus Christ
  spirit child of God, 11
  teachings of, 65–66
  wants us to serve others, 187–89
    statement on, by Spencer W. Kimball, 187

Joy, fulness of, 14

Judged
  by First Presidency and Twelve Apostles, 296
  by records, 295–96
  by Son, 296
  by Twelve Apostles, 296
  by words, works, thoughts, 295

Sacrifice, 171–77
Satan
  appears as angel of light,
    149
  cast out of heaven, 18–19
  and followers tempt us, 19
  fought against Jesus in
    heaven, 18–19
  and Millennium, 284,
    285–86
  opposes good, 23–24
  sought to take away
    freedom to choose, 18
  tempted Eve, 32
  wants us to break law of
    chastity, 249–51
Savior. *See* Jesus Christ
Scriptures, 52–56
  four books of, 52–55
  studying, 55–56
  what are, 52
Sealing, power of, restored by
    Elijah, 267–68
Second coming of Jesus
    Christ, 277–81
  statement on, by Brigham
    Young, 278
  signs of, 280
Service, 185–91
Seventy, office and duties of,
    90
Signs of the times. *See* Second
    coming of Jesus Christ
Sin
  all are guilty of, 122
  what is, 122
Smith, Joseph, Church
    restored through,
    110–113
Sorcerers, 149
Spirit, gifts of. *See* Spiritual

gifts
Spirit prison, 292–93
Spirit world, 289–93
  statement on, by Brigham
    Young, 289–90
  statement on, by Ezra Taft
    Benson, 289–90
  statement on, by Joseph
    Smith, 289
Spirits
  bodily form of, 290
  of men resemble Heavenly
    Parents, 11
Spiritual gifts, 141–49
  developing, 148
  a feature of true church,
    104–5
  Satan imitates, 149
Stake, 112
Stealing, 204–5
Strong drinks, 193
Sunday the Sabbath, 161

T

Talents
  developed in heaven, 13
  developing, 218–221
  statement on, by Heber J.
    Grant, 220
  statement on, by Marvin
    J. Ashton, 220
Tea, 193
Teacher, office and duties of,
    88–89
Teaching, gift of, 145
Telestial glory, 298
Temple, eternal marriage
    performed in, 242–43
Temple work, 255–61
  during Millennium, 283
Temples, 255–56